W9-BGE-148

PRAISE FOR *MEMES TO MOVEMENTS*

"Bridging scholarly research and street activism, this analysis shows how memes are so much more than an internet phenomenon. . . . In this incisive and illuminating study, the author shows how she appreciates the power of art, the power of the internet, and the intersection of the two."

—*Kirkus Reviews*, starred review

"*Memes to Movements* is essential reading. An Xiao Mina is one of the best people writing about memes today and unpacks with great urgency, understanding, empathy, and wisdom all the reasons why memes matter, how integral they are to the ways we communicate, and how they shape and change society. Memes are the essential unit of cultural exchange, and An's work demonstrates why we should be taking them seriously."

—JONNY SUN, author and illustrator of
everyone's a aliebn when ur a aliebn too

"Weaving together global cases of meme culture, activism, and misinformation, An Xiao Mina brilliantly reveals how internet culture, social movements, and political agendas are intimately entwined. *Memes to Movements* is essential for anyone invested in activism or geopolitics. By analyzing the evolution of digital social and political activity, this book offers a critical intervention at a moment when the public is anxious about technology and political life."

—DANAH BOYD, author of *It's Complicated:
The Social Lives of Networked Teens*

"The dumbest idea anybody ever had about the internet was that the serious stuff and the silly stuff are disconnected, that the frothy world of cat pictures can have nothing to do with the somber conduct of political dissent. No one does a better job than An Xiao Mina of tracing the deep connections between the inventive and playful culture of memes—those endlessly repeated and mostly humorous bits of ephemera—and political conversations among people who often lack other outlets for public speech. Mina is a unique voice, an indigenous member of multiple cultures, an artist and a scholar, and an observer and participant in networked politics. In *Memes to Movements*, she explains how the culture that leads to Grumpy Cat also allows people to express resistance to politics as usual. Wearing a hoodie is transformed into a political statement, mispronounced Chinese words become tools for evading censorship, and social networks become symbolic battlegrounds for supporting marriage equality. Mina shows, in terrifically engaging detail, that memes can be serious and silly at the same time. *Memes to Movements* is a fascinating and important look at the way that people are adapting internet culture to vital ends."

—CLAY SHIRKY, author of
Cognitive Surplus and *Here Comes Everybody*

"Internet sleuth An Xiao Mina takes readers on a journey around the social media globe. *Memes to Movements* is the quintessential guide for understanding the how and why of this social media phenomenon. Mina is a voice for social change—and a voice of reason—in this visually overwhelming world."

—ALICIA ELER, visual art critic/reporter at the
Minneapolis Star Tribune and author of *The Selfie Generation*

"A visionary and sweeping history of the internet phenomenon, Memes to Movements is a must-read for anyone concerned about how our wildly complex society can evolve with the tools technology has given us—for better or for worse. It is an all-too-timely book that shows how urgently we need to understand the impact of the algorithms, codes, and hidden structures that have become tools of both liberation and oppression. Whatever your thoughts about our digitized world, this brilliant and original book will challenge them to evolve."

—PAUL D. MILLER AKA DJ SPOOKY,
author of Rhythm Science

"An Xiao Mina is a wide-ranging explorer of the frontier where technology meets social change. Her keen understanding of the contrasting ways that social media operate in different countries means she is ideally placed to offer a global perspective on their growing social and political impact."

—TOM STANDAGE, deputy editor of *The Economist*
and author of *Writing on the Wall: Social Media—
The First 2,000 Years* and *The Victorian Internet*

"As internet culture has moved from niche to mainstream, and as it has developed into an unprecedented global force, we're evermore in need of incisive, clarifying work about what exactly we mean when we say 'internet culture.' It's a rare thinker who can look at the internet as it actually is—a spectrum that runs from memes and image macros to social movements and sophisticated forms of political speech—and draw conclusions that include the richness of that spectrum without shying away from the humor and playfulness of the web. But An Xiao Mina is just such a thinker. To truly attempt to understand internet culture, one must occupy many places at once. Mina lives across digital spaces and cultures, and she brings that perspective and authenticity to all her work and now, finally, in book form with *Memes to Movements*."

—SCOTT LAMB, VP of International, BuzzFeed

MEMES TO MOVEMENTS

MEMES TO MOVEMENTS

HOW THE WORLD'S MOST VIRAL MEDIA

IS CHANGING SOCIAL PROTEST AND POWER

AN XIAO MINA

BEACON PRESS ▪ BOSTON

BEACON PRESS
Boston, Massachusetts
www.beacon.org

Beacon Press books
are published under the auspices of
the Unitarian Universalist Association of Congregations.

22 21 20 19   8 7 6 5 4 3 2 1

This book is printed on acid-free paper that meets the uncoated paper
ANSI/NISO specifications for permanence as revised in 1992.

Text design and composition by Kim Arney

Portions of subchapters 2.2, "Behold, the Llamas," and 3.2, "Enter the
Pandaman," are adapted from An Xiao Mina, "Batman, Pandaman and
the Blind Man: A Case Study in Social Change Memes and Internet
Censorship in China," *Journal of Visual Culture* 13, no. 3 (2014).

Illustrations by Jason Li

Library of Congress Cataloging-in-Publication Data

Names: Mina, An Xiao, author.
Title: Memes to movements : how the world's most viral media is changing
social protest and power / An Xiao Mina.
Description: Boston : Beacon Press, [2018] | Includes bibliographical
references and index.
Identifiers: LCCN 2018018009 (print) | LCCN 2018027029 (ebook) |
ISBN 9780807056608 (ebook) | ISBN 9780807056585 (hardcover : alk. paper)
Subjects: LCSH: Internet memes—Political aspects | Social media—Political
aspects. | Internet—Political aspects. | Social movements.
Classification: LCC HM851 (ebook) | LCC HM851 .M5454 2018 (print) |
DDC 302.23/1—dc23
LC record available at https://lccn.loc.gov/2018018009

To my grandma, who taught me how to garden,
and to my grandfather and uncle SJ, who taught me how to see

CONTENTS

INTRODUCTION

■ ■ ■ ■ ■ ■ ■

HANDS UP, UMBRELLAS UP

IT WAS THE SUMMER OF 2014, and I saw two social media streams unfold on two different continents in two different languages. One stream emanated from events in a small, mixed-race city in the US heartland. Eight thousand miles away, another stream arose from events in a teeming, millions-strong metropolis along the South China Sea.

In the United States, Michael Brown, eighteen, had been shot and killed by police in Ferguson, Missouri, a suburb twelve miles southeast of St. Louis. Early reports suggested that he died with his hands raised in surrender. What the public knew for sure was that Brown was shot by a police officer and that his dead body lay in the street for four hours.[1] Demonstrators came out in droves—first in St. Louis and then suddenly in major cities around the country. They were angry and eager to voice their concerns about racial profiling and historic violence by the state and state actors.

As they raised their hands and fists, they also raised their phones—to document, share, and network with protests across the country. I watched my social media feeds flood with images of people with their hands showing, palms facing the camera. The photos reenacted, as a performative gesture, the chant that was quickly becoming synonymous with the Ferguson protests:

"Hands up!" the chant leader would call out.
"Don't shoot!" the crowd would respond.
"Hands up!"
"Don't shoot!"

Hands-up-don't-shoot photos of solidarity showed people in their homes, cars, places of employment, dorm rooms, cafes. Dozens of students at Howard

1

University, the most prestigious historically black college in the country, came together to take a large group photo of their hands raised. It went viral. A broad national dialogue on race, policing, and systemic injustices against African Americans would soon take hold, often under the mantle of #BlackLivesMatter.

Meanwhile, half a world away in the subtropical metropolis of Hong Kong, tensions were growing over issues of democratic rights and universal suffrage. A month later, in September 2014, the similarities became impossible to ignore: students' hands were raised to the sky in a gesture against police violence. City police had just weeks earlier released pepper spray and tear gas on students protesting in the city. Hong Kong, once a British colony, was handed over to China in 1997, and it operated ostensibly under a "one country, two systems" policy, which afforded the city considerable media and electoral freedoms in China. Protesters were concerned with what they saw as increasing encroachment on their democratic rights as the mainland government sought to exert its influence.

To shield themselves from the pepper spray, students unfurled bright, colorful umbrellas that made a striking image from above and below. Soon, just as the hands-up gesture became a symbol of the emergent #BlackLivesMatter movement, umbrellas up became the symbol of what would soon be called the #UmbrellaMovement. Photos of unfurled umbrellas appeared on social media, on such sites as Twitter, Instagram, and Facebook, as protesters chanted in Cantonese, "I want true universal suffrage!"

Hands-up gestures aside, little seemed to connect Ferguson and Hong Kong directly. The striking similarity of the hands-up gestures in both cities was more likely a reflection of common concerns about police violence. The events happened worlds away from each other, and though both groups of protesters sought substantive changes from the powers that be, the specifics of these demands differed significantly. One group called for an end to police violence; another group called for universal suffrage. Both worried about the harmful encroachment of the state into aspects of daily life.

On occasion there was deliberate crossover, as when Ferguson protesters donned umbrellas against the rain and cheekily thanked protesters in Hong Kong for the idea. Protesters in Hong Kong adopted some slogans from the #BlackLivesMatter movement, like "I Can't Breathe," a reference to the last words of Eric Garner, a man choked to death by police in New York City. In the case of

Hong Kong, "I Can't Breathe" was more metaphorical, suggesting the suffocating effects of limited suffrage. These gestures, though fleeting and infrequent, helped demonstrate solidarity as both movements made international headlines.

Andrew Kling @AndrewAKling #HongKong, thanks for the umbrella idea—turns out we needed them. **#FergusonOctober #Ferguson**.

1:08 p.m., Oct. 10, 2014[2]

Jigme @JigmeUgen Solidarity from **#HongKong**'s **#UmbrellaRevolution—#ICantBreathe** stay strong sister **@rosetangy #BlackLivesMatter #umhk**.

8:49 p.m., Dec. 17, 2014[3]

The internet was essential to the rise of both movements. It made them visible to themselves and to each other. It's nearly impossible now to think of a social movement without the internet, and as the world comes online, communities advocating for change are popping up globally, in places large and small, channeling their energies to the streets and to the web.

Social media allowed disparate cities participating in the #BlackLivesMatter movement to connect with each other. "Black lives matter" chanted at a march in Washington, DC, could be live-streamed and shared using the hashtag #BlackLivesMatter and made visible to a protest in St. Louis, where people might be chanting the same thing. An umbrella sticker posted on a lamppost on a busy street in Hong Kong could inspire someone to share a similar sticker in a Chinese diasporic neighborhood in Los Angeles.

The rise in popularity of selfies and hashtags has helped create a sense of physical co-presence.[4] A #HandsUpDontShoot selfie or a selfie with a colorful umbrella becomes a way of participating in protests around the world doing the same thing—a way of saying, "I'm part of this too." The physical and the digital blend seamlessly with each other, and they meet on online social networks.

Traditional institutions of power are adapting to digitized efforts, and the limits of what many networked movements have been able to achieve are becoming apparent. Years after the marches in Ferguson, many of its leading local protesters have been arrested and a number have even died at unusually young ages, suggesting the weight of stress and trauma. Others, such as Ramsey Orta, the man who filmed the video of Eric Garner, face regular harassment from police.[5] Across the United States, Blue Lives Matter laws have emerged to designate attacks on police officers (frequently dressed in dark blue uniforms) as a hate crime, thus increasing the potential consequences for anyone charged with this crime.[6] Counterprotesters have utilized such chants as "White lives matter" to repurpose the original phrase, most notably during a white supremacist rally in Charlottesville, Virginia, in 2017.[7]

Meanwhile in Hong Kong, Umbrella Movement activists have made a concerted attempt to occupy local seats of power by founding Demosistō (香港眾志), a prodemocracy political party. Nathan Law, a leader in the Umbrella Movement, became the youngest person elected to the Legislative Council in 2016.[8] He was eventually disqualified from office after a government lawsuit and, later, he was sentenced to months in jail for his activities in the movement, alongside Joshua Wong and Alex Chow. Their sentences were dropped eventually, but it came with a price: more stringent laws against civil disobedience throughout the territory.[9] At the same time, the general public started expressing discontent with the movement overall, and opposition groups have spread the color blue as a symbolic color of their own, reflecting support for the police, and the color red, supporting mainland China.[10]

Movements today are perhaps more complicated and open-ended than ever before. That the most creative aspects of social media culture have become so widespread within protest movements and their corresponding countermovements reflects the major role that digital culture plays in the twenty-first century. How the creative side of the internet is transforming these movements—and others like it—raises questions about whether the internet can really lead to positive social change, or whether it's simply encouraging people's worst appetites for narcissism, isolationism, polarization, hate, and propaganda. The past few years have made these questions only more potent.

ON JANUARY 20, 2017, I took the bus from New York City to Washington, DC, for what would be two major events in contemporary American history. The first, occurring that day, was the inauguration of Donald Trump, the first American president to come to office without any prior political experience, riding a wave of populist interest fanned by his now infamous use of Twitter and misogynistic, xenophobic rhetoric. Protests organized by such groups as #J20 Protest and Inaugurate the Resistance swept DC and much of the nation, while supporters like Bikers for Trump organized their own actions.[11] The second event, the Women's March, occurred the next day, centered in Washington, DC, with sister marches in such major cities as Chicago, Los Angeles, and Boston, along with smaller cities like Charleston, Virginia, and Nashville, Tennessee, and international ones including Southampton, England, and Berlin, Germany.[12] It was the largest protest in American history, with more than three million demonstrators across the United States.[13] Inauguration attendees at the National Mall in Washington donned bright-red baseball caps, hoodies, and T-shirts. "Make America Great Again" these items read, reflecting the unforgettable slogan of the Trump candidacy. The hat in particular became an icon, visible from above during rallies and on election night, and in countless red-hatted profile pictures posted online. The slogan frequently appeared on social media in acronym form as #MAGA, uniting supporters via social media as a rallying cry and an identity marker.

Many Women's March attendees donned knitted pink hats with little triangle ears on top. Each pink hat looked different, with slightly different shades of pink and slightly different materials and shapes. That's because the hats were made by countless individuals, many of whom were women, who gathered in knitting circles in the weeks and months before the Women's March. There was no one hat, no one hat style, but a general shape and form. The pink hats were "pussyhats," the brainchild of Krista Suh and Jayna Zweiman. As Suh noted in a talk at Barnard College, she wanted to reclaim the word "pussy."[14] Just months before, a recording of Donald Trump, talking backstage on the set of the *Days of Our Lives* soap opera, had leaked online: "And when you're a star, they let you do it. You can do anything," he said to a TV personality. "Grab 'em by the pussy. You can do anything."[15] On Inauguration Day and the day of protests that followed it, countless selfies of people in red MAGA hats and pink pussyhats flooded social media feeds. Each selfie was slightly different—sometimes in a group, sometimes in solitude; sometimes on the streets, sometimes at home; people of many genders, races, and ages. But the symbolism was the same and—for better or for worse—became a feature of the protests and a signal to supporters and the broader community: this is who I am, and this is what I stand for.

The symbolism was even more vividly represented in the signs people carried at the protest marches. At the Women's March, I stood in the middle of the

National Mall with a camera. I was documenting the signs people carried, and I came across one referencing the infamous This Is Fine dog. The dog, created by comic artist KC Green, casually sips coffee while surrounded by flames. "This is fine," the dog says in the original. "I'm okay with the events that are unfolding currently." As the comic progresses, the dog is engulfed in flames, its body melting and eyes bulging, a victim of its blithe optimism. In the sign I photographed, the dog took on a further iteration: he had become the newly inaugurated US president, Donald Trump, and as he sipped coffee, the White House was engulfed in flames. Another was honey badger, a meme sparked by a 2011 viral video claiming the honey badger's badassness. "Honey badger don't care," declares "Randall," the video's maker.[16] One woman wrote on a protest sign, "This honey badger gives a shit." Another image I spotted was the Nope Octopus, made famous in a GIF as it hops away quickly, saying, "Nope Nope Nope Nope," part of a larger internet vernacular of saying "Nope" to something you disagree with.[17] As if speaking in unison, groups of people carried Nope signs, which looked just like the original GIF and other memes circulating online.

The two days of red and pink hats and witty signs were just a microcosm of a larger phenomenon: memes are everywhere. It's difficult to overstate the spread of memes in all corners of life: from the streets to the offices of our political leaders, from the Right to the Left, scribbled onto signs, stenciled on our streets, worn on our heads and posted back online. Internet memes are one of the newest creative forms, born of digital culture and in dialogue with offline life, from such daily issues as complaining about a movie or cheering on sports teams to heavier issues about social justice and human rights. They draw on long human traditions of remix and remaking, from street art, hip-hop, and painting, manifested in a digitally connected world.

I think of an *internet meme* as a piece of online media that is shared and remixed over time within a community. Think of a funny picture of a cat being held up by its front legs, so it stretches out and looks quite long. (This is a real meme called Longcat, who is indeed long.)[18] Now imagine if someone else does the same thing with their cat. And someone else does too. And they share it with each other, and then someone else stitches them all together in Photoshop to create a team of three long cats. This is meme culture. Memes can be silly, they can be harmless, they can be destructive, they can be extremely serious, and they can be all these things at the same time. A meme is an invitation: "You can do this too." And in both Ferguson and Hong Kong, during the inauguration and during the Women's March, memes spread across borders and territories to involve much larger groups of people acting in solidarity than might previously have been possible.

I began writing about the internet's creative side in 2009 when I practiced digital performance art in New York City. I kicked off Art 2.1, a column on art and social media for *Art21*, a blog hosted by the popular PBS contemporary art series of the same name, and I've written pieces about newly breaking trends and compelling examples of social media art for *Hyperallergic*, a Brooklyn-based online art publication, where I continue to serve as an advisory editor.[19] Social media was seeping through the art world, and people were asking, "What does this mean for art? How can artists adapt their practices to this new creative platform? Can art on social media really be a thing?"

In 2009, I was the first invited artist by the Brooklyn Museum for the 1st Fans Twitter Art Feed, a series of commissioned performances on Twitter. I was interested in the history of communications technology, and so I used Twitter to post messages in Morse code.[20] It was an absurdist piece of sorts: why tweet using an outdated mode of technology? But at the time, Twitter was seen as a new milestone in communications technology, and I thought that by looking at the first telecommunications technology—the telegraph—we might be also able to learn a bit more about the future of technologies.

A few tweets into my monthlong performance piece, something happened: people started tweeting back in Morse code. And then they started tweeting to each other, also using Morse code, without involving me per se. I was removed entirely from the conversations. The project left my hands, and it turned into a (very small) meme, a networked practice cocreated by many. I was the artist and instigator, but I was no longer the sole creator of the piece. This fascinated me, and I founded an online artist collective called @Platea. *Platea* comes from the Latin word for "street," and in the Middle Ages, it also meant a "stage." It is the source of *plaza*, the Spanish word for public square. Our collective wanted to explore the power of public art in the digital streets of social media, and we created a series of projects that made art a collective, cocreated, and global practice on such platforms as Twitter, Facebook, Flickr, and Ravelry.

In 2011, I saw firsthand how this creative impulse can be a form of power in the face of traditional institutions of power. That year I had the privilege and honor of working at the Beijing studio of Chinese artist Ai Weiwei, an activist and artist who often spoke out against injustices in the country, even at the expense of his physical safety. Ai's internet art practice had first begun with blogs. He used blogs to talk about China and politics, but his continued exploration of sensitive issues led to internet censors taking down his blog in 2009.[21]

He later sought refuge in Twitter, where he quickly gained tens of thousands of followers. In China, local social media platforms are censored and Twitter is blocked, but he and many other Chinese people had found ways around the country's "Great Firewall" to access Western social media sites such as Twitter and Facebook. Ai created performance pieces on Twitter, like "Say Your Real Name," where he asked people to say their true name and where they lived.[22] This was an important action of visibility and courage, because so many internet users, aware of the gray area they occupied by using a site blocked in China, had pseudonyms so as to avoid government scrutiny. He offered T-shirts, documentaries, and even copies of his iconic porcelain sunflower seeds as a reward for participating.[23] It was the first of many online actions that Ai would spark and invite others to cocreate, and most important, it helped set a culture of creative action among his community, a culture that would soon help him in a profound way.

On April 3, 2011, Ai Weiwei was supposed to board a plane from Beijing to Hong Kong. But he never made it to the gate. While he was going through passport control, national security officials escorted him to a car and put a hood over his head, thus beginning an eighty-one-day illegal disappearance, one of hundreds the government was enacting in the wake of the Arab Spring, Occupy Wall Street, and nervousness that a fervor of activism might bleed over to China. This made many governments nervous, including China's, and hundreds of known activists were rounded up and detained, including Ai Weiwei.[24]

I woke up that day to chaos at the studio, as his Chinese assistants did their best to get the word out on social media. Their tweets made it to the broader world, but their posts to Chinese social networks were quickly censored. This is a common practice: in addition to disappearing activists, the government aims to remove mention of them from online platforms. It's a political practice as old as time—Roman leaders practiced *damnatio memoriae*, or an erasure of memory, when they sought to remove political enemies from history.[25] The Romans didn't have the internet.

Anyone who tried to talk about Ai Weiwei quickly found their words vanished, thanks to keyword search algorithms and human censors. They tried variations: "Ai Weilai" (爱未来), which means "Love the future," and "Tiger Cub Ai" (艾虎子), which in Chinese sounds like "Bearded Ai" (艾胡子). These rapid remixes aimed to stay one step ahead of censors, as concerned citizens made efforts to speak out about his disappearance. At the same time, the Fifty Cent Party, a team of internet commentators paid by the government, directed messages to Ai Weiwei supporters, including myself, pushing the idea that he had died of a heart attack while in custody.

Activists started to share pictures of sunflower seeds, a coded reference to his installation at the Tate Modern, which was a field of one hundred million porcelain sunflower seeds. People online transformed this food—a common snack in China—into a symbol for his release, and they posted a wide variety of photos, illustrations, and remixes of these seeds. Many corners of Chinese social media came to life around this ostensibly censored event, even when they couldn't use the words "Ai Weiwei" directly.[26]

Concerned supporters couldn't organize physically in China, but their use of the internet became a means to organize and show scale in a way that simply couldn't have been possible even just a few years prior. On the streets in other parts of the world, the global art community gathered outside Chinese embassies and advocated Ai's release. They sat in chairs peacefully outside the embassies in New York, Berlin, and London, among many other cities, and they made sure to leave an empty chair to symbolize and visualize his absence.[27] The action was a reference to the artist's seminal work, *1001 Chairs*, produced in 2007.[28] That year he gathered hundreds of chairs to represent 1,001 Chinese nationals whom he helped travel to Switzerland for Art Basel.

The memes and actions online even spilled over, quietly, into the streets of China. I saw portraits of Ai Weiwei's face in many parts of Hong Kong, where citizens had greater freedom for political expression, appearing as stencils and printed on paper strung up in the city. Even then, police tried to stop the spread of these images.[29] And as I wandered the streets of Beijing, I saw a few sunflower seeds stenciled on the walls of *hutong*, the famous alleyways at the heart of the city.

Eighty-one days after he was taken away, the artist was released under strict conditions—the government held on to his passport, and he was ordered to stay off social media. It was never made explicitly clear if the international pressure helped his cause, but some, such as Human Rights Watch's Phelim Kine, have argued it has.[30] Against government orders, Ai began tweeting a few months later and continued exploring internet-based provocations, such as live-streaming his home to the world as a response to the government's ongoing surveillance of his life.[31] He helped spark new memes, and his community responded with support. Four years later he would receive his passport back, and he moved to Berlin to set up a new studio.[32]

This experience raised more questions for me: What role do memes play in movements today? Why do people make so many of them? How do these seemingly simple media objects interface with other media, like blogs, television, and radio, and how do they engage such complex issues as the global refugee crisis, enforced disappearances, police brutality, and a rising tide of ethnosupremacy and nationalism? How can something so apparently ephemeral and frivolous support meaningful change? And can it be used to harm people too?

Five years after my work at Ai Weiwei's studio I stood in the middle of the newsroom at City University of New York as my colleagues and I watched the United States change on November 8, 2016. As director of product at Meedan, a technology company that builds tools for global journalists, I played a role in a journalistic project called Electionland, which focused on researching and reporting on voter issues on Election Day in the United States. We watched from the newsroom as it became increasingly clear that Donald Trump would be elected president of the United States. Shortly after the election, an international conversation about fake news came to the fore. What role had fabricated news sites and online propaganda played in disseminating false narratives about the candidates? What memes did people create—such as the idea that Hillary Clinton was gravely ill during the campaign—and how were these memes reinforced by media outlets and others?

The confusion and misinformation shared online reminded me so much of what I'd seen in China with the Fifty Cent Party. Whether it's being done deliberately as an act of political propaganda or through misunderstandings from people with good intentions, the effect is similar: Americans are quickly beginning to distrust traditional news institutions and anything they've heard on social media. Many have turned to the silos of friends, family, and niche media for their news diets, and it's become increasingly more difficult to build a single national narrative. In these environments, internet memes spreading misinformation are much easier to generate. And amid the confusion, the real policy issues can often be missed.

By necessity, this book takes a global and intersectional approach. In the coming pages I'll take a closer look at meme culture in such places as China, the United States, Uganda, and Mexico as case studies in memetic strategies in highly different contexts. I focus on China and the United States because these two countries have such radically different internet environments, and their citizens face such different issues. I also look at a selection of countries in the Global South, which are frequently overlooked in international media discourse due to linguistic and economic barriers, along with long-running postcolonial narratives that reinforce images of dysfunction and poverty. Citizens in these countries are swiftly coming online, and they face challenges with visibility on the global stage and basic connectivity in their local environments.

Many have written about the legal and technical aspects of the internet in facilitating or hampering social change, and there is a substantial body of literature about the societal role of the internet. Others have written about the power of the internet in developing skills and resources for enacting meaningful change. While touching on these aspects, this book aims to be a complement, looking specifically at the creative media that people create and share online, and how these media objects in turn help fuel fundamental aspects of contemporary social movements. Photo remixes, selfies, YouTube songs, hashtag jokes—this is the "silly" stuff of meme culture, and the focus of this book is how the silly and the serious are deeply intertwined.

I'm not aiming for a comprehensive, detailed history of memes in social movements, nor do I hope to offer a guidebook for movements more broadly. And while I try to discuss historic moments, I am not myself a historian. Rather, I examine the role of internet culture in a handful of movements in these localities as a way of helping shed light on broader issues and helping us refine the questions we ask about communicating today. As a rule, I only write about movements that I've observed in person in some way, because I believe the digital and physical must inform each other, but I turn a lot to primary and secondary sources to help understand what I've seen. I do my best to get the details of movements in this book correctly, but this is always a bit of a fraught exercise, as I am an outside observer to almost all of them. Any errors in representation are mine and mine alone. There are a number of important memes in movements—Occupy in the US, the Green Movement in Iran, violence against the Rohingya in Myanmar, the conflict in Syria and ISIS's global propaganda efforts, Idle No More in Canada, Ni Una Menos in Argentina and Latin America, the global #MeToo movement, and Fees Must Fall in South Africa—that I don't discuss, along with movements just emerging as I work on this book. That said, I take a global perspective because the internet is global in reach, and its global impacts have been uneven. Some places and issues are starting to manifest the potential for truly transformational change, and others have been swiftly crushed or co-opted. Asking why can help us understand what makes memetic activism effective and also where its weaknesses might need to be supplemented by other efforts.

You don't have to spend much time on the internet to know that it's changed society. Every purchase you make online, every television show that quotes social media, every corny joke forwarded to you by your great-uncle is made possible because of the internet. Many modern conveniences simply couldn't be possible without the networking and communications capacities that the internet enables. We shop, we read, we pay our bills, we find jobs, all thanks to the internet. We also watch funny videos.

For some people—those who've long lacked access to media and voice in society—the internet has been so much more than a medium for convenience. It's become a medium for expression, a place to write blog posts, share selfies, join in on hashtags, craft puns, and make memes. The same dynamic that helps cat videos and dancing babies go viral can also help push new perspectives and narratives, as people find their creative voice and join a chorus of others online and offline.

Memes are the street art of the social web, and, like street art, they are varied, expressive, and complex, and they must contend with the existing politics of our public spaces. Sometimes this is silly, sure. And that's pretty wonderful. Not so wonderful is that meme culture often reinforces the powerful, with sometimes terrifying efficiency. But sometimes, memes help make transformative, positive changes to society. This book is one small way to make sense of all this.

CHAPTER 1

■ ■ ■ ■ ■ ■ ■

THE REVOLUTION
OF THE CAT

"To begin with," said the Cat, "a dog's not mad. You grant that?"

"I suppose so," said Alice.

"Well, then," the Cat went on, "you see, a dog growls when it's angry, and wags its tail when it's pleased. Now *I* growl when I'm pleased, and wag my tail when I'm angry. Therefore I'm mad."

"I call it purring, not growling," said Alice.

"Call it what you like," said the Cat.

—*Alice's Adventures in Wonderland*[1]

CATS SEEM TO HAVE A KNACK for wandering into our technological revolutions. Some ten thousand years ago, human societies in what is now the Middle East invented agriculture, the ability to plant, harvest, and store grains and other foods. For millennia before then, most human societies were hunter-gatherers, wandering from place to place seeking food. This ability to store grains laid the groundwork for a different form of civilization, one based on cities and social classes, where a ruling elite could centralize its power over a working class. This led to new systems of inequality and arguably spurred the development of math and writing (to create ledgers and records), new forms of trade, and new forms of military might.

It was around this time that the great ancestor of the domestic house cat poked its head into a granary, eyes wide, whiskers quivering, tail flicking back and forth sharply. It sprang forth suddenly and pounced on a rodent nibbling on grains. From then on, feline and human society became forever intertwined, though the relationship has long been uneasy. Of all domestic mammals, cats hold a distinction for having chosen us and never quite being tamed—they could not care less that we're around, but we have long cared that they are.[2]

When I talk to people about internet memes, I often turn to cats. While cats don't rule the entire global web, they certainly occupy a major chunk of it, and almost everyone has seen and can remember a particular cat meme. Some cat memes are politicized, but many are shared simply for their hilarity. I have seen cat GIFs popping up on the Chinese web, with the same level of funniness and fuzziness as in the United States, and cat videos are said to roam Russia and much of the European Union too.

Which begs the question: why cats? Why does cat media appear to be so dominant on the web? This may seem to be a silly question, but looking at cat memes on the internet will illuminate deeper issues about the role of creative media online, and why this matters for socially engaged netizens. Cats, both deadly predators and cutesy snugglers, are a perfect symbol for how memes operate: erratic, unpredictable, and yet somehow attractive, they embody the free-spirited nature of the internet, which sometimes brings cuddles and sometimes brings claws. More than simply "a-mew-sing," they are key to illustrating how and why internet media gives voice to so many.

THE POPULAR HOUSE CAT HAS HAD A LONG, historical relationship with humans, including most famously with the ancient Egyptians. As cat historian Donald W. Engels has noted, the cat was a relative newcomer to our domesticated creatures, and it occupied a new sphere.[3] Dogs helped us hunt, cows and pigs provided food, and camels carried our loads. And as humanity began coming together in fixed settlements, cats kept away smaller creatures that could be found around the home. For centuries in Western culture, cats have represented freedom and, to a certain extent, women and femininity. Famously, they don't come when called, and their wandering, unpredictable nature reflects a freer spirit than the loyal dog, beasts of burden like donkeys, and livestock like sheep and cows. Roman motifs show women playing with cats, and an early Greek coin from 700 BC shows the founder of a Greek city-state dangling a piece of string above a playful cat.[4] The common motif is strikingly similar to all the GIFs of cats jumping and playing on the internet. Indeed, the roaming, freewheeling cat embodies Epicurean values of freedom and pleasure seeking, the opposite of more restrained Stoicism.

But despite these rosy beginnings in their relationship with humans, domestic house cats have also faced substantially more invisibility and stigma than dogs. The Chinese zodiac has a year of the dog but no year of the cat among the twelve animals (though there is a tiger year, to be fair). The lucky cat—the ceramic creature with a raised paw that's popular in many East Asian restaurants—may be a popular icon today, but cats were just as likely in medieval Japan to be depicted as evil, grinning beasts.[5] Regal Fu dogs guard the emperor's dwellings in the Forbidden City, and lions, phoenixes, and dragons occupy noble space in the Chinese canon of creatures. But the mighty house cat gets nary a mention.

Cats are also one of the few species in history to face religious persecution. During the horrors of the Spanish Inquisition and the subsequent witch hunts, the cat population in Europe took a serious plunge when they were made guilty by association with anyone, especially women, practicing pagan religion. Writing in *The Toast*, journalist Gabrielle Loisel offered an extensive view of cats in Western society, dubbing them "The Devil in Disguise." In 1484, Pope Innocent VIII excommunicated all cats, and a mass slaughtering of felines began in Western Europe. The scale of devastation was so vast that some speculate the bubonic plague erupted as a result of all the rats that could suddenly run free in cities, where they spread the disease-bearing fleas with them.[6] This stigma emerged again during the Salem witch trials, as witches were said to make their victims purr like cats; and as urban legend goes, no purely black cats exist anymore, as all were hunted to death.[7]

Cats took a second, albeit more moderate, dive in the United States in the 1950s, as the pragmatism and loyalty of dogs took center stage shortly after World War II. In the *Leave It to Beaver* era, such television shows as *Lassie* and the movie *Old Yeller* confirmed the adage that the dog is man's best friend. This was the decade that Monopoly introduced the Scottie dog piece, a symbol of an upper-class upbringing.[8] Later down the road, comic strips like *Heathcliff* and *Garfield* painted cats as mischievous troublemakers and their owners as neurotic losers like John Arbuckle or, as with *Cathy*, as crazy cat ladies. These are not isolated incidents: writing in *Slate*, Daniel Engber pointed out that canines have, for centuries, dominated printed literature, at a ratio of two to one with cats.[9] Before the internet, dogs were simply more represented in all media—and usually in a positive light. One might argue that there was a dog media hegemony, or at least a preponderance of canines in popular media at the expense of cat representation.

Why is that? It's complicated, but owning a dog is a public act, and institutions and media in Western culture have long supported dog lovers and their obsessions. Dog people typically have public parks and public streets, while cats have generally remained indoors or, when they do go outside, they are elusive and difficult to spot. The Westminster Kennel Club Dog Show and other such contests display the very best of dogs' nature: obedient, friendly, coordinated, and outgoing. They are loyal companions trained to hunt prey and protect human beings, and they are memorialized for their service to humanity in statues: Balto in New York's Central Park, a sled dog who delivered crucial medical supplies to head off a diphtheria outbreak in Alaska in the 1920s, and Greyfriars Bobby in Edinburgh, Scotland, who, according to legend, stayed loyally by his master's grave for years after his passing.[10]

Owning a cat, on the other hand, is more of a private act. Yes, there are cat shows akin to Westminster, but they present cats as docile, quiet, and aloof, a far cry from the buzzy eyes and frenetic jumping that characterize the typical cat video. This silliness is something most cat owners see only in their homes. More often than not, cats tend to hide when strangers visit. So much of the joy that cats bring comes only in quiet, tender moments—waking up to one sitting on your chest and purring in your ear, or coming home from a stressful day to one rubbing against your leg and curling up in your lap. Then there are the kookier moments, like when they peep their heads around a corner or jump into random boxes.

As those early Greek and Roman motifs suggest, people have long had fun with their pet cats, but before we had access to low-cost cameras, it would have been too costly for the average person to capture those moments. Cat lovers have always privately celebrated them but had no way to recreate those experiences of feline joy for others. By and large, portraits of cats before the twenty-first century show them with a quiet precision, literally showing cats at their most docile rather than their most expressive. These days, however, cat lovers can document first and think later. They can whip out their camera when their cats are zipping around the house and zoom in to capture all the strange facial expressions these critters are known to make.

This matters because cat memes represent the intersection of felines with a new technological revolution: the way media is made, remixed, and distributed. Photos and videos have historically served to document the world around us or to provide aesthetic experiences. This makes sense when one thinks of these forms of media as created by dedicated professionals at great cost. Media objects once took much longer to create and even longer to distribute, so they were left in the hands of people well trained to make them. Over the past two decades, however, with the proliferation of smartphones and the ability to share pictures quickly on a social platform like the internet, media also serves a communicative and social purpose, a way to bond with others. And with that comes more expressive uses of media.

Cat photos, cat GIFs, cat videos, cat songs, and other media all celebrate the feline. The influential internet meme site I Can Has Cheezburger is named for the popular Happy Cat, which is a happy-looking cat with bold text around it who is asking, "I can has cheezburger?"[11] According to Know Your Meme, a leading meme indexing site in the United States, the origins of Happy Cat are murky at best, likely first appearing on a user forum called "Something Awful," and its motivations for asking for said "cheezburger" unclear.[12] But it was enormously popular in early cat meme culture. Indeed, some iconic mascots of the internet have invariably been feline: the Pop Tart–bodied Nyan Cat, the permanently upset (and ever adorable) Grumpy Cat, the baby-faced Lil Bub, Brother Cream in Hong Kong, the gray animated Pusheen.[13] The Internet Defense League, a coalition of technology organizations dedicated to protecting internet freedom, set up a "cat signal" that people could embed on their sites to serve as a beacon for assistance when legislators might be considering laws that limit the internet.[14]

Cat images are an example par excellence of an internet meme. The word "meme" was coined by Richard Dawkins in his seminal 1978 work *The Selfish Gene*. The basic idea is that human cultural practices—tying one's hair in a ponytail versus tying it in intricate braids, wearing watches versus wearing extensive bangles, or holding racist views—spread like biological genes. Some memes take hold of the public's mind, proliferate quickly, and along the way morph and shift to the sender's viewpoints. The word "meme" picked up steam later in the 1970s, as Dawkins's work sparked an entire field, called *memetics*, to study these phenomena. The scholarship about memes is long and varying, with heated debates about what, exactly, constitutes a meme. Suffice to say, if you've ever sung the "Happy Birthday" song or clicked your tongue to show disapproval, you've participated in a meme. A meme, in other words, is a unit of culture.

Academia took hold of the word and used it for years, but it remained largely dormant in public discourse for decades until the internet rolled around. At that point, as scholar Limor Shifman has argued, it started taking on a new meaning. In her book *Memes in Digital Life*, one of the first academic texts on the subject of memes, Shifman says that internet memes should be seen in a specific light, treating them almost separately from the original Dawkins sense of the word. Internet memes have three key characteristics, and I find her view a helpful summary of how internet memes operate:

1. *"Internet memes are digital objects. They share common characteristics of content, form, and/or stance."* Think about remixes of the Nyan Cat Pop-Tart form: all of these memes are digital, and they share some basic characteristics. Each cat looks generally happy, while one has sunglasses, another has an Afro, and yet another is pink instead of gray.

2. *"Internet memes are created with awareness of each other."* All the Nyan Cat variations work because they (or their makers, at least) are shared in a milieu of mutual visibility. This is important: internet memes are often highly visible practices shared among internet communities. If a "meme" hits the internet but no one sees it, it's not quite a meme.

3. *"Internet memes are circulated, imitated, and/or transformed via the internet by many users."* Shifman's definition makes a key distinction between a meme and an object that simply goes viral. If a cat video gets shared widely and clocks one million views, it's clearly gone viral. If people imitate or transform it and add their own versions, they've made an internet meme.[15]

Shifman's definition is quite comprehensive. Another definition I find useful comes from Amanda Brennan, who serves as a meme librarian at Tumblr (yes, that's her official role): "Pieces of content that travel from person to person and change along the way."[16]

Internet scholar Kate Miltner, who wrote her master's thesis at the London School of Economics on the topic of LOLCats, or funny cat images, explored the serious side of these media, namely, their intricate cultural practices and implications for how internet communities operate. "I found that when it came to LOLCats," Miltner noted, "sharing and creating were often different means to the same end: making meaningful connections with others."[17] "Fundamentally," she argued, "people engaged with LOLCats for their own entertainment and to make meaningful connections with others" in pairs or in larger communities.[18] Indeed, as she observed, LOLCat language has its own grammar, with an internal logic.

This social role might seem silly (cats? really?), but its effects have been profound for the cat lovers among us. When the internet came along, social media platforms enabled cat owners to find each other and thereby break what sociologists call *pluralistic ignorance*—the mistaken belief by a group that their beliefs are not shared by their peers.[19] Pluralistic ignorance was more likely to occur before the internet, because the outlets for expression for the average person were limited. If you didn't see a cat peeping out your neighbor's window, how could you know he had an orange tabby with big green eyes? If your coworker carefully brushed off the fur from her dress each morning before work, how would you know she let her cat sit on her lap while she ate breakfast?

As internet theorist and *New York Times* columnist Zeynep Tufekci has noted, the expressive, symbolic value of online actions should not be underestimated:

> The rise of online symbolic action—clicking on 'Like' or tweeting about a political subject—though long derided as 'slacktivism,' may well turn out to be one of the more potent impacts from digital tools in the long run, as widespread use of such semi-public symbolic micro-actions can slowly reshape how people make sense of their values and their politics.[20]

This happens thanks to the community building afforded by internet expression and, by extension, how these forms of expression challenge pluralistic ignorance. This is no small feat; in Tufekci's assessment, it's "perhaps [the internet's] greatest contribution to social movements."[21]

After pluralistic ignorance is broken, new norms of behavior and belief can start to form through regular repetition and affirmation of messages—a process called *synchronization of opinion*.[22] What cat lovers had long faced was a powerful stigma. Men who loved cats were considered less than masculine and women who loved cats were considered spinsters. Curiosity kills cats, who shouldn't be nosing around other people's business. Cats get your tongue, keeping you from speaking. Fat cats take all your money. And when cats are away, mice can come out to play. All variety of negative connotations and idioms have historically been associated with cats in the English-speaking world. But thanks to the internet, the cat, you might say, is now out of the bag: cats are awesome, and that message is repeated, and thereby reinforced, quite frequently. The narrative changed.

It's not that no one loved cats before the internet—far from it, in fact. Millions of Americans have owned cats, and, based on sheer numbers of animals, Americans have owned more cats than dogs, making them the number two pet in the country after fish. Thanks to the internet, for the first time in history literally millions of cat lovers realized they were not alone, and, pretty soon, they realized that their collective meows were strong. And this is key: our love for cats was always there. The internet just gave that love an avenue for expression.

As it turns out, cat videos and images are no more common than dog ones. Jason Eppink, a curator at the Museum of the Moving Image, found that, together, media about these animals rarely exceeds 0.3 percent.[23] Exploring this in the popular exhibit *How Cats Took Over the Internet* (in which my research collective, the Civic Beat, took part), Eppink noted that it only *seems* that cats have taken over the internet. I think of this as the "Internet Cat Fallacy": members of a once-invisible community begin expressing their views, and it seems as if they have taken over the entire internet. They haven't; cats have simply claimed their place in a media environment that's long favored dogs.

The Internet Cat Fallacy proves that cat media isn't at all dominant on the internet—just that there's more of it now than before the internet existed. And so instead of asking "Why are there so many cats on the internet," one should really be asking "Why wasn't there as much cat media before the internet?" To answer this question is to tell the story of hegemonic media environments and how our relationship to these environments has been transformed by the twin powers of social media platforms and lower-cost access to media-making tools, like cameras and image editors.

It's highly doubtful, of course, that a pro-dog lobby was keeping cat videos from surfacing widely. That said, the fact remains that canine images and stories have long dominated our media environments, from those first dog paintings and statues that memorialized master and beast straight on to print and broadcast media. But then the internet enabled the cat lovers of the world to show that, yes, there are a lot of us, thank you very much, and furthermore, there's nothing at all wrong with that.

In 2011, fifty years after Scottie Dog started traipsing around Boardwalk and Park Place, Monopoly introduced the cat piece.[24] Before 2011, Animal Planet hosted only one show about domestic cats. Today, its cat and dog programming is roughly equal.[25] In one striking finding, Google X lab computers looked at ten million videos on YouTube in order to be trained to better recognize images. Due to the sheer number of cat videos available, the systems started to recognize cat faces above all else.[26] As cats have led the way, so has an entire fleet of cute animals, from baby goats to chinchillas to tiny rabbits. Flat-faced dogs that have been bred solely as companions, like pugs and French bulldogs, now have their own online communities of lovers alongside the more traditional hunting favorites like spaniels and hounds.

In this media diversity, it's not that the functional, heroic dog has toppled but that the media environment has *made room* for more fuzzy creatures in our lives. This is part of how the internet operates: making space for other groups and perspectives. Many of the fuzzy creatures popular on the internet now won't save a child from drowning or deliver needed medicines. They won't tell you when a strange individual is trying to get into the house or join you at the office for Bring Your Dog to Work Day. But they will be utterly quirky, strangely neurotic, wholly adorable companions who will bring you joy.

The silliness of cats may seem a world away from the seriousness of politics today, but the leap is never far. In the spring of 2016, as the United Kingdom considered "Brexit" (for "British exit"), a referendum that would legally remove the country from the European Union, a curious meme began trending on social media, especially Twitter: #CatsAgainstBrexit.[27] People posted pictures of their cats in various poses: curled up; pawing at the camera; looking wistfully outside the window; hiding in the sink. The meme started a few days before the referendum when UK academic Lilian Edwards posted her tabby looking forlorn and said, "My cat is sad because #Brexit. If you agree RT w[ith] your cat."[28] RT they did, hundreds of times, and many more began posting their own cats. A few days after #CatsAgainstBrexit hit social media feeds, citizens of the United Kingdom came together for the referendum on June 23, 2016. #CatsForBrexit also emerged, though it numerically had less popularity. Some posts reflected sincere support for Brexit while others included satirical quips that compared

Britons' desire to exit the EU to cats' desire to leave the house. After meowing and meowing repeatedly to leave the EU, the jokes went, they would end up just wanting to go back in. It's a joke only a cat owner could fully understand.

By a razor-thin margin, the United Kingdom voted to exit the European Union. The referendum revealed a country divided politically, and the reactions online were just as strong. As I wandered the streets of London the day after the referendum, I saw dour faces all around—most of the city had voted to remain— and their voices on social media reflected their thoughts.[29] #CatsAgainstBrexit couldn't stop the exit vote—much larger forces than memes influence how people in a democracy vote. But in the days after the referendum, many "remain" voters online continued to rally around their cats.

Why cats? Why dogs? Why are there so many darn animals on the internet, and what business do they have discussing politics? There's a simple answer: people own cats and people own dogs, and so it's natural that we take photos of them and share them on the internet. Human beings are complex creatures, capable of holding thoughts that are both serious and silly at the same time, and pretty soon, we start using animal images to talk about serious political issues. Internet memes help create space for conversation, whether that's about domestic pets marginalized in mainstream media or political viewpoints that are not regularly considered or made visible.

And herein lies the revolution of the cat: media at the margins moved closer to the center, revealing what was, in so many ways, always there to begin with. Taken in the context of a hegemonic media environment that has historically favored dogs, the rise of the cat on the internet can be seen as presaging the rise of citizen creative media and memetic expression for social change advocates and communities around the world. If one reads the tea—er, catnip—leaves, the creative culture that birthed cat videos, GIFs, image macros, and other media phenomena signals a shift in people's orientations to the media environments they had inherited. An obsession and practice that was once private—humans' love for cats—was revealed to be a lot more widespread than previously believed. Media that were once difficult and expensive to create were, with the help of technology, placed in the hands of millions to do with as they wished, and they now had the means to share their creations globally at a scale unique in history.

Importantly, technology has helped people create and share cat videos more easily, but they have become popular because we made them so. Their popularity has continued thanks to dedicated communities that amplify messages and support each other. These communities create a pipeline for participation that extends beyond the meme itself and into media environments like television shows and magazines, where new narratives have been built. Publishers and merchandisers have profitably come on board with celebrity cats and their owners, and opposition groups have tried to tamp down the spread of cat videos, equating them with a dumbing down of our culture. All the while, the culture continues to shift as cats become a regular part of discourse, with a steadily shrinking stigma.

As New York University technology theorist Clay Shirky has observed, the smallest, silliest creative act is still a creative act.[30] It's easy to dismiss cat videos as low culture, but their very accessibility is a transformative change from media consumption to media creation and public sharing. In his book *Here Comes Everybody*, Shirky notes that "We now have communications tools that are flexible enough to match our social capabilities, and we are witnessing the rise of new ways of coordinating action that take advantage of that change. . . . [We] are living in the middle of a remarkable increase in our ability to share, to cooperate with one another, and to take collective action, all outside the framework of traditional institutions and organizations."[31] And indeed early creative explorations, whether cats or otherwise, are often people's first step—a simple step, to be sure—in engaging with media critically and creatively. While we are learning to make and share cat videos with one another, we are learning to make and share media that better reflects our own values and perspectives.

This can start simply, as with the collective voice of the American internet, which in the late 1990s and early 2000s was largely white and middle class.[32] Through networked creativity, that internet population told a world that celebrated canines that felines are just as amazing. And as cat videos have expanded the media environment that celebrates the American canon of pets, so do other creative acts by citizens. After we've had a little practice with cat videos, it doesn't take long till we realize we can make videos about anything else, too, and get those out into the world for a community to find. And therein lies the revolution.

CHAPTER 2

. . . .

ALL ABOUT THE FEELS

The contemporary Internet was designed, in no small part, for the dissemination of cute pictures of cats.

—Ethan Zuckerman[1]

WHEN YOU THINK OF MOVEMENTS AND THE INTERNET, you might think of strategies and theories of change. But the internet is also awash with "feels," American internet slang for "feelings," and memes are like vectors of feels that help people find and affirm each other. The ease of sharing memes and their lightweight nature allow them to act as signals of identity and belief. This can be as simple as saying, "I like cats," and as complex as saying, "I believe in dismantling the racist power structures upon which society is built." Or it can be somewhere in between, as in, "I find this political candidate most compelling."

Through easy repetition, memes can become a constant stream of affirmation. Often taking the form of humor, memes help us laugh through extremely difficult times, on issues ranging from illegal disappearances to internet censorship. But not all memes are funny, and more important than humor is that they can be remixed and reshaped, imbued with the personality of the maker. Meme culture is inherently social. It says, "You can do this too, and here's a whole community of us doing this. You're not alone."

HOIST HIGH THE PROFILE PICTURE

Joe is running through the halls with a rainbow flagged
[sic] tied on like a cape high fiving everyone.

—@JillBidenVeep (parody account)[1]

ON JUNE 26, 2015, my internet feeds exploded with rainbows. The US Supreme Court ruled 5–4 that marriage equality is a constitutionally supported right for all people, and people had feels about that.[2] I logged on to various social media platforms and came across a funny comic. A gender-nonspecific cartoon character was leaning back from a computer as a ray of rainbowed light burst forth from the screen and engulfed the character's face in colors. Everywhere I looked online after the Supreme Court's judgment was announced, people's profile photos were overlaid with the rainbow flag, placed on top of their faces in celebration. Friends were sharing rainbows everywhere. It has become routine to show one's support and advocacy for a wide variety of organizations and causes by adding a colored overlay or sticker to social media. That happened after marriage equality was affirmed. The significance was especially resonant given the historic moment, and I and others took pictures and shared them online, amid the chorus of both digital and physical flags in social media and the physical world.

Rainbow flags have graced the streets of many United States cities long before the internet, most famously in San Francisco's Castro District, where a giant rainbow flag flies over the iconic gay neighborhood. San Francisco Board of Supervisors member Harvey Milk, the first openly gay politician to be elected in a major US city, encouraged artist Gilbert Baker to create a flag to represent their community.[3] Baker designed it in 1978, and he sought to generate a fresh new symbol, as he noted in an interview with the Museum of Modern Art:

> It was necessary to have the Rainbow Flag because up until that we had the pink triangle from the Nazis—it was the symbol that they would use [to denote gay people]. It came from such a horrible place of murder and holocaust and Hitler. We needed something beautiful, something from us. The rainbow is so perfect because it really fits our diversity in terms of race, gender, ages, all of those things.[4]

The creation of the flag also happened to fall near the ten-year anniversary of the Stonewall riots, which began on June 28, 1969, in response to a police raid on Stonewall Inn, a popular gay bar in New York City.[5] The riots drew increased national attention to LGBTQ rights and played a key role in sparking the modern LGBTQ rights movement. Since then, the flag has fluttered during Pride parades and outside establishments catering to gay, lesbian, bisexual, and transgender people. In a world without the internet, this was one of the most effective ways to signal a simple message: "We're of like minds, and it is safe to be here." Over time, it also became a symbol of celebration, as Pride parades gradually shifted from somber movements to include celebratory gatherings.

Several decades later, in 2008, the flag was flown prominently in cities like San Francisco and Los Angeles, where people of the same gender celebrated California's first official same-sex marriages. The mayor of San Francisco, a city that has been a longtime bastion of the queer community in the United States, even officiated a number of these weddings. The momentum for gay marriage across the state of California seemed strong, but by November 2008, that momentum seemed to come to a screeching halt. That month, many people in the United States were celebrating that the country had elected its first African American president in a landslide, as Democratic candidate Barack Obama swept the nation on a message of hope and change. However, while California had predictably gone "blue" and voted for Obama, the in-state propositions, or proposed laws and policies that citizens could vote on, had mixed results. One proposition in particular drew national attention: Proposition 8, which sought, by way of a constitutional amendment, to ban gay marriage and preserve the legal notion that marriage is between one man and one woman.

On the same day that Obama won the presidential election, Proposition 8 passed by six hundred thousand votes. Though Obama had won the state with 60 percent of the vote, 52 percent of Californian voters chose to ban gay marriage permanently in the state that day.[6] Despite what had been growing support for gay marriage in the country, many Californians had been blindsided by the more organized actions for Proposition 8, which used traditional door-to-door organizing, galvanizing supporters in counties likely to lean a little more to the conservative side of the issue.[7]

A few months after the election, photographer Adam Bouska and his partner, Jeff Parshley, started a photography campaign in response to Proposition 8, and they wanted to do something that might have greater reach than California. Social media seemed to be a likely answer, but it wasn't clear what would work. Twitter was still nascent then, and Obama had just over one hundred thousand followers, which at the time was considered large.[8] Facebook, while increasingly popular, barely had two hundred million users, two million of whom followed the new president.[9] The iPhone was so new that the *Sex and the City* movie, which came out that year, featured a scene in which the show's star, Carrie Bradshaw, looked completely lost when trying to navigate its interface.

Bouska and Parshley used the slogan "NOH8," a combination of the 8 in Proposition 8 and a statement against antigay hatred: "No hate." They also developed an eye-catching square logo with the N, O, and H in black and the 8 in red. NOH8 was a phrase geared for the emerging culture of hashtags on Twitter—something short and simple to write on a T-shirt or, as it turns out, a face.[10] Bouska gathered friends, celebrities, and members of the queer community in different spots—his studio in West Hollywood, nightclubs, bars, and other places—to sit for a portrait. The format was simple: people showed up in white T-shirts, and they had a piece of duct tape placed on their mouths. Bouska and Parshley then drew "NOH8" on their cheeks. It was a classic studio session, but the specific format—a portrait that contained a political statement—was uniquely suited for social media.

The NOH8 Campaign, as their organization came to be called, began distributing the photos online and encouraging people to spread them on newish social media sites like Twitter, Tumblr, Facebook, and Second Life, a virtual world popular at the time. Bouska, already a well-established fashion photographer, was also able to drum up celebrity support, and the slickly designed logo readily lent itself to T-shirts, hats, and other visually distinct objects that would catch attention in public places. Celebrities could easily show their support for gay marriage while out in public without saying a word.

Celebrities pushing causes and disseminating them through their visage is nothing new. Indeed, the idea of celebrity endorsements is built on the idea that people who have been following famous people's careers are more likely to trust that person and what they say. In the network of voters in the United States, celebrities have long been important nodes who can promote a cause and help bring it into the mainstream. NOH8 was well suited for that.

But in 2008, social media allowed for more people, not just celebrities, to become mininodes. This was especially true on Twitter, where people could amass followers and retweet sentiments, but it was equally true on sites like Facebook, where more intimate conversations could occur. That's when I started noticing new profile pictures in my social media feeds. I'd seen people using their profile pictures before—for instance, by applying a sticker to their profile photos on a site like Twibbon.com, which allowed them to visually support such causes as HIV/AIDS awareness and environmental protection. NOH8 reached a new scale, and Bouska's stylistic choices made an impact. People who had sat for his photos didn't just upload their NOH8 portraits to an album; they changed their profile pictures entirely.

This was important: because the photos were so visually distinct, they sent a clear message to others. Like a celebrity wearing a T-shirt out in public while shopping for groceries, people could post about anything—their lunch, the kind of day they had, how difficult work is, and so forth—and still be making a statement to their circle of followers and friends, because their profile pictures appeared alongside each message. Each post reinforced the message, and when you saw many people in your network posting with that same image, you started to see a network of supporters. Even people who weren't able to sit for a portrait with Bouska could order a T-shirt or hat online, ask someone to take a photo, and then post it online. The NOH8 campaign swept Los Angeles and, eventually, the rest of California and the country. By 2009, West Hollywood declared December 13 a day of NOH8, in honor of the organization and values it promoted.[11]

I spoke with Brosnan Rhodes, a West Hollywood–based barista at the time who was one of the first people to receive a portrait from Bouska. "It was a statement to my community for what I stood for, and also to my family. It opened up a conversation with people who might not have thought about gay marriage before, or how Proposition 8 affected me."[12] Rhodes joined others in marching in the city, chanting, "No hate, no on 8," reinforcing the message in the streets. The chants, the profile pictures, the marches, the phone calls all contributed to breaking down the idea that few people supported the idea of gay marriage, and "No hate" was a key catchphrase.

As tends to happen, people's profile pictures eventually returned to normal, and the photo project faded from public view. This is natural. Life goes on, and we want to record other life moments, not all of them political. As with our lives on public streets, our lives in digital spaces reflect the many facets of who we are. The profile picture is often the most public visual expression of our digital personas. To this day you can still see T-shirts at protests bearing the phrase NOH8, which now stands for a much larger conversation beyond marriage equality and includes homophobia, transphobia, and other forms of hate. It helps to remember what steps were necessary in the days before the internet to learn whether someone you knew supported marriage equality. Rainbow flags were generally flown only by LGBTQ-identified people, but what about those who didn't identify as such? You would have to ask outright about someone's views on same-sex marriage, but brokering that sort of conversation was risky—what if the person disagreed with you? Memes filled in a vital gap, helping to indicate to queer and nonqueer people alike what you stood for.

Organizations supporting gay marriage and LGBTQ rights began strategizing their plans of action. Some took a cultural approach—spreading awareness and education through on-the-ground organizing and journalism. Others pushed for policy changes. Multiple states held referenda on gay marriage; some allowed it, some banned it, and others supported civil unions, a legal status that gave all the legal benefits of marriage without the name. On March 25, 2013, five years after Proposition 8, the US Supreme Court began hearing arguments regarding Proposition 8, and their ruling would affect marriage rights nationwide.[13] The Human Rights Campaign (HRC), the largest LGBT advocacy organization in the United States, asked people to change their profile pictures to a special red and white version of their logo, which was usually a blue background with a yellow equal sign. This was a typical strategy of the HRC: in previous legal battles over the years, they had distributed T-shirts, bumper stickers, and laptop stickers for people to signal their support. The profile photo tactic was an extension of that strategy. They released a Facebook app that allowed people to quickly change their profile picture to any of these logos, and they encouraged people to use the hashtags #time4marriage (to share their stories) and #UnitedforMarriage, which trended nationally on Twitter.[14]

Changing one's profile picture to support marriage equality was, of course, nothing new, but in terms of technology, a lot had changed since the original NOH8 Campaign in 2008. For one, the iPhone finally had a front-facing camera, following the lead from other smartphones that had added the feature. A culture of selfie taking and sharing had exploded on social networks, including on the relative newcomer Instagram, which had fun and, perhaps most important, flattering filters. People had a much easier way to take and upload photos, and a much easier way to make them look great. Meme culture had also taken hold in broader circles, thanks to the popularity of image-editing tools such as Adobe Photoshop and Microsoft Paint and the rise of Tumblr, Reddit, and similar networks, which encouraged sharing and remix.

The HRC's simple logo and text overlay created something that might be called a *memetic template*. It was easy to replicate, easy to edit, and easy to share again, all the while making it recognizable to others as inspired by the original. In place of a phrase like "I am a lesbian, and I support marriage equality," people could easily add their text. More important, people already had a fundamentally different mindset toward digital media than they had in 2008, and they had many more networks on which to share their creations. The HRC logo quickly began spreading as national attention turned toward the US Supreme Court hearing. The new red and white logo began showing up on people's profiles across multiple social media networks, and people took selfies overlaid with the logo. Delaware senator Chris Coons posted a red and pink logo on top of his profile picture on Facebook, and after Hillary Clinton announced her support, a number of people distributed a photo of her with the logo.[15]

Others got more creative. As LGBT writer Sean Kolodji described in the *Civic Beat Reader*, an online magazine on memes that I cofounded and ran briefly, one group distributed the logo with the Statue of Liberty French-kissing Lady Justice, referencing the iconic Alfred Eisenstaedt photograph *V-J Day in Times Square* of a sailor kissing a woman.[16] Some use the equal sign of the logo to create a smiley face, like this =), and they used it as the place where Princess Toadstool, a popular video-game character from the Mario Bros. franchise, and a lover would walk. When laid out like a zebra crossing, the logo was also perfect for having the Beatles walk over it, evoking their iconic 1969 album cover for *Abbey Road*. Two strips of bacon on a red background could easily recreate the logo, as could two crackers, two pairs of white jeans, and, yes, two white cats.

So what changed between 2008 and 2013? According to the HRC, the red and pink logo appeared more than eighteen million times in social media feeds, a reflection of growing support for marriage equality.[17] Part of this success can be attributed to the HRC's reach, with a multimillion dollar operating budget and a disciplined national campaign strategy. Part of this is timing, of course, as national attention had shifted to the Supreme Court hearings. There's also a little bit of luck. It's always difficult to predict when the next big meme will erupt on social media; though in retrospect, it's always clear that a variety of factors contributed.

Also, the success of the logo remixes and their spread can be attributed to people outside the LGBTQ community showing their support. As Kolodji said to me while he was preparing his compilation of memes, it was like a coming out party for straight people. The fun of the logo, and the fun of making and sharing remixes, was a simple way for many people to participate. It provoked conversations on Facebook and helped people show their support for a cause that they might have privately believed in but had few avenues to support publicly.

In offline campaigns a ribbon or bumper sticker serves as a symbol of solidarity tied to one's self and one's car (which in the United States is often an extension of one's self). In the twenty-first century, profile pictures often serve as people's most public self-expressions, making ourselves visible not just to those around us in geographic space but also to anyone in our social network who sees it, regardless of where they live. There's something special about observing someone, especially a queer person, watch these memes as they float through their social media feeds. People smile, they laugh, they are filled with joy, even for a brief moment.

From the outside, any one image looks small and fleeting. But for someone watching their community of friends and family sharing these images, the power is in the aggregate, in seeing the network and the community coming together for support. It's the same reason some of us raise rainbow flags in a neighborhood—we want to show what the community stands for and supports.

The impact is potentially greater when a loved one participates in the meme. The aggregate has the ability to boost people's emotions and, over time, even shift narratives in a powerful way.

In 1973, economist Mary Rowe posited the idea of a microaffirmation, the small, often subconscious show of support for a marginalized person: smiles and nods, looking them in the eye when they're speaking, verbally acknowledging their work. Rowe's theory built on earlier work by sociologist Chester Pierce, who had developed the concept of microaggressions, which are small actions that over time produce feelings of inequality among those being marginalized.[18] For a queer person, this might be as simple as hearing a hateful word such as "faggot" thrown around in casual discourse or being ignored by straight waitstaff at a restaurant. Each of these actions is hurtful, but none of them by themselves is overly significant. They are often fleeting and, in theory, could be readily forgotten and brushed off. It's the aggregate that matters. Each rainbow flag, each HRC logo, each NOH8 sticker serves as a microaffirmation; for a queer person, the overwhelming show of support can be extremely meaningful and powerful. By shaping the logos and flags and fusing them to their identities online, supporters send an important message not just about what they stand for but also about who they are as individuals: they are people who support marriage equality for all people.

On June 26, 2015, all the legal battles of the previous seven years reached a zenith, and the Supreme Court announced its ruling. A parody account of former vice president Joe Biden's wife, Jill Biden, @JillBidenVeep, tweeted, "Joe is running through the halls with a rainbow flagged tied on like a cape high fiving everyone."[19] The account added a few hashtags, including #LoveWins, which was the big hashtag of the day, as supporters around the country celebrated the historic and groundbreaking victory. Photoshopped images of Joe Biden wearing a rainbow flag as a cape circulated on social media, as did a wide variety of rainbows in other situations: the Apple logo bursting from a rainbow, Obama on a unicorn shooting rainbows out of his hands.

Acknowledging the power of the profile picture for this movement, Facebook officially rolled out a tool that made it simple for anyone to overlay the rainbow flag on their profile picture, and Facebook CEO Mark Zuckerberg posted a photo of himself as an example.[20] For each of these flags in digital space, there seemed to be more in physical space. The flag flew high throughout Pride marches across the country, as people handed them out, hung them from their car windows, and carried them in marches. People took photos of those actions and events, and they uploaded them to social media and to their profile pictures, continuing the cycle. Between 2008 and 2015, the country had changed: marriage equality was the law of the land, and supporting marriage equality put one on the right side of history. All along, we had the profile pictures to prove it.

BEHOLD, THE LLAMAS

Strong grass mud horses, how beautiful they are
They run in the direction of sunrise, unyieldingly
and without fear.

—Grass Mud Horse Cartoon and Rap[1]

PART OF THE LONG-TERM POWER of the symbols and memes about marriage equality is because they drew on historical images. The red equality logo tapped into a larger cultural symbolism of red, which stands for HIV/AIDS advocacy, and the rainbow flag profile-picture overlays reflected the deep roots of the flag in physical space. What happens when a new social-political issue arises, for example, internet censorship, and when that issue arises in an authoritarian context? On the internet and offline, censorship is designed to keep communities in the dark about what they might collectively believe. By stamping out public expression, authorities ensure that people remain in a state of ignorance, receiving only a singular view, frequently from state media.

This was the strategy of the Chinese government in 2000 when it started the Golden Shield Project. Seeking to grow its economy, the country made efforts to develop the infrastructure for the internet, while at the same time taking steps to control the information that flowed through it. Over time the project focused on content-filtering firewalls, moving from general content control to surveillance of individuals. The project became more popularly known as "the Great Firewall of China," or GFW for short, and it allowed the government a great deal of leeway in censoring the internet for some content while opening it up for other content.[2] As China's internet population rapidly grew, users also grew accustomed to not being able to access certain sites or to seeing content deemed unacceptable disappear.

From this environment of censorship a little animal emerged, poking its head out through the GFW, determined to find a way out. Tucked away in the dark corners of China's internet, deep in the Gobi Desert, there roams a fuzzy creature known as the *cǎonímǎ* (草泥马), "the grass mud horse."[3] It is a gentle, noble beast, roughly resembling an alpaca llama, with a long, graceful neck and sturdy legs suitable for both fast running and carrying large burdens. The Gobi Desert is a dangerous and forbidding place, filled with hot sands and empty of water. It's unclear how such a furry creature survives in a hostile environment—it is not especially adapted to the Gobi, but it certainly makes do, always with a wry grin and friendly demeanor.

Like the cat, the grass mud horse is a fuzzy creature that makes funny faces and gets into absurd situations. It is a popular creature on the Chinese-speaking internet, making up GIFs, stickers, emoji, and even plush toys. In China, cat and dog pictures circulate widely on the internet. Many Chinese people keep these creatures as pets, and, as in the West, their love for these fuzzy animals extends to online culture. Brother Cream, a popular cat meme in the Chinese-speaking world, is a classic example. A bookstore cat in Hong Kong, his cute faces and loveable demeanor make him a staple on the Chinese internet.

But while cats roam much of the global internet, the grass mud horse holds a special place in Chinese activists' hearts. Indeed, upon hearing the Chinese name for the grass mud horse, a fluent speaker would almost immediately know what is going on: the grass mud horse and the land it dwells in are profane puns. As Mandarin is a tonal language with limited phonemes, puns are commonplace, especially puns that change meaning through tones. *Cǎonímǎ* written with one set of characters and tones means "grass mud horse." But *càonǐmā* written with slightly different characters and pronounced with slightly different tones is the more familiar colloquial phrase roughly translated as "fuck your mother." And Ma'le Gebi—the Gobi Desert—sounds remarkably like another Chinese phrase meaning "your mother's cunt."

The grass mud horse cannot rest easily in the desert. It faces a mortal enemy, the dreaded *héxiè*, or river crab. This pinching creature descends into the Gobi Desert and chases after grass mud horses, who must run for their lives. The *héxiè*, as it were, sounds similar to *héxié*, or "harmony." "Harmony" here refers to a 2006 proposal from former president Hu Jintao to develop a "harmonious socialist society."[4] In the context of the internet, such "harmony" meant further censorship under the Golden Shield Project, the Great Firewall, which was capable of filtering content from the outside world based on source and even keyword. Thus, the *hexie* is the crabby embodiment of a censored, "harmonious" internet, the antithesis of the fuzzy, freewheeling grass mud horse. Together, the river crab and the grass mud horse are some of the most enduring memes of China, embodied as both puns and digital animals. They emerged as early as 2009 when the Chinese government launched a censorship campaign against pornography and any material they deemed insensitive.[5] Even the *New York Times* wrote about it that year, citing *China Digital Times* editor Xiao Qiang's declaration that the meme has "become an icon of resistance to censorship."[6]

Like any good internet meme, countless remixes of the river crab and grass mud horse exist as netizens engage in a constant effort to outdo each other's creativity. Any image of a llama can in fact become a grass mud horse, and, by extension, an outcry against China's stringent censorship. There are grass mud horse plushies and cartoons, and even a fake Happy Meal toy. A group of netizens created a fake Chinese character composed of the radicals, or visual components, for "grass," "mud," and "horse," and they debated online about how best to pronounce it. One popular proposal was that it should be pronounced "fock," a phoneme that does not exist in Mandarin but certainly seems appropriate. The most impressive of these interpretations, in my mind, is the grass mud horse theme song, a remix of the Chinese-language theme song of the Smurfs. Coupled with a cutesy tune and slow-motion videos of llamas prancing around and spitting, the lyrics go a little something like this:

> Oh lying down Grass Mud Horse
> Oh running wild Grass Mud Horse
> They defeated river crabs in order to protect their grass land
> River crabs forever disappeared from Ma'le Desert[7]

Pronounced differently, with slightly different tones, the second half of these lyrics could be read as "Harmony forever disappeared from your mother's cunt." An animated hip-hop version tells a mournful tale of the grass mud horse's plight.

Their catchy tunes and lyrics linger on in Chinese cyberspace similar to car dealership jingles (just imagine this rapped, with a fun beat in the background):

> Strong grass mud horses, how beautiful they are
> They run in the direction of sunrise, unyieldingly and without fear[8]

Soon the horse and the crab found other punny companions. On Baidu Baike, a Wikipedia-like service on Baidu, China's leading search engine, the grass mud horse became just one of the Ten Mythical Creatures of China's internet. Among these creatures could be found the French-Croatian Squid, whose Chinese name, *fa ke you*, deliberately sounds like the English language "fuck you."[9]

The puerile humor, the profanity, the misogyny (one mythical creature references rape), and the wacky animals would all be familiar to anyone using the internet outside China. Within China, these memes took on a distinctly political character with a clear stance against internet censorship. As with many internet memes, the grass mud horse and its menagerie of companions is a form of in-joke. At least until it became too famous, its friendly face and punny name meant it could slip past the scrutiny of internet censors while inspiring hilarity among its users. It looks harmless in image form, but for those in on the joke, it's a profane outcry against the policies that forced it to become a secret symbol. To be clear, these creatures are by no means the only memes in China. In a country with now more than seven hundred million internet users and an active social media population, there are countless memes, many of which center on cats and dogs, with cute animations and oddball language.[10] Some are nationalistic, and most seem to have no overt political undertone. Indeed, the vast majority of youth internet activity in China is apolitical, and memes make up just one part of a larger repertoire of youth expression and identity formation online.[11]

Such sites as Sina Weibo, in fact, encourage lots of imagery, with embeddable photo and video features and the ability to simply repost a message in a fashion similar to a retweet on Twitter or a share on Facebook. The site is popular among urban Chinese youth and is only one of many *weibo*, or microblogs, that have emerged on the Chinese web. Though these sites bear a resemblance to Twitter with a 140-character limit, this limit allows for nearly a paragraph or two of content in the Chinese language, where most words are as short as one or two characters. On other platforms, for example, WeChat, character counts go much higher, allowing for people to essentially create blogs. WeChat evolved first as a one-to-one messaging app, but over time, it's allowed for a mix of public posts and games. This media-rich environment makes it easy to share images, text, and video, giving space for a vibrant meme culture.

The phenomenon of the grass mud horse offers an opportunity to look at the many different types of media that make up internet memes. There's a popular misconception that internet memes are only image macros, in other words, images with text superimposed above and below, or that they are only cats and dogs. But memes can take many forms and exist on many types of media, and it's these many forms that give them their richness.

IMAGE MEMES AND IMAGE MACROS

When someone shares a picture of a llama photoshopped onto a car, they are sharing an image meme. Many internet platforms encourage photo embeds, because human beings are visual creatures, and so image memes tend to do particularly well. Image memes can have text on them, and in those cases they're called *image macro memes.* The popular meme format in the West, of creating an image and adding text above and below it to make a statement, is a good example of an image macro.

TEXT MEMES

The many puns circulating about the grass mud horse are an example of text memes. They are, technologically, the easiest to create, and they're most familiar in the Western context as hashtag memes, like #BlackLivesMatter and #MakeAmericaGreatAgain. The grass mud horse plays a similar role, making up the text of songs and sentences, and even serving as an identity marker: when activists want to signal to others that they stand for a free and open internet, they might say, "I am a grass mud horse."

VIDEO MEMES

Video memes are the most technologically and creatively demanding to create, but often also the most virally popular. Length doesn't matter so much—some video memes can be quite long, while others can last just a second or two. The grass mud horse theme song may sound like a Smurfs song, but it takes a lot of technical knowhow and talent to organize a resinging of the song and then to splice and edit imagery to make a compelling video. GIF memes can be considered a subgenre of video memes. GIFs operate effectively under lower bandwidth conditions and, through repetition, often reinforce a message or make a humorous statement.

PHYSICAL MEMES

When the grass mud horse leapt from the screen and into phone stickers and plush toys, it went from a purely digital meme to a physical one. Not all these toys were actual grass mud horses; indeed, many people just repurposed existing plush dolls of llamas to make a statement. Regardless, the ability to remix or make a physical object to produce a memetic statement is quite common. Thanks to smartphone cameras, anything done in the physical world can quickly enter the digital world, and thanks to rapid production cycles, anything made popular on the internet can quickly become a physical product disseminated through online stores.

PERFORMATIVE MEMES

In 2011, the Chinese artist Ai Weiwei posted a photo of himself jumping naked while holding a grass mud horse to cover his crotch. When he did, he was participating in a performative meme, using his body to generate a version of the meme circulating on the Chinese web at the time. The joke was once again a pun, this time with an even more explicit political message: "The grass mud horse covers the center"—*caonima dang zhongyang* (草泥马挡中央)—sounds a lot like "fuck your mother, Central Party Committee." This performative meme took aim at one of the most powerful institutions in China, and it asked citizens to embody their political stance through performance.

SELFIE MEMES

Selfie memes are a common subgenre of performative memes that deserve special mention. When people post photos of themselves cuddling a grass mud horse, they are posting selfie memes. Thanks to the advent of both front-facing cameras on smartphones and social networks like Instagram and WeChat that encourage photo sharing, selfies have swept the digital world. As with "Coca-Cola" and "taxi," "selfie" is a word that rarely requires translation in other languages.

When someone says "internet meme," you might think just of cats, but the panoply of interpretations can actually be quite diverse. Just as the meme's usage can be silly, so can that silliness be transformed into powerful political messages. Indeed, in a country like China, internet memes have force in an authoritarian state that seeks to enact control over all broadcast and internet media. To understand why, it helps to go deeper into how China's propaganda and censorship system works, and how memes have worked around that. In China, the state promotes messages that serve its interests and censors those that do not, but it does so in a sophisticated, targeted way. As Anne-Marie Brady, a researcher on the history and evolution of Chinese propaganda, noted in an interview with me for *Change Observer*, the strategies borrow heavily from Western democratic models of political persuasion. Nevertheless, the propaganda still comes from a single agenda and purpose, with messaging and censorship guidelines circulated weekly to media outlets.[12]

The manifest expressions vary depending on the audience. During the ninetieth anniversary celebrations of the Communist Party's founding, for instance, I documented everything from party-friendly avatars for gamers to classic red and yellow banners for construction workers.[13] These different forms of expression resembled more of a segmented marketing strategy, with different messaging for different audiences. For the most sensitive topics, however, such as human rights abuses, the messaging rarely varies, and censorship is often the preferred course of action. In these cases, too, the state may choose to spread disinformation through strategic newspaper editorials or paid internet comments.

Hu Jintao, then president of China, used the phrase "harmonious society" to articulate a guiding policy that led to further censorship under his leadership. The grass mud horse and river crab menagerie reflect a similar deftness with language, with the absurdity and humor operating contra the famously humorless visages of the Politburo. Even the popularity of the grass mud horse song can be seen as a riposte to monotonous Party music, historically blared on the radio and in public spaces and played during state television broadcasts. The song gives people upset with the system of censorship a chant they, too, can rally around.

The country also controls the technology on which the internet operates. By ensuring legislative and, by extension, technical control of all servers located within its borders and keeping a tight lid on the data pipelines that allow information into and out of the country, the Chinese government's goal is to allow the internet to flourish for commerce and entertainment while deadening its use for political organizing or expression. The Great Firewall ensures control of the data, but it is just one part of a larger system of censorship. All Chinese social media platforms employ some form of keyword-search algorithm that blocks terms deemed sensitive by the government. Furthermore, major platforms like Sina employ human censors, rumored to be in the thousands, who monitor all content and fill in the gaps that the algorithms miss. In addition, the government employs professional commentators to spread progovernment propaganda on social media platforms. These individuals are known popularly as the Fifty Cent Party (五毛党) because of the rumored fifty cents in Chinese currency that they receive for each comment they leave.[14]

Those who cross a line can expect to see their messages deleted or their entire account frozen. The former has happened to me a number of times, with a simple, disquieting message on my Weibo account noting that the post was removed. More egregious violations can lead to an account being deleted entirely or, in more extreme cases, an unpleasant police visit, popularly known as *hecha*, or "drinking tea." That the threshold is often unknowable is part of the strategy—with netizens uncertain as to how much they can speak out on a given topic, the government ensures a certain level of self-censorship.

Why does such stringent censorship exist in the first place? The cost-benefit analysis of this policy should be understood in the framework of the "Cute Cat Theory of Digital Activism," proposed in 2008 by internet theorist Ethan Zuckerman. The theory begins with two basic assumptions. First, the original internet was made for sharing academic papers, scientific data, and the like. "Web 1.0," as Zuckerman calls it, was largely utilitarian in scope. However, as the internet has become more of a popular medium, it exists now for sharing amateur media:

> The web, as designed by Tim Berners-Lee at CERN [the European Organization for Nuclear Research], was intended to let physicists share research findings online. As innovators commercialized the web, it became a space for commerce and distribution of content by established publishers. With web 2.0, the web became a space for the creation and dissemination of amateur content. The contemporary Internet was designed, in no small part, for the dissemination of cute pictures of cats.[15]

The ideal world for an authoritarian government would be one in which the internet populace does nothing but share cute cat pictures and other amateur content. "Bread and circuses" for the masses, as the old Roman phrase goes. Keep the people fed and entertained, and they will not get too involved in politics. However, unlike circuses, which can be centrally controlled, the internet operates more like a freewheeling forum. The challenge an authoritarian government faces is that a platform that facilitates the rapid spread of cute cat images is one that can also facilitate the rapid spread of activist messages.

Zuckerman described a situation in Tunisia where activists uploaded videos of the presidential airplane in use to draw attention to government misuse of funds. The first video was seen by a relatively small number of people, but when the government moved to block the entire hosting site for the video, they disrupted the circus and ended up upsetting far more people, people who were not previously politically engaged. The Chinese censorship machine is, in theory, designed to prevent something like that from happening. With targeted controls, it should be able to pinpoint activist messages while allowing others to flourish. Blanket censorship this is not; with such a crisp level of precision, censors can control the flow of information based on topic, easing up on and tightening censorship depending on the time of year.[16] The scale of censorship is vast and impressive, with likely thousands of people employed around the clock and with complex algorithms that never get tired.

It is in this environment that activism about the most sensitive topics had to adapt. In Zuckerman's theory, there is a difference between an activist message and a cute cat. But in China, at least regarding the most censored content, spreading a straightforward activist message is rarely effective. Thus, instead of referring directly to the travails of internet censorship, the multiple puns of the grass mud horse menagerie skirt the topic while allowing the user to publicly express an opinion. Even to a trained human censor, deciding whether a picture of a llama is politically subversive or just a photo from the zoo is not entirely clear-cut. Deleting too many of the latter would cost political capital.

In this way, a number of Chinese activists have employed the best qualities of internet memes—their rapid virality, their irreverent sense of humor, and their participatory quality—and transformed them into online actions. These puns and images slip past both machine and human censors through coded verbal and visual language. Faced with stringent and targeted censorship, activists embed their messages within the cute cat. And in so doing they created a channel for expression and affirmation, helping people find each other despite the strictest enforcement of internet censorship in the world. The humor played an important role in disrupting the power of silence in China: if censorship is intended to generate "feels" of fear and uncertainty by separating people from each other online, humor disarms those feels with laughter and shared community.

In China, many internet memes evade censorship in a tactical way, by shifting and morphing to avoid keyword-search algorithms or by avoiding words altogether, using the power of in-jokes to avoid censors' scrutiny. And they do something even more important: they break the silence of self-censorship through an addictive participatory culture, while making people with similar concerns and issues visible to each other. Their messages alone may not be deliberately designed to foment a social movement or even advocate a cause, but they are powerful nonetheless. Just as rainbow profile pictures and red equality logos signaled support for marriage equality in the United States, grass mud horse pictures and selfies made people in China visible to each other for the first time and, through sheer repetition, affirmed and reinforced a commonly held belief. Memes like these face outwardly, too, getting more people to pay attention through their novelty.

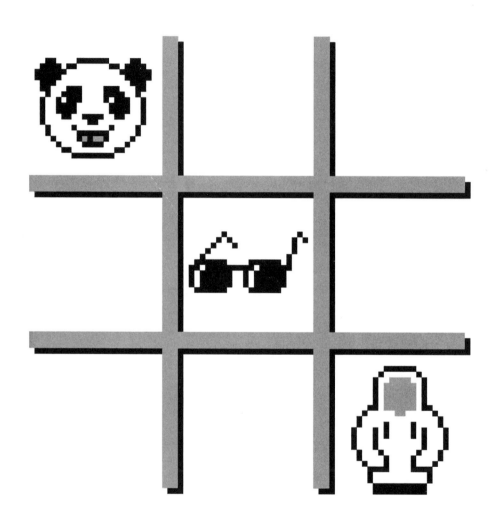

CHAPTER 3

■ ■ ■ ■ ■ ■ ■

AHEM, ATTENTION PLEASE

I'm not interested in reading messy information like
some of that anti-government stuff.

—Fang Binxing, father of the Great Firewall[1]

WE LIVE IN A WORLD OF DISTRACTION, of entities competing for our attention, whether that's banner ads, billboards, television shows, people singing on the streets. In a world where information is everywhere, attention becomes a more critical deciding factor about a society's values. As the previous chapters demonstrated about funny cat videos, llama remixes, and rainbow flag profile pictures, memes acquire charisma through regular remix and iteration, and they drive attention to groups' causes through connecting with media and other influencers.

Operating by themselves and within closed communities, memes are already powerful, but as they spread outside the communities that created them, they gain their power through the work of influencers—movie celebrities and super-connected people in media, like bloggers, journalists, broadcasters, radio personalities, and politicians. Memes draw attention through the use of symbols, catchphrases (often in the form of hashtags), performative gestures and selfies, and other forms. When masses of people post selfies with sunflower seeds, they drive attention to their actions, which in turn drives attention to the cause they are fighting for. This has proven to be extremely useful for marginalized communities in both industrialized and developing contexts, challenging some of the traditional flows of media influence. And it can start simply, with a hashtag.

FROM SPAIN TO UGANDA AND BACK AGAIN

> Spain is not Uganda.
>
> —Mariano Rajoy[1]

> Uganda is not Spain.
>
> —Multiple Twitter posts

THIS STORY ABOUT EAST AFRICA starts with a text message in Western Europe. Years before much of the financial and social turmoil that struck the European Union in the late 2010s, there was the 2012 Spanish bank bailout. Struggling with the need for additional financial support from the EU, Spanish prime minister Mariano Rajoy sent a reassuring text message to his finance minister:

> *Aguanta, somos la cuarta potencia de Europa, España no es Uganda.*
> Resist, we are the fourth power in Europe. Spain is not Uganda.[2]

The words were picked up in international media, making a few headlines. Rajoy seemed to be suggesting that although Spain might be struggling, at least it's not a poor country in Africa. In another era the response might have come and gone quickly, a turn of phrase with a flash of interest before being quickly forgotten. But the response on social media was speedy, and it came from what at the time seemed an unlikely source: Ugandans themselves. Posting a video on YouTube, Ugandan journalist Rosebell Kagumire called out the remarks and started a hashtag trend on Twitter that would echo throughout social media: #UgandaIsNotSpain.[3]

Samuel Ouga @Ougasam why **#UgandaIsNotSpain**: In the last 5 yrs, average Ugandan's income has risen 15%. The average Spaniard's has contracted 6%.

3:24 p.m., June 18, 2012[4]

Chris Wolf @ChristineWolf Agreed! Beautiful national parks, mountain gorillas, and some of the kindest people on earth! **#UgandaIsNotSpain**

11:00 a.m., June 17, 2012[5]

The Professor is in @WilGafney #Spain you wish you were as solvent and stable as **#Uganda**. **#UgandaIsNotSpain**

11:03 a.m., June 17, 2012[6]

The brash, quirky humor caught many by surprise, and international media outlets quickly picked up on the response. After covering the many biting responses, *BBC News* compared the economies of the two countries, and *Al Jazeera* pointed out the absurdity of the comparison, noting the rapid economic growth Uganda had experienced. *Foreign Policy* hosted an opinion piece from Ugandan journalist Jackee Batanda:

> When the world looks at emerging markets, it is the countries like Uganda that offer hope for the future of growth. It is therefore important to correct the perception that Uganda is a lost cause. That's a long way from the truth. Uganda is a resource-rich country with a vibrant culture.[7]

The hashtag provoked a round of public soul-searching on the part of both Spanish and Ugandan media. Spaniards expressed dismay about their leader, while others took pride in their country's health-care provisions and overall GDP while pointing out the country still had many systemic problems.

These sorts of conversations are typical now when a social media outburst pokes at people in power. But the most remarkable aspect of this story is that, for a rare moment, people from a historically overlooked nation (how many people outside East Africa can point out Uganda on a map?) were able to drive the conversation on international media. Spaniards joined in on the hashtag conversation, commenting:

Ibai Trebiño @ibaitrebino *Rajoy fascista y maleducado. No nos representas. Hastag anti rajoy, gran iniciativa ugandesa.* #UgandaisnotSpain [Rajoy is a fascist and uneducated. You don't represent us. A hashtag against Rajoy, a great Ugandan effort.]

6:06 a.m., June 13, 2012[8]

Sara @greenpeeptoes *Vergonzoso y desafortunado comentario. ¿Cómo nos van a tomar en serio con semejante ignorante en la presidencia?* [A shameful and unfortunate comment. How are they going to take us seriously with such ignorance in the presidency?]

1:49 a.m., June 13, 2012[9]

What Ugandans on YouTube, Twitter, and in the media managed to achieve, in a matter of days, was attention. Kagumire, a trained journalist with an understanding of social media dynamics, clearly recognized a moment of opportunity, and she sparked a hashtag that remixed the prime minister's reported choice of words. This hashtag, in turn, drove attention to the clever tweets that people posted, which international media picked up on, thus sparking another conversation. The reason it worked relies on a number of factors. The world was already watching the issue and discussing Rajoy's poor choice of words. Ugandans were then able to leverage the existing attention and judo it to a conversation about misguided assumptions about both countries.

What also mattered here was technological access. Compare this cross-language, cross-continental back and forth on Twitter to how things might have unfolded before social media. Historically, news outlets have relied on letters to the editor and phone calls to understand reader responses. By the time an international newspaper reached Uganda, someone in the country, upset by how his country was portrayed in the news, could write a letter or make a phone call. But delivery could take weeks—and by that time the news cycle would almost certainly have moved on. A phone call might have worked, until you considered the cost: a few cents per minute for one person to call in could easily add up and be prohibitively expensive. Further, one person can be ignored. Without social media, few ways existed for a significant number of people to show their disagreement with Rajoy's framing of Uganda.

In 2009, SEACOM, a submarine cable company, laid a 10,625-mile data cable that connected East Africa with high-speed broadband, reducing the cost per megabit by more than 90 percent and connecting countries in the region to both Europe and India.[10] Today, it snakes along the bottom of the Indian Ocean and Mediterranean Sea until it reaches Mombasa, Kenya; Djibouti, Djibouti; Dar es Salaam, Tanzania; Maputo, Mozambique; and Mtuzini, South Africa, among other cities. From there, underground and overland cables extend throughout much of Kenya to Uganda and Rwanda, landlocked countries to its west.[11]

This cable, followed by a number of other broadband cables, has had significant effects on internet use in East Africa. Within seven years of the initial installation, the number of internet users in Uganda grew by 600 percent, from two million users in 2008 to nearly twelve million by 2016, largely centered in Kampala, the country's capital city.[12] People were especially likely to connect via mobile phone, thanks to the proliferation of low-cost internet capable phones from manufacturing hubs in China. These phones have tapped into a wide variety of mobile phone towers dotting the country, thanks to investments from carriers such as MTN and Airtel.

In the 1980s, when Mariano Rajoy began his political career, Uganda was facing more difficult times.[13] After Yoweri Museveni took power as president of the country, Joseph Kony, a military leader from northern Uganda, led the Lord's Resistance Army (LRA), known for its cultlike culture and ruthlessness, to challenge Museveni's rule.[14] When Kony began the resistance, the internet was little known, but he, too, would become a meme of sorts.

Just months before #UgandaIsNotSpain took off, another hashtag about Uganda had taken hold of the world, driving attention to the country and, more specifically, to the LRA. In March 2012, Invisible Children, an NGO (nongovernmental organization) and advocacy organization based in California, released a video about Joseph Kony. "For 26 years, Kony has been kidnapping children into his rebel group, the LRA, turning the girls into sex slaves and the boys into child soldiers," noted Invisible Children founder Jason Russell in *KONY 2012*, a thirty-minute video that quickly went viral. In the film, Russell speaks to his son. "He makes them mutilate people's faces, and he forces them to kill their own parents."[15] The video was combined with a digital outreach campaign on multiple social media channels, all organized using hashtags such as #StopKony and #Kony2012.

The campaign took off. Millions of social media posts later, Invisible Children was able to drive a stunning range of international attention to their cause, compelling the United States, the African Union, and the United Nations to pledge troops and resources to hunt down and capture Joseph Kony and stop the LRA from committing any further abuses.[16] The goal of #StopKony didn't quite come to fruition—Kony himself had long since left Uganda and relocated to the Central African Republic, a few hundred miles northwest of Uganda.[17] But the campaign served as a model for many Western organizations as they sought to drum up attention and support for often-overlooked issues.

Occurring in 2012 about the same country, both #StopKony and #UgandaIs NotSpain serve as a useful comparison for how something as simple as a hashtag can drive a conversation. Through sheer scale of users, hashtag trends can involve many more people, who gather online in a form of digital public assembly, than traditional physical organizing. In addition, the joking and one-upmanship of these trends, as people compete to make the best quip or joke, serves as a useful way to drive attention. This is not simply because of the number of posts. Rather, the variety of posts and the range of remixes serve as a sort of Darwinism of attention, where only the best and fittest posts float to the top, thanks to multiple shares decided by multiple people. University of Michigan communications professor Amanda D. Lotz has noted that intentional overproduction is a key strategy in traditional media, which deliberately create multiple shows, commercials, songs, and other media, because they never know which one will quite take off. She writes:

> The primary strategy for dealing with the uncertainty of success is intentional overproduction. Television, film, and recording industry executives all work in a universe in which they know full well that more than 80 percent of what they develop and create will fail commercially. The key problem is that they don't know which 10 to 20 percent might actually succeed. So, while it is painful from a resource-allocation standpoint, the strategy has been to produce far more creative goods than might succeed and then see what works.[18]

Hashtag culture functions in a similar way, but the overproduction is created by many people, riffing off of each other. Algorithms like Twitter Trending catch them and highlight them in a section on the site that is visible to many, which in turn drives more attention. People outside the group might see it trending on Twitter and start asking, "What's going on here?" And soon local media and then international media catch on, followed by an international conversation about the issue.

In online culture, the # sign has long been an important symbol to indicate topicality. On Internet Relay Chat, an open source, open access chat system popular in the 1990s, chat topics and channels are indicated with a # preceding the word, like #books or #election1997. In some programming languages, developers use multiple # marks to indicate when they're leaving a semantic comment for a human, rather than a computer. If the @ sign is often used to represent people, whether in email addresses or user handles, the # often indicates topicality or information.

In 2007, designer Chris Messina coined the term "hashtag" on Twitter, a portmanteau of the words "hash" and "tag."[19] In British English, *hash* refers to the # sign. The idea of a hashtag was to organize content and information to make it searchable, especially for technology conferences. So someone could tweet "The coffee in the lobby is great #barcamp," and the #barcamp would indicate for others that the person posting the tweet is at a conference called BarCamp. In addition, anyone could search for tweets containing #TED (for the TED Conference) or #HurricaneHarvey to see everyone else conversing about that same event. It's a useful tool that's easy for humans to read and understand while still being accessible for computers to do searches and organize information. Since that time, hashtags have evolved from a way to organize information online to a form of expression in their own right. The designs of many social media platforms, most notably Twitter and Facebook, highlight trending hashtags by giving them a prominent place on their site, which in turn helps drive further attention to the hashtag and conversations within.

One helpful way to understand the role of hashtags—and, by extension, much of meme culture online—is to think of them as oral culture written down. It's the iterative, repetitious culture of hashtags that makes them resemble oral culture traditions more than written. Although online discourse takes a written form, it looks more like the spoken word: repetitious, iterative, and informal.

Writing about GIFs, technology theorist Britney Summit-Gil's comparison of oral culture with digital culture rings true for other media like hashtags:

> Because the stories, theories, and pedagogies of oral societies exist only in people's minds, they are stabilized and canonized far differently than in literate societies. Memory is necessary for knowledge preservation, and mnemonic skills like repetition, metrical speech, and rhyme become key to knowledge transmission. Expression relies on formulas and epithets to guide memory: not the "princess" but the "beautiful princess"; not the "oak" but the "sturdy oak." These mnemonics are not only practical, but an integral part of making performance pleasurable and engaging.[20]

And just as oral culture is iterative and repetitious, so is digital culture. The repetition of the phrase "I can has cheezburger" stands in as a mnemonic for a certain range of internet users. When evoking this phrase, one can riff on it a bit: "I can has iPhone?" "I can has pizza?" Knowing and understanding this phrase thus enters cultural consciousness and indicates to others that you are part of this corner of digital culture and know its norms. It's this culture of iteration that allows online communities to create not just new content on hashtags but also new hashtags entirely. Each new meme has spin-off memes and subcommunities dedicated to those memes, and then sometimes the memes get mashed up. Like oral culture, digital culture never stays still, and these practices cross text, media, video, and some amazing cartoons, and they get people to sit up and start paying attention to something long simmering just beneath the surface.

ENTER THE PANDAMAN

I seek light, and I seek truth.
—Multiple posts online

ATTENTION CAN BE A DOUBLE-EDGED SWORD. It drives media conversations, but its effects must always be understood in the context of existing power structures. Two hashtag memes about one country—#UgandaIsNotSpain and #StopKony—show that looking at how people and organizations respond to attention is just as important as the attention happening at all. Sometimes attention can have ripple effects on the other side of the globe. In 2011, the world's attention focused on the so-called Arab Spring in countries like Tunisia, Egypt, and Syria, which were gripped by protests and acts of civil disobedience after years of repressive rule; and toward the Occupy movement in the United States, which sought to challenge the capitalist power structure of the most powerful country in the world; and on to the birth of the Podemos party in Spain. It felt like a year of global protest and occupation.

That year China doubled down on its censorship of the internet and control of public spaces. Likely fearing that the rising global fervor of revolution would reach the country, government leaders also cracked down on activists, disappearing hundreds and placing many more under heavy surveillance. The famous artist Ai Weiwei was one of them, as were well-known activists like lawyers Teng Biao and Li Tiantian.[1] Ai Weiwei was one activist among many experiencing particularly harrowing conditions, but in the suffering he and his community faced, something else became evident to those of us paying attention: the power of memes to remind us of his and our shared humanity and to construct an alternative story.

Sentenced to prison for four years for his human rights work, the blind law-yer Chen Guangcheng was already a leading light in activist circles and had developed a steady following by 2006. He entered prison while the internet was relatively nascent in the country, used primarily among urban elites who chatted on messaging boards and small social networks. By the time Chen was released, in 2011, Chinese-bred social media sites like Sina Weibo and WeChat were beginning to take hold, thanks to the sheer volume of mobile phones, digital cameras, and smartphones that were both manufactured and consumed in China. China's internet population had exceeded five hundred million, and it was growing rapidly.[2]

Chen would initially encounter little of this. After his release, he faced a new nightmare, as his wife and daughter were then held in illegal detention in their own home. As with most dissidents in the country, the government sporadically censored any mention of Chen's name and related terms online.[3] At the time of his detention, he was one of the most famous dissidents in China, and yet he was effectively rendered a nonperson. When *Guardian* reporter Tania Branigan called the local police office in early 2011 to inquire about Chen's status, the officer replied, "We are not sure what you are talking about. We will get back to you."[4]

Despite this, technology helped amplify Chen's and his wife's voices almost immediately. In a harrowing video smuggled out of his home and posted to social networks, he and his wife described the systematic attempts to prevent their communication with the outside world. They were kept in their home as guards stood not just outside the house but also outside the town to make sure no outsiders tried to visit. They barred him from accessing any phones or computers that could be used to get the word out. Officials went so far as traveling one hundred kilometers to detain his brother, who had bought a SIM card for Chen's phone.[5] In the context of China's wider abuses against activists and dissidents, the situation increasingly seemed dire.

In October 2011, the anonymous Chinese comic artist Crazy Crab (his moniker refers to the river crab of Chinese internet lore) organized an online action asking netizens to send in pictures of themselves wearing sunglasses so he could post them to a central website, Dark Glasses Portrait. The sunglasses directly referenced Chen's iconic sunglasses.[6] He also encouraged netizens to post the pictures to their own social media accounts. As a visual image, the *zipai*, or selfies, were brilliantly constructed, tapping into an existing selfie culture in China that arguably predated the rapid growth of selfies in the West. They were also easily replicable and remixable, relying on a prop that almost everyone had that also directly evoked the individual in question.

In many ways these selfies served a dual purpose. First, they seemed innocuous enough to censors, who weren't clued in to the sunglasses reference. Participants' photos could look like any common photo of a person wearing sunglasses. For some people, this helped them keep their privacy, too, as big sunglasses obscured their faces. Second, like the selfies used in the movement for marriage equality, they showed scale for the in-group in a powerful way. As Crazy Crab reported in an interview with me, more than six hundred people (a large number for China, where even a small fraction of that number would never be allowed to gather in physical protest) shared their photos with him, and countless others participated online.[7] This became a way of showing scale and numbers in a context where physical gathering simply wasn't possible.

The meme took off, spreading in less than a week, according to Crazy Crab's account, from mainland China to Hong Kong to Chinese overseas and then more broad international self-portraits, and he collected formal submissions on a dedicated blog. The sunglasses meme eventually turned into a performative one when it took the form of a flash mob in China. Concerned citizens and supporters gathered in Longyang, a city near where Chen was being held, and donned sunglasses in the public square.[8] These actions both online and offline created temporal and digital street art, reclaiming the public spaces of the internet for a political cause. Crazy Crab was inspired by the French street artist JR, whose Inside Out Project consisted of portraits in public spaces. Unable to do that safely in China, Crab enacted a portrait project that existed in the only way it could: in the public space made possible by the internet.

Chen Guangcheng memes and images existed before the sunglasses meme, and Crazy Crab tapped into this, activating a community of supporters. The memes about Chen became increasingly more diverse thereafter, mutating regularly to keep ahead of censors. Chen's handsome, sunglassed face—instantly recognizable and easy to evoke and reproduce—appeared online in sketches and cartoons. It showed up on T-shirts, stickers, and faux postage stamps. Activists rallied around hashtags like #FreeCGC (Free Chen Guangcheng) and #CGC自由 (ziyou, meaning "freedom"). Some came up with poetic phrases like 要光要诚 (yao guang yao *cheng*)—"I seek light, and I seek truth"—referencing the two characters of Chen's given name—*guang* and *cheng*—which mean "light" and "truth," respectively.

The #FreeCGC hashtag grew in popularity and was itself censored. As one of many strategies to sidestep the ongoing censorship, the phrase was then slapped onto cars and motorcycles with a picture of Chen designed to look like Colonel Sanders from Kentucky Fried Chicken. In China, KFC and its imitators are extremely popular fast-food chains, so the Free CGC stickers looked like an offer for fried chicken. As with the meme in digital space, these offline memes became an in-joke for participants and supporters while allowing them to more safely express themselves in physical space. Thanks to digital cameras, online pictures of the cars and motorcycles sporting the stickers allowed the meme a second wind.

The dark humor took a turn when actor and *Batman* star Christian Bale attempted to visit Chen in December 2011. Visits like his had become a performative meme of sorts, as netizens sporadically organized groups to provoke guards. These performative actions were done deliberately with an eye toward documenting the experiences on Weibo.[9] Participants already knew what was going to happen—they'd be turned away, and, in some cases, threatened with physical harm—and the act of public documentation would show the brutal conditions Chen was living under. Bale was, like everyone else, immediately turned away. Video released by CNN showed him and his companions being chased by a rotund man in a green coat, and they drove away quickly before he could do more.

Online comic artist Remon Wang noticed that the rotund man, with his peculiar face and green military jacket, resembled a panda. He distributed a poster online of a fictitious film dubbed *Batman vs. Pandaman*. It launched scores of other memes that imagined Chen Guangcheng in a superhero movie, from highly illustrated images to more rough Photoshop cuts. Netizens also began inserting Pandaman into out-of-context photos, facing off with Kim Jong Un, the president of North Korea, and standing among China's Politburo. He became so popular that Chen, in a video released on YouTube shortly after his escape, made direct reference to the would-be villain (referring to him as "Green Coat," another phrase used by netizens to describe the man) and identified him by his real name.[10]

The secret detention of Chen Guangcheng and censorship of his name was designed to cultivate fear among activists and sympathizers while rendering Chen invisible to the general public. It's no accident, then, that Remon Wang's comic of Batman versus Pandaman took off: amid terrifying, disempowering stories of the blind Chen's suffering, this funny meme painted him as a super-hero in his own right, while his captor was transformed into a harmless panda. Humor has always served the function of telling difficult truths. In the midst of the heartbreaking realities of Chen's detention, these memes made the situation a little bit easier to handle, even when amplifying and disseminating the clear abuses he experienced. In contrast to the official silence the government attempted to enforce, these memes allowed a creative flourishing of references to Chen's name and face, and they encouraged frequent repeating of his story and living conditions. They affirmed his humanity through the humanity of others.

By spring 2012, almost miraculously, Chen escaped. The story reads like a plot from a movie. Waiting for cover of night, when he would have the advantage, he hopped the two-meter wall surrounding his home and made his way through the woods over the course of a few days, passing through a reported eight layers of defense. He met a friend in a getaway car at a prearranged location, and they drove to Beijing, where he eventually made his way to the US embassy.[11] Censors increased their efforts to prevent any mention or discussion of Chen, going so far as to censor words like "CNN"—which was covering the event—and "pearl"—a reference to the woman who helped Chen escape.[12]

Even in this repressive communication environment, memes about Chen continued to slip through. Crazy Crab jumped in with an homage to a still from *The Shawshank Redemption*, a film about a wrongfully accused man who makes a dramatic prison break. In Crazy Crab's comic, which circulated on Sina Weibo, bewildered guards in the form of pigs from the video game *Angry Birds*, stare down the hole through which *Shawshank*'s protagonist escaped. Another creative netizen remixed the original movie poster into the "Dongshigu Redemption," swapping in the name of the town in which Chen was held. The maker of the fake poster even photoshopped dark glasses onto *Shawshank* protagonist Andy Dufresne, cleverly referencing the activist's signature shades.

When censors caught on to the reference and blocked searches for the Chinese word for the film, users began posting quotes from the film in English. "Some birds aren't meant to be caged," went one that I found, because "their feathers are just too bright." Messages like these were few and far between, but they had managed to escape censorship. In his video message post-escape, Chen happened to be wearing a Nike jacket. "Just do it," says one image, with a picture of Chen deftly avoiding escape like Michael Jordan. And another meme was born.

The memes, importantly, helped keep Chen in the public eye. While China censors its local media, activities in the country don't happen in a vacuum. Indeed, stories of hundreds of people posting pictures of sunglasses amplified the movement's message, receiving coverage in important China-focused news outlets like *Shanghaiist* and *China Digital Times* before then being circulated in major Western outlets like the *Atlantic* and the *New York Times*. The Pandaman story and cartoons drove another set of conversations in international media, while the sunglasses reached the halls of the US Congress. Chen's escape represented an incredible symbolic victory—from memes to freedom in less than a year—and given the ongoing international reach of many of the attention-driving memes, memes similar to it likely contributed to a growing international awareness of Chen's situation.

As Crazy Crab explained to me, he wanted to provoke a conversation and a slower, more internal transformation of participants and observers: "Even if there are people who didn't send pictures because of fear [of reprisal], a type of inner experience is also a part of the activity. The treatment [of Chen] is unjust and fearful. I believe they cannot forever remain silent." In the case of severely censored topics like Chen Guangcheng, memes make the difference between no mention of him and hundreds of messages about him, between fearful silence and raucous laughter. When evaluating the impact of this meme, the focus should not be on the billion who did not speak; rather, it should be on the hundreds who found a voice for perhaps the first time. Collectively they created a new narrative that better matched participants' own understanding of the truth; they pierced a small hole in the blanket of official silence enforced by the state. The very act of speaking out is a matter worthy of attention, and Crazy Crab and others clearly understood the double-edged sword of attention—helping bring light to Chen's story while also increasing the risk of government scrutiny.

The longer term impact of these memes is sometimes difficult to assess. Indeed, the memes seemed to have little to do with the actual activities that helped him secure his freedom. Rather, it was the work of a small circle of activists, skillful negotiations on the part of the US State Department, and the resilience of Chen and his family that eventually got them out of detention and into safety. Although Chen was freed, secret detentions, which were already a common practice in China, were officially made legal under "Article 73."[13] The international attention succeeded in creating much-needed visibility in the singular case of Chen, but the broader story of activist detentions in China looks more dire.

Indeed, the country's system of censorship would soon adapt to meme culture. Chen no longer lives in China, but other activists such as Li Tiantian, Teng Biao, and others whom mainstream media may never cover remain in constant risk of being disappeared. Writer and activist Liu Xiaobo, who received a Nobel Prize for his efforts to bring democracy to China, contracted liver cancer while in custody and died in a hospital shortly thereafter while on medical parole.[14] Today, hundreds of lawyers, writers, and activists remain disappeared or under constant surveillance without meme-worthy stories or iconic sunglasses that can inspire artistic responses.

3.3

THE HOODIE THAT
SPARKED A MOVEMENT

Looking back, that was really scary for me. I was thinking,
"Wow, what if we didn't do this. What if the story had died?"

—Daniel Maree[1]

A FEW MONTHS BEFORE CHEN GUANGCHENG'S ESCAPE, while he was held in Donshigu, another event in another small town on the other side of the world sparked a strikingly similar series of memetic strategies to drive attention: the shooting of the African American teenager Trayvon Martin in Sanford, Florida, on February 26, 2012. Public reaction to the shooting speaks to how attention to marginalized people operates in the freer media environment of a democracy, and how attention laid the groundwork for a much larger movement.

At some point during that February day—maybe in the morning, maybe later in the evening when it got chilly—Martin put on a dark hoodie. It was an unassuming one, the sort of hoodie popular in the United States among young people, from Facebook founder Mark Zuckerberg to skater Tony Hawk. Martin walked down to the corner store to pick up some Arizona Tea and a bag of Skittles, paying cash at the register. He would never make it home.

According to documents released by a Florida prosecutor, Martin was shot to death after a physical altercation.[2] The assailant, George Zimmerman, was a gun owner and member of the neighborhood security council. On a 911 record of the incident, Zimmerman is recorded as saying, "These assholes, they always get away," and he soon hung up, in pursuit of Martin.[3] The death of Trayvon Martin came and went, with very little attention. "Boy, 17, Shot to Death in Sanford During 'Altercation,' Police Say," read the headline of the *Orlando Sentinel*, a local news outlet.[4] About a week later, the story emerged into national news via Reuters, CBS, and others, along with blogs such as *Color of Change* and *Black Youth Project*, thanks to a dedicated media push by the Martin family.[5]

What if you could draw a line from the first tweets about Trayvon Martin to the media stories about him? Massachusetts Institute of Technology (MIT) researchers Erhardt Graeff and Matthew Stempeck did just that. Using a tool called Media Cloud, they searched all the social media that mentioned Martin, and they were able to code these results and track the strands of conversation about his death. Watching the chatter, they traced a clear path between what was happening on social media and, eventually, the mainstream media conversations about him. With each major mention from a particularly strong node, they saw spikes. For instance, responding to the news, Barack Obama noted, "If I had a son, he would look like Trayvon Martin."[6] A spike in conversation occurred online, as news outlets covered both the conversation and Obama's words.

The Dream Defenders, a Florida-based activist group that had been operating for years, organized marches and sit-ins that were critical to driving attention on the state and national levels.[7] What also helped was a powerful new symbol. As the Trayvon Martin story started gaining steam in national media, digital strategist Daniel Maree was watching the news unfold, before it slowly tapered away. There was already a growing amount of chatter on social media about Martin, and a hashtag had started to organize news and information about his death and the aftermath. Just a few days after news stories about Martin appeared, the stories seemed to be tapering off.

"Looking back, that was really scary for me. I was thinking, 'Wow, what if we didn't do this. What if the story had died?'" said Maree in an interview I conducted with him for the *Atlantic*.[8] Maree, a black South African who immigrated to the United States, told me he could see himself in Martin. To understand this fear, it helps to understand some of the imagery associated with hoodies in the United States. While hoodies are common among skaters and techies, they've also been demonized in media. Initially associated with positive attributes, like the hardworking eponymous hero of *Rocky* wearing a hoodie, its casualness was gradually overtaken by its associations with criminality, especially for youth of color. "Often hoodies will be used to suggest sinister motives," explained semiotician Michael Thomas Mills in an interview with NPR in the aftermath of

Trayvon Martin's death, "usually with the perpetrator pulling the hoodie over his head before entering a house."[9]

In *Ebony* magazine, L'Heureux Lewis-McCoy pointed out the racialized aspect of the hoodie and other ways that black people's sartorial choices can be associated with criminality:

> As news outlets go on a witch-hunt for pictures of Trayvon looking "thugged out," they are hoping to argue one's dress reflects one's character and worth. Nothing could be further from the truth. A tailored suit does not mean innocence, nor do sagging pants or a hoodie mean guilt. Justice is not just for those who live angelic lives and dress in socially conservative ways, it is equally for those who have been muddied by the world's injustices and dress as they prefer.[10]

Maree, concerned about the dropping media attention, felt he had to do something. On social media many people were already talking about the hoodie and how it might have contributed to perceptions of Martin. Did his hoodie make him look more dangerous than he was? Did it feed into a long-running visual stereotype about black men in hoodies? Maree went on YouTube, put on a hoodie, and called for a march.[11] The video quickly picked up steam, the date was set, and people grabbed their hoodies. As Maree told me later, he was determined to transform the hoodie from a stereotype to a symbol of unity.

Even before people marched on the street, they also began posting pictures of themselves, and they attached brief statements to these photos. Each selfie resonated on social media, with such hashtags as #millionhoodies, #trayvonmartin, and #IAmTrayvon. As the march proceeded down New York City's main avenues and other marches took place in many cities across the United States, it also proceeded on social media. These selfies, like the sunglasses selfies used to raise awareness of Chen Guangcheng, served a dual purpose: they helped draw attention to Trayvon Martin's death, and they also invoked an image that symbolized him. This collective action, combined with the marches, YouTube videos, and outreach efforts, helped drive national attention.

The hoodie was not the only image that people latched on to. The Skittles candy Trayvon Martin held in his hand also transformed into a meme. Popular in the United States and many parts of the world, Skittles are small beads with a sweet flavor, and they come in multiple colors: green, yellow, orange, purple.

Though primarily purchased to be eaten, they are sometimes craftily used as a tool for arranging and building collages, and in that regard, they are also a fitting symbol of unity. People posted pictures of themselves holding Skittles in their hands, dropping Skittles on the ground, painting Skittles on protest signs. A few creative artists arranged Skittles into a portrait of Trayvon Martin, evoking his recognizable face clad in a dark hoodie. The hoodie meme and the Skittles meme converged.

Shortly after the wave of protests online and offline and the growth of a Change.org petition made by Martin's parents, news stories about Martin began picking up again. Maree's strategy was working: while the march didn't literally have one million people—in New York City, it was closer to hundreds—it garnered significant attention, and mainstream media outlets were talking about Martin in a different way: rather than just his death, they started highlighting the possibility that his being killed was unjustified, and even more, was an example of strong racial bias.[12]

In 2012, the idea of using Twitter as a source for news and information was still relatively new. Jeff Jarvis, a professor of journalism at the City University of New York, had observed the trend of journalists turning to social media for news and also of using social media platforms to disseminate news. The radical notion behind Jarvis's explanation is simple: rather than a mode of broadcast, *networked journalism* on social media platforms makes journalism more of a conversation. Journalists are just one part of a larger whole online that is discussing critical issues, and they frequently work in a collaborative fashion.[13]

To understand the Trayvon Martin story, and to understand how a story that in the era before social media would have quickly disappeared from the national conversation reached critical mass, it helps to understand the entire media ecosystem that Daniel Maree and other digital activists operated in. Yes, they were interfacing with mainstream media outlets, who collectively have an audience reach of millions. But mainstream media didn't immediately pay attention: some of the earliest writing about Martin came first through blogs focused on covering issues about people of color.

And it's important to remember that on social media, not everyone is equal. Some have argued that social media has a flattening effect, giving a voice and platform to people who might traditionally have been silenced. But while everyone has the same profile picture and same character count restriction, they have different numbers of followers. Think about a big web of intersecting lines, crisscrossing through space and interconnecting at different points with other lines. This is a classic network graph: each line represents a connection, and each intersection represents a person or a node. Some nodes might be small—maybe made of just two lines. Some nodes, on the other hand, can be quite large, connecting a wide variety of lines and strands. Run a drop of water along one strand, and as soon as it hits the node, that water fractures and splits into many more strands. In network theory, these people are called *supernodes*, people who are able to share and disseminate their message to a wider variety of people. The average person might call them celebrities.

Celebrities such as MC Hammer, Diddy, and Amber Rose were critical to the success of the Million Hoodies March.[14] Some attended the march, but they also posted pictures. When they posted pictures, they shared those on the hashtag. Millions of followers collectively saw them, and they shared them across networks like Facebook, Twitter, and Tumblr. The celebrities helped draw attention on the network and off, driving further media attention. Not all of it was positive. If we imagine networked journalism as a conversation about a topic of attention, we have to remember that conversations are often messy. People say things they don't mean. People argue and disagree. People fight. And just as some news outlets called out the apparent injustices in Martin's case, other outlets cited vigorous disagreement. On *Fox News*, for instance, commentator Geraldo Rivera said that young men of color shouldn't be wearing hoodies. People took offense with his idea, noting that he ultimately placed the onus of stereotypes onto those being stereotyped.[15] It seemed an awful lot like blaming the victim.

And just as protesters wore hoodies as a show of support, another hashtag emerged—#Trayvoning—and it took the form of a performative meme. Before I describe this particular meme, I want to take a step back to the performative meme type it emulates. In 2010, for example, "planking" took hold of social media, starting in the United Kingdom.[16] It's the odd sort of meme that makes sense in the often random world of social media. People posted pictures of themselves and friends horizontal and perfectly straight, often balanced on an object like a trash can or a railing. The more impressive your plank looked, the more likes and shares it got. Planking was soon followed by "owling," a practice of crouching on a high object and making an owl face.[17] The "-ing" meme turns many nouns into verbs—"Tebowing," which refers to football player Tim Tebow kneeling down in prayer and resembling Rodin's *Thinker*, and "dabbing," which refers to a dance move called the dab where you stretch out one arm and point your face into the elbow of your other arm—and in so doing, it transforms those noun-verbs into fun and participatory memes.[18]

#Trayvoning emerged to transform the symbols central to #IAmTrayvon and turn them into something else: a mockery. Performers put on hoodies, lay flat on the ground as if shot, and scattered Skittles and an Arizona Tea can around them. While die-ins are a common protest tactic, where activists lie on the ground to protest deaths from a war or from police violence, this particular action was designed to make fun of the way Trayvon died. These performative memes came and went quickly, but they also got the attention of media outlets, many of which criticized the actions. "Congratulations internet!" wrote *Mic* reporter Nicholas Demas. "You have once again found a new and innovative way to be extremely offensive."[19] But even as some in the news media criticized these actions, the actions were the source of the stories. Journalists entered the social media conversation and contributed to it, even when they disagreed, because the memetic actions themselves were novel enough to drive attention.

How did activists for Chen Guangcheng and Trayvon Martin come up with such strikingly similar strategies for galvanizing attention to people whose stories and experiences might previously have been swept under the rug, whether by overt censorship or by general lack of interest? Understanding how attention works on social media platforms is a critical part of this story. In *The Attention Merchants*, scholar Tim Wu has argued that "technology doesn't follow culture so much as culture follows technology. New forms of expression naturally arise from new media, but so do new sensibilities and new behaviors."[20] Wu wrote about this in the context of why we seek to present images of ourselves so frequently on social media, and that social media platforms are shaped to encourage these behaviors. Instagram in particular rewards and encourages self-display with mechanisms such as "favs" and "likes" that create "for untold numbers an addictive form of self-affirmation."[21]

That selfie memes for both Martin and Chen became popular forms of activist expression is because social media platforms in both the United States and China optimize for certain forms of expression that drive attention. These forms of expression, like selfies, were already emergent practices in both cultures, thanks to such sites as Sina Weibo, Twitter, and Instagram (at the time of Chen's detention, the last wasn't blocked in China). Activists learned to operate within the dynamics of these spaces and leveraged social media–based attention to get people talking about their respective causes. Wu also writes specifically about Instagram and microcelebrity with words that could apply to a number of visually oriented social networks:

> But what of all those many among us busily keeping up an Instagram feed with no hope of ever reselling the attention? For most, the effort is an end in itself, and the ultimate audience is the very subject of the camera's interest. Understood this way, Instagram is the crowning achievement of that decades-long development that we have called the "celebrification" of everyday life and ordinary people, a strategy developed by attention merchants for the sake of creating cheap content.[22]

Wu's book deserves a deeper deconstruction that looks at how the structures of the internet shape and drive how we as a culture express ourselves and, by extension, how activists in a variety of contexts leverage those structures to drive attention to their causes. If public streets and squares shape the capabilities of protests to get attention—for instance, there's a reason many protest actions involve blocking cars from driving—so do our digital public spheres. When we see global convergences of strategies in social media–driven activism, we are frequently seeing how activists shape their tactics to operate within their constraints and leverage key modes of gaining attention on these platforms.

On July 13, 2013, amid intense national attention, George Zimmerman was declared not guilty of murdering Trayvon Martin.[23] In retrospect, this became a galvanizing moment for organizers. "There is an extra amount of, I guess, bitterness that comes with this," said Elon James White, host of *This Week in Blackness*, a popular online radio show, "because at the moment we are being served up that America is this meritocracy, racism is over, and all you have to do is pull yourself up and you'll be fine. And we're learning, day by day, night by night, that this is consistently not true."[24]

#HoodiesUp, people declared on social media. They took to the streets once more, decrying the verdict, which they felt did not serve justice for Martin and his family. All the while, marches in the streets were filled with hoodies, and social media was filled with hoodie memes. The anger and frustration were palpable, with reports of violence and marches in Los Angeles, Miami, and other cities. More than one hundred thousand people signed an NAACP petition to call for a Justice Department investigation. The Dream Defenders organized a record-breaking, thirty-one-day sit-in at the capitol building in Tallahassee, Florida.[25]

With a not-guilty verdict, what exactly had the marches accomplished? They drew significant international media attention, but the marchers' central demand—that George Zimmerman face jail time for his actions—had failed. But if we look to just this outcome, we ignore the wide range of media conversations about the death of Martin. We ignore the politicians' comments, the media stories, the blog posts, the celebrity videos, the SMS threads and listserv conversations, the Trayvon posters, the #millionhoodies T-shirts and baseball caps, the artwork and open mics. In other words, we miss the conversation happening both online and off about Trayvon, a conversation that might not ever have happened in the first place had there been no Million Hoodies March. And that was the power of this particular meme: it sparked a national discussion about Martin and violence at the hands of law enforcement.

In the aftermath of the Trayvon Martin verdict, another conversation was going on, an exchange so small it received, at the time, almost no media attention. Los Angeles–based prison justice activist Patrisse Cullors connected with her friend Alicia Garza, an activist in Oakland, about the verdict. Garza wrote:

black people. I love you. I love us. Our lives matter.

Cullors responded in turn:

declaration: black bodies will no longer be sacrificed for the rest of the world's enlightenment. i am done. I am so done. trayvon, you are loved infinitely.[26]

It was a post so compact, it felt as if her grief was contained, like a thick sponge squished small, absorbing her pain while aching to expand and release it all. Cullors would reflect later on this moment: "I remember just feeling that that couldn't be the period to the story. That George Zimmerman couldn't just go home and that's how history books were going to be written."[27]

She ended the post with a hashtag no one had seen before and few paid attention to, but that felt apropos to the moment. It contained the narrative framework of a then-emerging movement: #BlackLivesMatter.

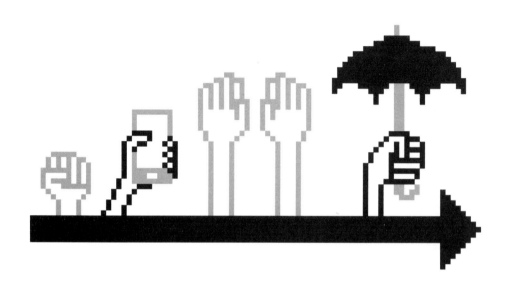

■ ■ ■ ■ ■ ■ ■

CHAPTER 4

NARRATING
OUR WAY TO POWER

All the world's a stage,
And all the men and women merely players;
They have their exits and their entrances,
And one man in his time plays many parts

—William Shakespeare,
As You Like It, act 2, scene 7

MEMES CONTAIN THE SEEDS OF NARRATIVES that can grow into stories much larger than themselves. Indeed, it's the creative milieu of meme culture that is conducive to narrative building. Attention can be short term or long term, occupying our minds as consumers and creators for a few minutes or a few months. Narratives last much longer, and they form the framework through which human beings see the world and tell stories to each other. Some of the most powerful narratives in twenty-first-century society emerged out of meme culture through a long process of iteration and experimentation. This is not an accident: the creative practice of meme-making means people can expose each other to narrative ideas and remixes. Some ideas float up, others sink, others stay in our minds and shift the conversation.

This is a process called *intentional overproduction*, and it's a familiar one in the advertising and entertainment industry.[1] I call it the spaghetti method: throw a bunch of things to the wall and see what sticks. In the context of an authoritarian state that aims to censor content, this creative milieu allows people to evade censorship and at times find a narrative that's deemed acceptable by the powers that be. In a more free media environment or in the international media context, finding the right narrative means setting a media and national agenda through which numerous stories, programs, and actions flow.

ATTENTION TO NARRATIVE

The single story creates stereotypes and the problem with stereotypes is not that they are untrue, but that they are incomplete. They make one story become the only story.

—Chimamanda Ngozi Adichie[1]

MORE THAN VECTORS OF AFFIRMATION AND ATTENTION, memes contain the kernels of narratives and the ability to challenge narratives. If attention strategies guide us to talk about something in the moment, narrative strategies guide us to new frameworks about society, about the world around us, driving attention in the longer term and shaping conversation for months and years to come. The study of narratives has a long, complex history in literature that has begun emerging in political conversation too.[2] One of William Shakespeare's most famous passages comes from *As You Like It*, in which the cynical Jaques compares life to a performance on stage, with distinct points that punctuate a person's life. This oft-quoted passage resonates with ideas that preceded Shakespeare and continue to influence us today: narrative is a powerful way through which we see the world.

Narrative, in simplest terms, is a story. Narratives have plots; a set of actors; areas of tension that captivate us; morals and lessons; a beginning, an end, and a series of middle points. Narratives give us a way to connect isolated events and frame them in a larger story. They have tremendous power politically and socially, wielded by activists and the powerful alike, as a strong narrative can shape perceptions about reality and, equally important, channel emotions that might propel action. Duke University professor Frederick Mayer has written about the importance of narratives, observing that humans are "story-telling animals":

> We make sense of, form beliefs about, and establish our stances on issues such as climate change less on the basis of reason or experience and more on the basis of the stories we subscribe to. Moreover, the news media are, whatever else they are, purveyors of story, always on the lookout for a narrative angle that will capture the attention of viewers, listeners, or readers.[3]

To understand how memes channel attention into narratives, let's look back on #UgandaIsNotSpain and #StopKony. Hashtags and memes created in a context of social change often serve as micronarratives. Stop Kony. Uganda is not Spain. Chen Guangcheng will defeat Pandaman. Trayvon Martin faced systemic racism. Hoodies are powerful. Through satire and repetition, social media users are able to shape and define a narrative, and through intentional overproduction, they start arriving at narratives that have the potential to resonate more broadly. Each new hashtag, as it gets picked up, has the potential to create yet another narrative. In so many ways, the battle for attention online means a battle over narratives.

Narratives are surprisingly sticky things. They are adapted for the human mind, which loves stories and imbues stories with emotional power. The stories we tell ourselves drive us forward or push us backward, and stories are built on top of cultural and political narratives that are much larger than ourselves. So much of what Mariano Rajoy, KONY 2012, and Western journalists were responding to was a long-running narrative about countries in Africa. That narrative includes stereotypes like ethnic violence, military conflict, and child soldiers. The Nigerian writer Chimamanda Ngozi Adichie has called it "the single story." In a TED talk, she argued that "the single story creates stereotypes and the problem with stereotypes is not that they are untrue, but that they are incomplete. They make one story become the only story."[4]

Sometimes, as with KONY 2012, a hashtag-driven narrative can reinforce an existing narrative by drawing attention to its particulars in a given country. This can come at the cost of accuracy—namely, that Kony was still operating in Uganda—while benefiting from the increased attention it garners. Other times, hashtags can help reshape and re-form a narrative. Other narratives, like the story of Chen Guangcheng, fit into multiple narratives: the long-running narrative that China oppresses human rights activists, and the heroic narrative of a blind man overcoming his conditions. The latter draws on long-running stories of blind men overcoming challenges that precede Chen, like *Daredevil*, the blind superhero in the Marvel universe, and *Zatoichi*, about a blind swordsman in Japan.

Most striking, hashtags shape narratives across great distances, leaping geopolitical boundaries to drive conversations in other countries' media. By themselves, they can't change people's minds, but they can get the ball rolling, connecting with media and politicians to challenge their views. Sasha Costanza-Chock, a technology professor and activist at MIT, has written on the subject. Addressing the role of creative uses of technology for social movements in the twenty-first century, Costanza-Chock noted that successful movements utilize something called *transmedia organizing*, a process that "denotes cross-platform, participatory media making that is linked to action and, ideally, accountable to the movement's social base." In other words, successful movements today make media across a wide variety of platforms and spaces—the internet, television, comic books, music, YouTube videos, and more. And they get their participants to make media too.

Costanza-Chock says more:

> Social movements are becoming transmedia hubs, where new visions of society are encoded into digital texts by movement participants, then shared, aggregated, remixed and circulated ever more widely across platforms. Despite persistent digital inequality, the praxis of critical digital media literacy can produce subjects able to fully participate in transmedia organizing. Transmedia organizers take advantage of the changed media ecology to mobilize networked social movements. Participatory media-making can help strengthen movement identity, win political and economic victories, and transform consciousness.[5]

For participants, the messages are no longer taken for granted or quietly critiqued but instead can be publicly challenged with regularity through internet meme culture, blogs, and other citizen media. Social change memes, then, take their place in the long line of activist art and culture—from street theater to graffiti—which aim to disrupt and challenge narratives in public space. Creative media activism shifts the media environment for individuals—in the case of internet memes, their digital media environments—and allows individual and small community expression about issues that matter most to them. What is new here is how the culture and structure of the internet have facilitated their rapid spread to newer and broader communities.

Indeed, memes allow us to more quickly develop the visual and verbal language around which movements organize. Think about the rainbow flag, the raised fist, and the yellow ribbon for women's suffrage in the United States. These symbols were designed and developed over time, and they were used as signals of support for different social causes. These signals of support in turn function as identity markers—"I support gay rights," "I am a conscientious fighter for racial justice"—that strengthen a movement's core. The iterative, remixable process of memes helps create, define, and amplify new symbols at a faster pace, transforming something as innocuous looking as sunglasses into a symbol of defiance and an expression of concern about an individual's humanity.

The narrative-shifting, emotion-affirming power of memes is a major contribution to movements, a contribution that can help sustain movements through challenging times. These media objects help marriage-equality advocates see, for instance, that they are not alone in supporting the right to marriage for people of all genders. By posting memes to our social media feeds and profile pictures—some of the most important representations of ourselves in digital public life—we begin to identify more strongly with the cause. As internet culture and media scholar Negar Mottahedeh told me in an interview for *Los Angeles Review of Books*:

> When you see a child at play, they are recreating the world, mimicking what is, leaving their mark on it, changing it in the process. Play creates the world anew. Many of the revolts were flash mobs that creatively circumvented the government's restriction. They did it playfully and oftentimes joyfully. People were revolting against what was and, in the revolt, created something new.[6]

Mottahedeh spoke in the context of the Green Revolution in Iran, but her words resonate broadly for meme culture: it's in the playful aspects of meme culture that movement narratives can be found. Memes help us envision another world, a practice known as *prefigurative politics*, and in creating space for the imagination, they can help motivate action.

The incumbent narratives being countered are often different, but the ability to shape and form a new narrative is critical to any movement. In China, that might mean the state media narrative; in the United States, that might mean longstanding cultural mores; and in Uganda, that might mean dominant Western media depictions. It's a common misconception that memes are ephemeral. A hashtag trends, a selfie meme circulates widely, and then they disappear as quickly as they seem to have emerged. But many of these memes are part of something longer term, which is a political narrative, and these narratives are driven by memes that go viral, garnering responses from people on the street, the media, and the world's most powerful politicians.

STORIES AND HISTORIES

Our ancestors were sold here! Our ancestors were sold here!
—Hands Up United protest, St. Louis, Missouri

I STOOD OUTSIDE the old St. Louis Courthouse one day in the sweltering summer of 2016, as protesters from the local Black Lives Matter community began gathering. On the front steps of that same courthouse, for much of the nineteenth century, more than five hundred African slaves were sold as property.[1] New purchasers would examine them and their bodies, haggle over their worth, trade deeds to indicate ownership. In that same courthouse, the enslaved Dred Scott and his wife, Harriet Robinson Scott, began a series of historic lawsuits arguing for their freedom. Dred Scott would eventually lose in a landmark US Supreme Court decision, and an earlier legal battle in St. Louis yielded a devastating decision: Scott was a slave first and foremost.[2] A century and a half later, St. Louis, and more specifically the suburb of Ferguson, would become the center once more of the nation's fight for racial justice.

The goal of the local Black Lives Matter activists that day in July 2016 was to disrupt Netroots Nation, a progressive conference founded by the *Daily Kos*, with a number of conference attendees joining them. I attended the Netroots Nation conference to help oversee translations of their social media feed into Spanish and to help diversify access to their social media, and I also spent time getting to know the conference and events on the ground. Black Lives Matter protesters marched from the courthouse and into the streets, with white people and nonblack people of color marching in solidarity, including along the freeway briefly—a technique frequently used to block traffic—and over to America's Center Convention Complex, where the Netroots Nation conference was being held. Speakers from a group called Hands Up United reminded marchers of the racial injustices of this country and that, when they went back to their respective locations, they should fight for racial justice and black lives in their own localities.

Starting the protest at the Old Courthouse was not an accident. While I'd long been aware of the historic racial injustices of the United States, standing in the courthouse and seeing and hearing the narrative the activists were drawing between slavery in the nineteenth century and racial injustices and abuses in the twenty-first century sent chills down my spine. They sang songs from the civil rights era, like "Keep Your Eyes on the Prize," and hung a banner that said "Racism Lives Here" while holding up their fists, invoking the Black Power salute of the 1960s. I sat on the steps of the courthouse to take a breather as the protest continued inside, and I imagined families and loved ones torn apart as they were sold on the front steps.

The evocation of history is a powerful technique used to build narratives. History extends time, showing that one incident is not isolated but part of a people's larger trauma, or a nation's larger pattern of abuse. While looking to the past, history necessarily makes us think about the future, and how things might change—or perhaps stay the same. Indeed, the English word "story" comes from "history," which derives from the Latin *historia*. A number of Black Lives Matter protests have made this connection to historic events and places, such as one march I attended in Oakland. Protesters gathered around the Alameda Courthouse where, in 1968, the Black Panther Party had also marched, at that time in support of Huey Newton, a cofounder of the party.[3] The march called for black people to lead and everyone else to follow, and people's T-shirts and signs referenced #BlackLivesMatter (cofounder Alicia Garza is based in Oakland), Trayvon Martin, hoodies, Eric Garner, and other recent symbols of the movement.

The national conversation about Trayvon Martin reminded me of the story of Rodney King in Los Angeles in 1991. Video of King being beaten severely by police officers took the nation by storm. When the officers in the video were acquitted, people took to the streets of LA to protest, and for four days, the city suffered tremendous violence and property damage. In A&E's documentary *L.A. Burning*, people noted the reason for the riots: they were fed up with police violence, and they were frustrated that, when they finally had video evidence, justice was still not forthcoming.[4] A national conversation about race ensued, but at that time connecting the dots was more difficult—how many other Rodney Kings were out there? How many other examples of police violence existed?

In 2014, St. Louis resident Michael Brown, eighteen years old, was shot and killed in Ferguson, a suburb of St. Louis, by Officer Darren Wilson.[5] Unlike the story of Trayvon Martin, in which only the words of George Zimmerman were available as witness, video and photos posted shortly after the Ferguson incident depicted Brown's body lying in the streets for four hours.[6] The imagery began circulating on social media, first among the St. Louis community and then nationally, in a now familiar pattern: a core group promotes an image, video, or story, and then other influencers help amplify it beyond its original geography. Videos on social media showed the protests in action and the police, armed with military gear, lining up to confront the protesters.

One of the core chants in Ferguson was "Hands up! Don't shoot!" The chants echoed early testimony that had suggested Brown had died with his hands up, and when a grand jury decided against indicting Officer Wilson, protesters in Ferguson took to the streets and social media.[7] "Hands up, don't shoot" became their common refrain, chanted and performed on the streets. It transformed into a hashtag, #HandsUpDontShoot, and a performative action: holding your hands up to the camera. The practice quickly went national. Around this time, the BlackLivesMatter hashtag circulated widely on social media. Led by professional activists Patrisse Cullors, Alicia Garza, and Opal Tometi, #BlackLivesMatter became a rallying cry on social media and in the streets as people chanted, "Black lives matter! Black lives matter!"

Examining both hashtag activity and content on BlackLivesMatter.com, which was established after the killing of Trayvon Martin, media scholars Deen Freelon, Charlton D. McIlwain, and Meredith Clark observed that "Brown's killing and subsequent media activity and groundswell of grassroots activism propelled BLM from infancy to maturity."[8] The hashtags were critical to fostering conversation among a wide variety of actors that ranged from activists and protesters to media observers and politicians; the Black Lives Matter website was directly connected to a majority of important websites, from *Truthdig* to *Snopes* to Public Radio International to the *Atlantic*. This savvy media approach combined with a strong groundswell of support on social media and in the streets ensured a clear pipeline of attention linking events on the ground to mainstream media, who in turn amplified videos and reports from protests and deaths. Soon, protests began erupting across the United States, and a new narrative emerged, the larger Movement for Black Lives. Leaderful, youthful, and national, the Movement for Black Lives as a coalition drew from the hashtag #BlackLivesMatter. It consists of organizations like the Million Hoodies Movement for Justice, cofounded by Daniel Maree and now run by veteran activist and cofounder Dante Berry; the Dream Defenders; and the Oakland-based Center for Media Justice.[9] It and the BlackLivesMatter hashtag are distinct from the organization, Black Lives Matter, which hosts multiple chapters to help local organizers build political power.[10]

Some of the most important innovations of the Black Lives Matter movement were in the seamless transfer of hashtags to the physical world. Hashtags and chants serve similar functions: they are inherently social and participatory, and they grow stronger in their repetition. When Staten Island resident Eric Garner was choked to death by police officers in Staten Island, New York, video of his death showed him saying, "I can't breathe" multiple times while they held him down. This inspired a chant and a performative action. Instead of holding their hands up, protesters held their hands to their throats and chanted, "I can't breathe." This chant also took the form of a hashtag, #ICantBreathe. I attended a number of rallies in the Bay Area, in both San Francisco and Oakland, and watched as people chanted and carried signs with all these hashtags on them. There were T-shirts and hats, posters and stickers. Protesters carried the names of victims of police violence, who had become popular hashtags: #TrayvonMartin, #PhilandoCastile (who was shot and killed during a traffic stop), and #SandraBland (who was found hanging in jail after being arrested).[11] Most striking to me as I watched protests in Oakland were the moments when people raised their fists and raised their phones, documenting what they saw before them and sharing the videos to social media.

Hong Qu, a visiting Nieman Fellow at Harvard University and a technologist working in journalism, observed that events driven by social media frequently lead to an intersecting range of actors. He looked at the 2013 Boston Marathon bombings as a case study.[12] There's the event, and frequently that event circulates on social media first. Given the sheer presence of cameras among potential witnesses, this is increasingly likely. Some influencers on social media in turn drive local bloggers and writers to amplify the message, which in turn gets attention from celebrities on social media. Mainstream media pays attention at different links along the chain, and this reaches both online news outlets and broadcast media.

Network mapping is a useful tool for tracking the news cycle that occurred after Michael Brown's death and after each killing of a black person that circulated on social media. With denser social networks among African American activists on social media, the ability to amplify an individual death, regardless of where it occurred in the country, ensured that more deaths could be recognized. Activists could link deaths around the nation and develop a narrative about endemic police violence against African American men and women. This ability to create a network across geography *and* across time is what makes the movement particularly powerful as a narrative.

When I consider what makes "Black lives matter" as a phrase, a chant, and a hashtag particularly effective, I think back to the article cofounder Alicia Garza wrote in *Feminist Wire*: "#BlackLivesMatter doesn't mean your life isn't important—it means that Black lives, which are seen as without value within White supremacy, are important to your liberation."[13] Hers was a call for a conversation about systemic racism, to include single individuals and understand how their lives are affected by larger structures. #BlackLivesMatter doesn't just drive attention, and it doesn't just affirm. It is itself a narrative. The implicit assumption of the phrase is that black lives are dangerously undervalued in American society.

This narrative, in turn, provided a frame for news media, advocates, policy makers, and others, and it set the national agenda for months and years to come. The *Guardian* published an interactive series that counted the deaths of black people at the hands of police, and television series emerged to look at the issue of police violence. In Latin America the chant of "*Vidas negras importan*" (Black lives matter) emerged, as people of black African descent challenged historic discrimination against their communities.[14] Communities of color started hashtags in alliance, for example, #Asians4BlackLives, and ethnographer and researcher Christina Xu began a letter-writing campaign, called Letters for Black Lives, which gave young people a template letter for immigrant parents who may not fully understand the movement's goals and aims.[15] At the University of Missouri, activists evoked #BlackStudiesMatter as they sought to raise awareness of systemic inequalities at the university after a couple of black students were called the N-word.[16]

The broader media impact is also palpable. Major films such as *Selma*, directed by Ava DuVernay and depicting the 1965 march across the Edmund Pettus Bridge led by Martin Luther King Jr., tapped into history. Books like Michelle Alexander's *The New Jim Crow* helped provide an intellectual and historical framework for the current prison industrial complex and its roots in slavery. Television shows and documentaries—for example, a reboot of the series *Roots*, which traces multiple generations of an enslaved family and a series of documentaries of the Los Angeles uprisings—have all evoked the history of the United States' racial injustices. In a short film about the opening of the new African American history museum in Washington, DC, the *Atlantic* highlighted the museum's long take on history, from Thomas Jefferson owning hundreds of slaves to Alicia Garza's original Facebook post: "Our lives matter."[17] To be clear, these major initiatives were not caused by the emergence of a hashtag—many were efforts being led for decades by their respective makers; rather, it's that they participated in a broader national conversation about race that the hashtag helped foster.

While hashtag activism is frequently derided as a form of "slacktivism" that achieves little, one of its most powerful roles is in driving attention and shaping narratives. One reason, perhaps, that it's frequently derided is because it appears to achieve little visible structural change—black people are still being shot by police and the American criminal justice system continues to show hallmarks of systemic racism. Another reason is that it seems to be simplistic—#HandsUpDontShoot and #BlackLivesMatter are hardly nuanced policy statements. But it's important to look at the broader narrative impact and milieu of media to understand the impact of hashtag activism when done effectively. Racial justice is an extremely complex issue with many levers and influences, with a long historical agenda; as history has shown, achieving equality in the face of great resistance will take many generations.

But it's also critical to remember that #BlackLivesMatter, a movement named after a hashtag, has successfully helped shift the national agenda for broadcast media, providing a framework for discussion about police violence and larger structures of racial inequalities. In the United States, crafting narrative has been a key lever for communities of color to bring their issues to the top of the agenda in a way that sustains these narratives. This is not an easy task, and it frequently requires iteration and an interdisciplinary approach.

Among Native Americans, for instance, #NotYourMascot provided a powerful rallying cry to end the practice of using Native American symbols, slurs, and images in sports mascots. Driven by the Eradication of Native Mascotry, a coalition of Native American activists founded by Diné Ihanktonwan journalist Jacqueline Keeler, the hashtag connected Native American communities around the country in calling for sports teams in their localities to change the names of their mascots. The national actions targeted the Washington Redskins in particular, but the focus on the issue helped local activists drive change. All in all, hundreds of teams have begun changing their names.

The action started as #ChangeTheName, calling for the Redskins to change their name. As Keeler recounted to me, the hashtag was randomly taken over by people in India who were campaigning for something completely unrelated. This forced Keeler and the group to pivot to #NotYourMascot, which was much more specific ("Change the Name" could refer to any name, really) and helped establish a clear narrative. The phrase and hashtag helped frame the conversation. For me, as someone who doesn't pay much attention to sports but had certainly heard of teams such as the Chiefs, the Redskins, and the Indians, it made me wonder why Native Americans and their culture are so frequently used as mascots when other ethnicities are not. One meme floating around suggested team names like the "San Francisco Chinks" and the "New York Jews" to highlight the absurdity and imbalance of this practice.

Keeler, who coined the word "mascotry," which the new hashtag evokes, described her motivations in an interview with me for the *Civic Beat Reader*:

> I want to take the focus away from the static image of the mascot. That image can be noble looking and it can be somewhat okay. But it's the cultural practices around having a native mascot: dressing up as Indians, playing Indian, donning red face, making up fake chants. These stereotypical actions are demeaning to Native people.[18]

Understanding the twin swords of narrative, Keeler explained that the strategy of focusing on mascots was not accidental.[19] Given an existing lack of interest in covering Native American issues in the United States, she knew that a narrative of resistance to a major sports team, one with national standing, would garner more attention and stories. Indeed, hundreds of stories have been written about the Redskins' name, the team, and its mascotry, even reaching the cover of the *New Yorker*.[20]

A similar strategy was operating when media activist April Reign kicked off #OscarsSoWhite after the 2015 Oscar nominations were announced.[21] Many people noticed that the films and the actors nominated were predominantly white. The Oscars, like American football, already garnered a great deal of attention, and the catchy hashtag took off. It helped generate a national media conversation about the racial composition of the Oscars committee and the historic underrepresentation of people of color among those receiving awards from the Academy of Motion Picture Arts and Sciences. That year's host, Chris Rock, referenced the hashtag and, more important, the issue a number of times during the televised awards ceremony. By 2017, *Moonlight*, a film with a black director and black acting leads, won Best Picture, and a more diverse array of people from the film industry were added to the Oscars board, with a stated goal to double diverse representation on the board by 2020.[22]

This is not to suggest that narrative is all that is needed. A powerful narrative can blind us to the other actions that we need to take to effect meaningful change. Indeed, Harvard legal scholar Lawrence Lessig has described four types of constraints that govern human behavior: law, social norms, markets, and architecture and infrastructure. He argues that these constraints also affect behavior on the internet.[23] But what makes a narrative more powerful than attention is its capacity to set a framework for conversation about legal, market-based, and infrastructural changes. Narrative helps shape new social norms. Whether that's the shootings of black people in the United States or the use of Native American imagery in mascots, narratives help people draw connections between seemingly unrelated incidents and chart through lines for productive conversations about underlying issues.

Also, with a new national agenda comes a new national debate; for every narrative, there is a counternarrative. As Black Lives Matter rose to prominence in American discourse, it also provided a framework for disagreement, such as the appearance of the hashtags #AllLivesMatter and #BlueLivesMatter. In the former, detractors frequently issued support for organizations that Black Lives Matter challenged, arguing that the movement ignores the lives of other people.[24] Supporters of #BlackLivesMatter note that systemic violence against black people in particular in American society necessitates clearly articulating the importance of black lives. With the #BlueLivesMatter hashtag, supporters of police have pushed for hate crime legislation that covers police and firefighters in protected categories, arguing that violence against the police is a systemic problem.[25] Indeed, the narrative structure of "black lives matter versus X lives matter" has proven to be particularly sticky. "Do black lives matter or do all lives matter?" emerged as a question for candidates in the Democratic Party debates during the 2016 election, while "Blue Lives Matter" bills have been passed in a number of districts, adding police officers and firefighters to the list of protected groups in hate crimes legislation.[26]

The capacity for generating narrative is not limited to those on the Left. On the American political Right, the Tea Party movement received its symbology from a memetic performance in 2009. Stock-trader Graham Makohoniuk galvanized people strongly opposed to the newly inaugurated President Obama and his administration to take pictures of tea bags that they then mailed to members of Congress.[27] Tea bags appeared on a number of signs, both as drawings and as physical objects pasted onto them.[28] Repurposed and remixed, tea bags came to symbolize resistance to the progressive administration and progressive politics. It drew on the long history of tea as a symbol of protest in the United States and effectively channeled a narrative of resistance, given that the original Boston Tea Party during the American Revolution was an act of resistance against British rule.

Narratives give us a structure to talk about incidents in a broader context, to help draw connections across seemingly unrelated incidents, and to drive a national and international media agenda. But how do we arrive at our narratives and symbols in the first place? Frequently this is a long process of iteration, remix, and experimentation that's endemic to meme culture. Perhaps counterintuitive, it's not dissimilar to how professional media organizations promote an ad or brand. Let's take a closer look at a movement just across the Pacific, in Hong Kong, where for many years activists have been building a narrative of resistance to the increasing influence of mainland China.

SYMBOLS OF ITERATION

If censorship exists, isn't it because aesthetics is perceived—at least by those in power—as a very real threat to the social and political order?

—Gabriel Rockhill[1]

IN JUNE 2017, shortly after Carrie Lam was elected as the new chief executive of Hong Kong, President Xi Jinping came to the city for an official visit. That would have been largely unremarkable but for one observation: prodemocracy protesters were not to be allowed near the areas of his visit, and symbolism related to their movement had to be removed, including, notably, a picture of President Xi holding a yellow umbrella. This effort echoed attempts by Xi to bar umbrellas around him during a visit to Macau in 2014.[2]

At the peak of the Umbrella Movement a few years prior, in 2014, an image of Xi was remixed to show him holding a yellow umbrella. The picture, obviously photoshopped, circulated widely on Chinese social media. A cardboard cutout appeared on the streets of Hong Kong, allowing anyone to take pictures with the president and his umbrella. Umbrellas, especially yellow ones, were once seemingly innocuous, just useful devices for carrying around town in this subtropical environment, where sudden rains are common. Suddenly umbrellas contained symbolism so strong that their circulation had to be prevented. How this happened is a story of the power of symbols crossing back and forth between the physical world and the digital world, driving a narrative so sensitive it was worthy of state censorship at the highest levels.

Let's step back a few years. In 2013, a few dozen students set up camp in the Central District, a neighborhood of Hong Kong, inspired by the words of Benny Tai Yiu-Ting, a law professor at the University of Hong Kong. They dubbed it Occupy Central with Love and Peace.³ The name, which also appeared as the hashtag #occupycentralwithloveandpeace, was an obvious reference to the Occupy movements that had swept much of the West. The Central neighborhood of Hong Kong is a bit like Wall Street in New York City: bustling with well-dressed business people and filled with commercial spaces. It's considered an important hub and therefore a suitable symbolic target for an occupation.

Hong Kong protesters resisting Beijing's influence had already shown a capacity for symbolic actions that proliferated on the internet. Just a year prior to the occupation, a group called Scholarism, founded by a young student named Joshua Wong, organized a campaign against mainland China's insistence that certain books be taught in schools. Scholarism activists dubbed their protest "Against Brainwashing." Participants (mostly students) took action by distributing stickers in subways and throughout the city, declaring that they were against brainwashing. They also practiced a performative gesture, familiar in Chinese culture, of crossing their arms atop their heads, which means "no" (it's roughly embodied in the "no" emoji: 🙅). These actions spread as selfies and in protests, including with cartoon remixes.⁴

Writing about the power of narratives in social movements, Harvard scholar Marshall Ganz notes that "stories map positive and negative valance onto different kinds of behavior. They thus become what [the philosopher] Charles Taylor calls our 'moral sources'—sources of emotional learning we can access for the courage, love, hope we need to deal with the fear, loneliness and despair that inhibits our action."⁵ Ganz went on to note that stories are more than words themselves: they are also performances, and as performances, they receive power from the speaker and context.

Hong Kong operates under an official "one country, two systems" policy. Despite being the territory of the People's Republic of China, it continues to operate with many of the same systems in place as when it was a British colony: certain forms of democratic representation, a free media environment, and an uncensored internet. During the handover to China in 1997, many citizens expressed concerns about Beijing's influence on Hong Kong, potentially stripping away key freedoms that they had grown accustomed to under colonial rule. Authoritarianism rarely enters a region immediately—it typically comes in the form of subtle concessions over years and even decades. In many ways, Scholarism was designed as a vanguard of resistance against subtle changes over the years. It started with resistance against a change in the education system and moved into the next issue: erosion of democratic representation.

On August 31, 2014, China's legislature announced that, while there would be a popular vote for Hong Kong's chief executive, all nominees would have to be chosen by a smaller selection committee. In Hong Kong, the chief executive has been traditionally elected not directly by the people but by a selection committee. In the new model, not much changed.[6] This time it was immediately clear that all the candidates would be Beijing supporters, which essentially told citizens they could choose their representative, as long as they chose one who supported strengthening relations with mainland China.

Citizens' frustration with this situation combined with an existing Occupy Central occupation led to an important shift. Scholarism and others put out a call to action for a student strike, and people started gathering to protest.[7] This raised considerable attention, but a turning point happened when police pepper-sprayed and teargassed protesters to get them to dissipate. The protesters held up umbrellas to shield themselves from the pepper spray (the umbrellas would be ineffectual against tear gas).[8] News outlets, already covering the events, captured from above images of waves of colorful umbrellas held up in the city's streets. Footage from the short documentary *Umbrella Dreams* shows the uncertainty and tension of the moment, as protest leaders called for people to gather in the streets on the grounds that most Hong Kong citizens don't get their news from the internet.[9] As the documentary progresses it becomes clear that the umbrellas were carried for defense: "Stop charging or we use force," declare the police. Soon protesters carried banners of their own: "Stop charging or we unfurl umbrellas."

New Yorker Adam Cotton dubbed it "the Umbrella Revolution," and news sites around the world captured iconic images of people holding umbrellas, in what was arguably the first major protest movement to gain international attention since mainland China took control of Hong Kong.[10] Memes quickly emerged showing umbrellas in a variety of situations: yellow umbrellas in different logo-like formations—one made to look like a gun, one like a peace sign, one as if it were being held by a rabbit. Why yellow for the memes? Protesters had already been wearing yellow ribbons to symbolize universal suffrage, drawing on its symbolism from related campaigns in the United States, including those for women's suffrage. In this fusion of color, art and visual expression became central to how this movement established the yellow umbrella as a key symbol of resistance.

At this point, it helps to step back and consider the role of Western media in naming global movements. The Arab Spring, a series of protest movements that swept a number of Arab countries, was of Western coinage, as were the names of numerous color-invoking movements in Eastern Europe, such as the Orange Revolution. Sometimes, the moniker makes sense as a word but is less useful as a way to accurately represent an entire movement with complex origins and motivations. With the Arab Spring, for example, the movement's name implied that it affected the entirety of the Arab world, when in fact it affected only a handful of countries in the region.

Channeling many people's disagreement with the idea of revolution, Jason Li, a Hong Kong designer affiliated with the University of Toronto's Citizen Lab (and the illustrator of this book), expressed umbrage with the "revolution" framing of the Umbrella Revolution. In *88 Bar*, a blog we both write on, he observed that the movement had never started as a revolution, and calling it such was counterintuitive.[11] In a move similar to what Ugandans online had done to challenge narratives from Europe, many in the Hong Kong movement proposed a remix: #UmbrellaMovement. Today, this is the official Wikipedia entry name for the movement, even if you search explicitly for "Umbrella Revolution."

And just as there were digital memes, so were there physical ones. The yellow umbrella, which as a symbol for universal suffrage united occupations in distinct parts of Hong Kong—Central, Admiralty, Causeway Bay, and Mong Kok—became a powerful part of the narrative about promoting democratic rights in the city. Journalist Becky Sun describes the variety of images and actions in detail for London's Victoria and Albert Museum:

> Next to the giant banners of illustrations and slogans articulated with duct tape and paint, strings of yellow origami umbrellas are flowing down the sides of the Tim Mei Avenue footbridge straddling Connaught Road, wavering in the wind. Sheets of computer designed posters, hand sketches and doodling are plastered on the walls, balustrades and any surfaces within reach around the Hong Kong Central Government Offices in Admiralty. Opposite the projection from "Add Oil Machine for HK Occupiers" and the "Lennon Wall," which is an

external staircase of the premises covered in supporters' and demonstrators' multi-coloured post-it messages, stands the "Umbrella Man" sculpture, whose outstretched arm with an open umbrella is mimicked by a performance artist next to it in full tear-gas proof protective gear.[12]

I followed the protests online from afar and arrived in Hong Kong a few months after the peak of the occupation, when a small occupation still existed in the Central District and people gathered nightly with yellow umbrellas on the other side of the bay, in Mong Kok. Most striking to me was how familiar it all seemed—the visual and verbal language that I'd been following on the internet and the photos and videos circulating on social media all came to life. Yellow umbrella stickers with the hashtag #UmbrellaMovement and "I want true universal suffrage" (我要真普選) could be found throughout the city. I spent a few days documenting them, slapped onto walls and street poles, each with different designs. When I visited the Occupy site in Central, I walked by a little box containing origami umbrellas. The box had a sign on it declaring "Free umbrellas!" In exchange, the makers told me, I should take a photo and share it online so that everyone would know that the umbrellas are there and the occupation still present. "They can shut down this camp, but they can't shut down the movement," they told me. I picked up a few umbrellas, took pictures, and then brought them home with me.

The most common format was a yellow umbrella icon on a simple black background, but the wide breadth of variation suggested the work of multiple designers and sticker makers. It's important to understand these stickers in their context—they existed alongside an extensive variety of commercially oriented stickers throughout Hong Kong. As with the T-shirts and hats of the Women's March in Washington, DC, the infrastructure for creating commercial advertisements could be easily repurposed by the movement to create stickers, ticker tape, and T-shirts that expressed the symbols and slogans of the movement. And there were the actual, functioning yellow umbrellas, repurposed with printed #UmbrellaMovement hashtags. I watched as some activists decorated their yellow umbrellas, which they'd simply purchased in department stores, by placing custom stickers and tape on them.

I met with Chung-hong Chan, a researcher in media and communications at the University of Hong Kong. Chan developed an algorithm to analyze dozens of Facebook pages and their commenters, and he found that people used a wide variety of symbols in their profile pictures, most notably the yellow umbrella and the yellow ribbon. Cartoon renditions, especially Mr. HK People, a direct reference to the popular Mr. Men children's books by British author Roger Hargreaves, also occupied these profile pictures.

The bright yellow-on-black background, the umbrella theme, the call for true universal suffrage—all of these things combined into a number of forms of expression that seamlessly transferred online and off. Student-oriented cafes in Hong Kong referenced the symbolism, signaling what the people in those places stood for. Books about the movement and about the question of democracy in Hong Kong used the imagery. When Yau Wai-Ching and Baggio Leung ran for legislative council, the students held up banners saying "Hong Kong Is Not China," and Leung Kwok-hung, aka "Long Hair," held up a yellow umbrella.[13] The symbol, though not as omnipresent as it once was, continues to have influence. With news of further encroachments of mainland China on daily life, protesters gather under its mantle.

Shaped in the vision of the protesters' words and beliefs (from Umbrella Revolution to Umbrella *Movement*), this narrative drove both Hong Kong and international discourse. The invocation of this symbol, remixed and amplified through meme culture, created a new narrative of resistance to Beijing, a narrative difficult to find in Xi Jinping's China, where repression of journalists and activism increased, creating a culture of fear and silence. Activists in Hong Kong still recall with great trepidation the summer when a number of booksellers disappeared after they sold books critical of the Communist Party. The story of an encroaching China was matched only by the story of students standing up to the party, a classic David and Goliath narrative that has long resonated with the human psyche. The umbrella, a tiny device that holds back the heavens, was a fitting symbol in so many ways, and its fusion with the yellow of suffrage rights gave it extra narrative power.

"It was a logistical, legislative issue," noted poet and scholar Henry Wei Leung in an interview with me, referencing the "I want true universal suffrage" rallying cry:

But summed up in it is the issue of voice, of self-representation, of integrity and dignity. The Movement began (before the arrests, the pepper spray, and the teargas) as a teach-in. Some people have described the protest camps as the envisioned living room of Hongkongers. Now I wonder if it was like a campus. Imagine the arts, creative media, stickers, songs, lectures, gatherings, plus things like flyering and canvassing—on a mobile university campus. Not hard to see the importance of the medium then. But even with division, the Movement as a historical moment was a divergence point, a point of common reference.[14]

What about the conversation in mainland China? It's complicated. Discussions about the events were lively, but researchers looked more closely: a select set of items was being censored, namely, those in support of the protesters. Instead, the majority of the online conversation was framed in pro-Beijing terms, with thousands of reposts for anti-Occupy posts and just six hundred reposts on a post related to the protest.[15] This suggested new censorship techniques and a dampening of the narrative's power in mainland China. Also, Instagram, which had been blocked intermittently in the mainland, appears to have been permanently blocked in October 2014, as it was popular with Hong Kong activists.[16]

Were the protests in Hong Kong successful? It depends on how you define success—since the original protests, new factions have emerged. Now a blue ribbon represents opposition to the protesters and their yellow ribbons, with blue symbolizing solidarity with the police. A red ribbon, though less popular, symbolizes Chinese nationalism and the red flag of the People's Republic of China. The flip side of Chung-hong Chan's research has shown that Facebook seems to be driving increased polarization in Hong Kong, especially among young people, as the gap between blue ribbons and yellow ribbons grows, a phenomenon aptly dubbed *cyberbalkanization*.[17] Chan pointed out in conversation with me that green ribbons—blue and yellow mixed together to produce green, or a unity of the two groups—have declined in popularity.

Many of the protesters were fined severely months afterward, after the press attention moved elsewhere, and leader Joshua Wong was eventually sent to jail, along with fellow leaders Nathan K. Law and Alex Chow.[18] A pro-Beijing chief executive was still elected, and there remains the ultimate timeline: 2047, when China's agreement to allow the one country, two systems policy officially ends. "Hong Kong is a city whose autonomy has already been signed away; it will be absorbed into mainland China by 2047," writes Henry Wei Leung. "One consequence of this foreknowledge is a form of protest with more reflexive than reformational properties, in which the appeal to outside forces is overshadowed by the closed circuit of self-affirmation, a clamoring 'here I am' which requires no response from higher authorities in order to be meaningful."[19]

Paradoxically, this seemingly impossible situation is also likely the thing that makes the story of Hong Kong activists' resistance to Beijing that much more compelling in many people's minds; it created a narrative with an unclear outcome, a form of narrative tension that drives many to pay considerably more attention. "Plot is the logic that makes meaningful the events that precede the story's conclusion. Without plot, events would be mere occurrences, discontinuous and separate moments, rather than episodes in an unfolding story," noted researcher Francesca Polletta in talking about narratives in social movements.[20] Indeed, the human need for story is something wielded powerfully by activists who understand how a narrative can be nurtured and grown, reaching the highest levels of media and government. Through narrative, we make sense of the world, and the seeds of a narrative start with small things like hashtags and profile pictures, which have the potential to spark a larger conversation.

I think back to the censoring of yellow umbrellas. Censorship, as it attempts to dampen narratives and symbols, serves as an indicator of their potential for lasting influence. Writing in the *Los Angeles Review of Books*, cultural critic Gabriel Rockhill reflects on the power of art and symbolism in the face of power:

> The very act of censorship implies, or so it would seem, that the censors resolutely believe in the political and social power of the arts. If they did not, why would they bother to police what people can see, hear and touch? Does not the very existence of censorship prove, in reverse so to speak, that art is a sociopolitical force to be reckoned with? In other words, if censorship exists, isn't it because aesthetics is perceived—at least by those in power—as a very real threat to the social and political order?[21]

If censorship reveals the political potential of memes, symbols, narratives, and affirmations, then it is worth reviewing them in another lens: through the eyes of governments and opposition groups.

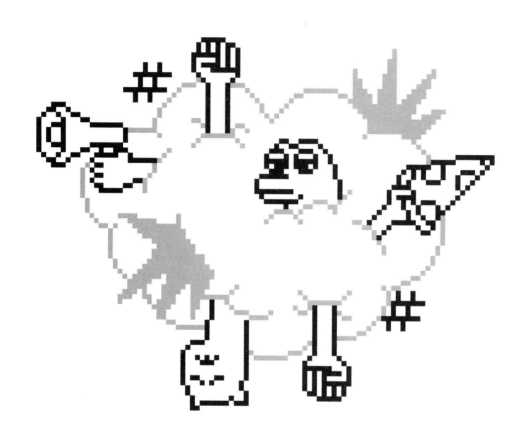

CHAPTER 5

. . . .

CHAOS MAGIC

> The point of modern propaganda isn't only to misinform or push
> an agenda. It is to exhaust your critical thinking, to annihilate truth.
>
> —Garry Kasparov[1]

MEMETIC STRATEGIES CAN CHALLENGE POWER, but the opposition adapts.
Nothing in the previous chapters suggests that memes can be useful only to those
with progressive, antiauthoritarian aims. Rather, memes are a media strategy
above all, and like any media, they can be used to communicate different kinds
of messages. The ability to quickly generate narratives on the internet reflects
a strength and a weakness: rather than simply censor overtly, governments and
countermovements can create alternative narratives based on rumors, falsified
information, and distraction, generating media popularly known as "fake news"
but that perhaps more accurately should be called misinformation, disinformation, and propaganda.

Moreover, there are many forms of power in addition to circulating powerful narratives on the internet. In China, for instance, punishing virality and
spreading rumors are ways to control bodies when the internet has proven to be
too difficult to control fully. Further, the easy remixability and context specificity of memes are also a weakness: existing memes can be co-opted, challenged,
and discredited. Like #BlackLivesMatter and #AllLivesMatter, as memes seep
into everyday life, they become sites of contention and, in some cases, violence
and oppression.

THE MEME ELECTION

The deep story was a feels-as-if-it's-true story, stripped of facts and judgments, that reflected the feelings underpinning opinions and votes.

—Arlie Hochschild[1]

"WHAT A NASTY WOMAN." In the middle of the third US presidential debate, while the Democratic Party nominee, Hillary Clinton, was in the midst of explaining her views about Social Security, Republican Party nominee Donald Trump smirked, raised his finger, and uttered the words. In an era before social media, viewers at home might have balked and yelled at their television screens. Talk show hosts might have thrown out a joke here and there, and op-ed columnists might have offered their take.

The collective memetic outcry overshadowed any nuance in Clinton's discussion of Social Security benefits as Trump's interjection was instantly tweet-worthy. Within seconds, Clinton supporters on social media took what was supposed to be an insult thinly veiled with misogyny and reclaimed it as their own. The hashtag #nastywoman emerged and began trending on Twitter. GIFs of Trump uttering the phrase began floating around, and pretty soon, so did image remixes. "I'm With Nasty," declared one sticker, riffing on Clinton's "I'm With Her" campaign slogan. Another image fused Clinton's face and the body of Janet Jackson from the musician's iconic *Nasty* album cover from the 1980s.

One of the most pointed responses was the hashtag campaign #Nasty WomenInHistory. People began sharing examples of assertive political women, like former US secretaries of state Madeleine Albright and Condoleezza Rice, who, if they had been debating Trump, might also have been called nasty. The posts appeared as image macros—photos with large text above and below them—reminding others of these women's accomplishments. In American English, "nasty" has long had a history of being used to criticize women, while also being used as an act of reclamation—hence the Janet Jackson reference, as the famous musician helped popularize the practice. The word "nasty" is often used like "bitch" and "slut" to penalize women for being too forthright about their sexuality and about being assertive in general.

Within hours some of these jokes and images started appearing on T-shirts, as the meme leapt from social media and onto the streets. Using websites such as Threadless and Teespring, online companies that streamline T-shirt production and distribution, people took the #NastyWoman trending topic, crafted a few designs, and uploaded them. The sites handled the rest, and the companies automated the process, with quick print runs and online templates. This ability to easily create and share physical objects is as important as the rise of Photoshop and social media tools: in 2016, designing and distributing shirts was almost as easy as purchasing them online. Within seconds of Trump's debate utterance, hashtags appeared; within minutes, images appeared; and within hours, shirts appeared. Within days, those shirts could reach their buyers, giving buyers a chance to post selfies, inspire friends to buy the shirts, too, and continue the viral life cycle. T-shirts, mugs, cloth bags, stickers, and pins circulated in the physical world like cousins of the digital world.

Text jokes, image remixes, video takes, and T-shirts and hats visually dominated the 2016 US presidential election. These memes took on a distinctly American character: expressing a plethora of often contrasting and incompatible views, as Americans from many walks of life weighed in with their perspectives. On the Right and the Left, for both those engaged in mainstream electoral politics and those voting for other parties, or no party at all, memes expressing a multitude of views floated around the internet.

A few months before, #Deplorables was the trending topic of the day, inspiring both digital memes and remixes, along with a suite of T-shirts and hats. Describing Trump's supporters, Clinton noted that many were sincere people with genuine concerns but that many also belonged in a "basket of deplorables."[2] The odd phrasing struck Trump supporters in a similar way as "nasty woman" had for Clinton supporters. Soon tweets about being a deplorable emerged. Some folks began describing "deplorable" values such as taking a pro-life stance, owning guns, and wanting to secure the national borders. Others turned the phrase around to chastise Clinton's "deplorable" actions, like maintaining a private email server or charging six figures for speeches at meetings of the investment giant Goldman Sachs.

A number of news outlets dubbed 2016 the "Meme Election." *Los Angeles Times* writer Carolina Miranda observed the broad range:

> Our endless electoral slog has produced viral images and animations of Florida Sen. Marco Rubio hitting a kid with a football during the primaries, New Jersey Gov. Chris Christie looking defeated as he endorsed Donald Trump for the presidency and the moment in which a bird landed on Sanders' podium during a stump speech in Oregon—leading an entire Internet contingent to dub the candidate "Birdie Sanders."[3]

Others observed that GIFs became the new sound bite, and indeed Clinton's and Trump's expressive faces lent themselves to GIFs.[4]

Memes in the election took a serious turn in September 2016, just months before the election, when the Anti-Defamation League (ADL), a civil rights organization with a particular focus on Jewish civil rights in the United States, added Pepe the Frog, a funny frog meme popular for its odd faces and phrases, to its list of hate symbols.[5] Pepe made history as the first visual internet meme to appear on this list, alongside more well-known hate symbols like the Nazi swastika and the white hoods of the Ku Klux Klan.

The co-optation of Pepe was the brainchild of the so-called alt-right, short for "alternative right," introduced to the world during the 2016 elections as an amalgam of right-wing communities with internet savvy. According to the Southern Poverty Law Center (SPLC), the phrase *alternative right* was coined in 2008 by Richard Spencer, who runs the National Policy Institute, a white nationalist think tank, and was described by a high school classmate as an "icon for white supremacists."[6] The SPLC describes the alt-right as "a set of far-right ideologies, groups and individuals whose core belief is that 'white identity' is under attack by multicultural forces using 'political correctness' and 'social justice' to undermine white people and 'their' civilization."

One alt-right technique is to turn otherwise innocuous images of cartoons like Pepe and milk (a decades-old symbol of white supremacy and Nazism) into expressions of white supremacy and thereby attempt to gain influence in public media.[7] Alt-right activists do this through meme culture, making and remixing images until one finally sticks. They are responsible for popularizing the words "cuck," a derogatory term with racist overtones referring to a weak male politician and a derivation from "cuckold"; "Kek," the Egyptian god of chaos and a deliberate typo of LOL (laughing out loud); and "snowflake," an insult for liberals that refers to the more common insult of calling someone a "unique snowflake."[8] If the opaqueness is confusing, that's part of the point: members of the alt-right aim to distance themselves from "normies" (normal people) who don't share their values, and using the meme language creates a group lingo.

Still, Pepe the Frog's life before 2016 was far less ominous. Created by Matt Furie in 2005, Pepe was a popular character in Furie's slacker comic *Boy's Club*, sparking countless silly memes as people mixed and remixed Pepe into a variety of other scenarios far beyond Furie's control. Pepe took on forms like sad Pepe and smug Pepe. Pepe spread throughout message boards and MySpace alike. Even Katy Perry tweeted with Pepe to complain about jet lag.[9] That Pepe would become a meme seemed inevitable. He's a funny animal, and funny animals tend to do well on the internet. He also has an expressive face with an air of mischief suited for many irreverent corners of internet culture. Whether laughing, crying, or grinning, he can be used to express emotions that words alone fail to capture. What seemed less likely was that Pepe would become a vehicle for white supremacy. Even Hillary Clinton's campaign website posted about Pepe, noting his associations with hate.[10]

Pepe's transformation was relatively recent. Indeed, a quick search online reveals Pepe in a white hood; Pepe's signature smug grin outside a concentration camp; Pepe with Hitler's toothbrush mustache, declaring "Kill Jews Man." This latter phrase co-opts Pepe's original signature quip of "Feels good man." Anti-Defamation League CEO Jonathan A. Greenblatt released a statement in response to the alt-right's usage: "Pepe was never intended to be used as a symbol of hate. The sad frog was meant to be just that, a sad frog."[11] Teaming up with Pepe creator Matt Furie, the ADL disseminated a series of comics to #savethefrog and take back Pepe as a symbol of chill. Later, Furie even began filing lawsuits against people using Pepe for hateful purposes.[12]

How, in the midst of a historic and contentious election, did a frog meme become a part of national political and social discourse in the United States? I spoke with researcher Caroline Sinders, who documents and analyzes right-wing memes.[13] In 2017, Sinders cofounded, with artist Susie Cagle and technologist Francis Tseng, Viz Lab, which collects and visualizes memes as sources of misinformation. In my interview with her, Sinders pointed out similarities between the frog's form, with its big lips and sly grin, and long-running depictions of minstrels in American society. Minstrels are entertainers in blackface—the practice of putting dark makeup on white people to make them look black—who mock African American society. As Sinders noted, Pepe's Hispanic name only reinforces his otherness. Furie has made numerous and vigorous condemnations of using Pepe as a hate symbol, but these unfortunate associations were twisted beyond his control.

Researchers Alice Marwick and Rebecca Lewis documented and analyzed the alt-right's techniques in a paper for Data and Society, a think tank focused on social and cultural issues about technology. "The term 'alt-right' is a neologism that puts a fresh coat of paint on some very long-standing racist and misogynist ideas," they wrote. They continued:

> The term "alt-right" is accommodatingly imprecise. On one hand, it describes an aggressive trolling culture present in /b/ and /pol/ [channels in 4chan, a popular social media forum] that loathes establishment liberalism and conservatism, embraces irony and in-jokes, and uses extreme speech to provoke anger in others. On the other, it denotes a loosely affiliated aggregation of blogs, forums, podcasts, and Twitter personalities united by a hatred of liberalism, feminism, and multiculturalism.[14]

Pepe was mainstreamed by then-candidate Trump's use of the meme, when he retweeted an image that remixed the poster for the film *The Disposables*, creating "The Deplorables." One actor's image was transformed into Pepe. This triggered discourse on both the Clinton and the ADL websites, which then further confirmed Pepe's use as a white supremacist symbol. Would Pepe still be used broadly if not for these acts of legitimacy? It's difficult to say—sometimes memes stick without any further institutional validation—but what is clear is that the meme received additional strength and amplification, and it appeared on signs at a number of Trump rallies too.

Of course, 2016 was not the first time memes were deployed during the federal elections. In the 2012 elections, during a debate between President Barack

Obama and Republican Party nominee Mitt Romney, Romney famously declared his support of women: "I have entire binders full of women who can fill my Cabinet."[15] The internet took hold—posting pictures of binders with women inside, tweeting along on the hashtag #bindersfullofwomen, and even drumming up a quirky YouTube song. An entire conference—BinderCon—emerged to support women writers in New York and Los Angeles, and the conference continues to go strong year after year (where I myself have been a speaker).

But if the Obama campaigns of 2008 and 2012 will be remembered for their innovative use of the internet, the Trump and Clinton campaigns of 2016 will be remembered for embracing the internet in full force, using Twitter, Snapchat, Reddit, Facebook, text messages, and other social networking platforms to reach potential voters. Part of the shift can be explained by the general integration of the internet into people's lives. By 2015, 68 percent of American adults had a smartphone and that percentage increased to 86 percent for people eighteen to twenty-nine.[16] In other words, young people of voting age with mobile internet technology represented an especially important voting bloc in the 2016 election.

One thing that bloc knows is what internet culture researcher Marley-Vincent Lindsey wrote while discussing Pepe: "Networks of memes never reach a moment of stability."[17] They almost invariably take on a life of their own, and there will always be another remix, on top of the remixes of the remixes, creating a seemingly endless tree of variation that snakes back in on itself. This is part of what makes meme culture work—it's a shift away from static notions of media consumption toward more dynamic ones of both consumption and production. Sometimes this allows marginalized communities to challenge dominant narratives and shape new ones. Other times, like during elections, a multiplicity of memes appears with no clear consensus. This especially reflects life in a democracy, where competing views and perspectives are not just expected but also encouraged. In theory, this is what should make a democracy function. *In theory*.

Every day during the 2016 election, there seemed to be a bevy of new hashtag memes. #TrumpANovel emerged one day to poke fun at the candidate's unusual way of speaking, with clever titles like *Belittle Women* and *The Gropes of Wrath*.[18] Others, such as #TrumpBookReport, composed book reviews in the voice of Trump.[19] Critiques emerged not just from the Right and Left but also from those seeking racial justice. Early in the primary season, #NotMyAbuela memes responded to a Clinton-campaign blog post titled "7 Things Hillary Clinton Has in Common with Your Abuela." Latinx communities online took umbrage with the idea of Clinton as a Latina grandmother.[20]

What made one meme disappear as quickly as dust in the wind and another meme continue on for much longer? There is, of course, the mysterious x factor of social contagion that taps deep into people's minds and catches the cultural zeitgeist, aided by strong emotions and punchy language. But behind any long-standing meme is an organization or individual who drives it.

And so we come to the most significant meme of the 2016 election: "Make America Great Again." The central slogan of the Trump campaign was abbreviated on social media as simply #MAGA, and it dominated the conversation about this historic election. The phrase's ambiguity left it open to many interpretations. Many news outlets called out the implicit messaging behind the slogan: Great for whom? they wondered aloud, thinking back to the days before the civil rights era, when citizens of color, especially African Americans, Native Americans, LGBTQ people, and women had far fewer rights and far greater restrictions on their lives, livelihoods, and mobility. Other outlets used the opportunity to talk about the country's failing infrastructure and rising epidemic of methamphetamine addiction. In this view, "Make America Great Again" spoke directly to Americans' economic struggles and concerns, even if many disagreed strongly with Trump's policies overall.

What makes MAGA perfect meme material? As with many famous political slogans—Barack Obama's "Change" comes to mind—"Make America Great Again" was specific enough in sentiment but vague enough in substance that supporters could project onto it any meaning they wanted. It's a memorable phrase that doubles as a rallying cry, first of all, much in the same way other great memetic phrases—"black lives matter" and the "grass mud horse" (remember, the latter also sounds like "Fuck your mother" in Mandarin Chinese)—have shown. It's a template, second, and that makes it easy to share, reproduce, and modify. And it had the backing of a powerful political party, giving it the lasting power than many flash-in-the-pan memes don't have. It drives attention to Trump and crafts an implicit narrative: "America isn't great anymore, but it used to be. We can fix that." This powerful narrative evoked a nostalgic past in much the same way as the Tea Party had, and even more so than the Reaganism to which it alludes.

What MAGA spoke to more than anything was what University of California, Berkeley, sociologist Arlie Hochschild calls the "deep story." Hochschild spent half a decade interviewing Tea Party supporters in southwestern Louisiana, many of whom would eventually vote for Trump. She writes: "Running beneath [political] beliefs like an underwater spring was what I've come to think of as a *deep story*. The deep story was a feels-as-if-it's-true story, stripped of facts and judgments, that reflected the feelings underpinning opinions and votes. It was a story of unfairness and anxiety, stagnation and slippage—a story in which shame was the companion to need."[21]

The deep story is a powerful framework, capturing the long-running undercurrents that memes interact with. If memes seem ephemeral, it is only because they are the like the scattered seeds of a story with deep roots, informed by culture, geography, upbringing, and a wide variety of other factors. The deep story is difficult to quantify and difficult to bridge between Left and Right, but it cannot be ignored.

It's important to remember that "Make America Great Again" is itself a remix, tapping into modern American history. In 1980, as Republican nominee Ronald Reagan sought the presidency against Democratic incumbent Jimmy Carter, he campaigned on the promise of turning the United States into a shining city upon a hill. His slogan captured the wonder and excitement of this imagery: "Let's make America great again."[22] Reagan campaigned on the promise of a better yesteryear and the possibility of returning the country to a vague vision of its past. In 2012, as he prepared for his run for president, Donald Trump applied for a trademark for "Make America Great Again."[23] In so doing, he recalled the Republican Party's most influential president in recent history and also channeled a growing anxiety among his base that the United States had lost its way. By cutting off Reagan's "Let's," Trump's tagline lent itself to easy hashtagging as an acronym (#LMAGA doesn't quite have the same ring to it).

Reagan's slogan was plastered onto lapel stickers, buttons, posters, and bumper stickers, tools of the broadcast era that allowed citizens to signal to others which candidate they supported. Before such production was readily affordable, messaging was mostly a one-way street: the campaign machine had enough money and resources to create and disseminate these media at a national scale. Trump's campaign had semblances of this type of production, too, especially as it took the form of an iconic red baseball cap, declaring "Make America Great Again" for all to see. Easily recognizable in a crowded street, I suspect the cap was a smart move for another reason: selfie culture. It could be easily added to a profile picture, either via

Photoshop or by actually wearing it on one's head, and then broadcast to others. It was the physical manifestation of a practice seen before—transforming one's profile picture on social media into a signal of support for a social cause.

During campaign season, Trump's team made variations of the phrase, engaging and supporting the possibility of remix: "Make America Strong Again." "Make America Win Again." Each of these iterations drew from the initial anchor and offered an additional iteration. The meme formed an easy template for dropping in synonyms for strength and greatness, all in support of the candidate. Indeed, MAGA became a central organizing theme for the Republican National Convention. Each day a different purported goal was addressed: on Monday, for instance, it was "Make America *Safe* Again," and on Thursday, "Make America *One* Again."[24]

Shortly after the red cap grew in popularity, immigrant rights activists in the United States remixed it, directly challenging Trump's anti-immigrant rhetoric. Journalist José Antonio Vargas, an undocumented immigrant and founder of #EmergingUS, a platform that looks at immigration and the growing racial and ethnic diversity of the United States, changed his profile picture to that of a red baseball cap stating: "Immigrants Make America Great."[25] Activist Jeronimo Saldaña, working to support the Arizona-based Latinx organizing group Mijente, created a series of red hats. One, "Make America Mexico Again," referred to much of the history of land in the American West and Southwest, which once belonged to Mexico.[26]

A number of other hats emerged, all riffing on the theme of "Make America Great Again." Some of these challenged Trump, some of these supported him, and others, well, they were just random: "Make America Deplorable Again." "Make America Native Again." "Make America Green Again" (in support of Green Party candidate Jill Stein). "Make America Grate Again" (in support of cheese makers, I suppose). Once, while I was catching a taxi in New York City, I spotted a young man on a bicycle with a black baseball cap reading "Make America Goth Again." The remixes continued, and they were as endless as the debates about what, exactly, it means to make the country great once more. The simplicity of the phrase, the reproducibility of the hat, and the popularity of selfie culture all came together in a perfect storm that took the hat and slogan from that of a single presidential campaign to campaigns of both support and resistance, with a little nonpolitical humor thrown in.

One way to look at this is to argue that the remixes feed a global capitalist order and represent the further commercialization of political discourse in the United States. You wouldn't be wrong to make this argument, especially given the sheer number of sales of physical products tied in with any emergent meme. As with the bumper stickers and posters of previous eras, memes reflect an important signaling mechanism about one's political beliefs and values. If you're living in a part of the country surrounded by like-minded people, that might just mean a show of solidarity. But if you're around others who disagree with your politics, promoting certain memes can feel more like an act of courage. In either case, using such a personal meme means lending one's self-identity to a group identity. These sorts of signaling actions are important, even when their quantitative impact is difficult to measure.

What's even more important is recognizing that efforts to resist Trump through parody still placed him and his words at the center, whether that's a MAGA remix or a pink pussyhat (a reclamation of his infamous words "Grab them by the pussy"). These memes are part of a larger story, namely, that his mastery of attention in the age of social media and online polarization all but made him the center of conversation, even among those who opposed him. The data bears this out. According to a study by Harvard's Shorenstein Center on Media, Politics, and Public Policy, Donald Trump received significant negative coverage during the campaign (more so than Clinton, though both received negative coverage), a trend that has continued into his presidency.[27] Despite this, he received three times as much coverage as a usual president, and among the Republican Party, Trump continued to see enormously high ratings, even while greatly upsetting the opposition.[28]

Internet sociologist Penny Andrews, a postdoctoral researcher at the University of Leeds, has noted that Trump above all understood how to work within the new communications environment, which demands novelty and the perception of authenticity. Like Kim Kardashian, Trump was the one you loved or loved to hate, and his meme-ready communications style guaranteed attention from fans and antifans alike. In an interview with me for *Civicist*, Andrews says:

> For me, fandom is a really useful way of looking at the way people respond to politicians and political parties in a contemporary context—not just because politicians are celebrities of sorts, but because the old ways of understanding politics have broken down. We had the post-war consensus, then

the (neo)liberal consensus, and now we are somewhere else entirely—what I call a digital dissensus, quick to jump to outrage and fragmented into echo chambers. People don't necessarily vote based on their class, their employment or other traditional factors. A lot of people don't vote at all.[29]

After the election, when Donald Trump was declared winner of the electoral vote, another twist on the MAGA meme emerged. A spike in hate crimes was reported across the country, jumping up 67 percent against Muslims.[30] Some of these incidents involved physical attacks on racial, religious, and sexual minorities. Others were verbal incidents. But some took the form of media, spray-painted on walls: "Make America White Again."[31] In these cases the phrase transformed into an overt show of support for white nationalism, often appearing alongside swastikas and other historical symbols of white supremacy. This specific iteration of the phrase had been used frequently on social media prior to the election results being announced, but its emergence in graffiti was striking: more than fifty years after Martin Luther King Jr., Rosa Parks, Fannie Lou Hamer, and others built the civil rights movement, the US was seeing a growth in vocal white supremacy. This form of hatred had been hiding in plain sight in the memes all along, but it grew extra teeth with physical acts of violence against people and property.

On *This American Life*, host Zoe Chace interviewed an attendee at an inauguration celebration party called the DeploraBall, a play on the word "deplorables." "We did it," said the attendee. "We memed him into the presidency. . . . We shit-posted our way into the future. . . . This is true because we directed the culture."[32] ("Shit-posting" means what it sounds like. Know Your Meme, the meme indexing site, defines shit-posting as "an Internet slang term describing a range of user misbehaviors and rhetoric on forums and message boards that are intended to derail a conversation off-topic.")[33]

There are many complex reasons a person becomes president in the United States, and it's hard to say that memes by themselves brought Donald Trump to power. On the other hand, meme culture helped center Trump in a way few had seen before, helping set the terms of the debate both online and in broadcast media, both in GIFs and on T-shirts. And Trump, a former reality television star and a tabloid fixture, knew more than his opponents how to capture attention. His meme-ready utterances, whether deliberate or not, were fodder for an environment of dissensus, and his basic techniques have continued into his presidency, introducing a new communications style that combines modern entertainment and fandom with political power.

The meme about America's greatness had achieved greatness itself, helping propel a controversial but engaging celebrity from the most underestimated candidate of the Republican Party into the office of the most powerful person in the world. The alt-right called the election the result of "meme magic," but there was no magic.[34] A TV star by training, Trump knew and understood the ecosystem of broadcast media, social media, and news media that such celebrities can masterfully navigate. It is through his omnipresence as a brand and his ability to inspire his fandom as a TV star and then a candidate that Trump was able to dominate the media landscape.

ON JANUARY 20, 2017, the United States saw the inauguration of its forty-fifth president. Donald Trump reshaped the communications style of a presidential candidate and now a president, showing that the full embrace of meme culture, even at the expense of one's overall popularity, offers enormous opportunities for media power.

In his inaugural address, Trump invoked the now iconic phrase, remixing it once more as the world tuned in:

> Together, we will make America strong again.
> We will make America wealthy again.
> We will make America proud again.
> We will make America safe again.
> And, yes, together, we will make America great again.[35]

5.2

BODIES AND MINDS

You don't want the world to know what happened?
What are you afraid of? I am not afraid of you. I
took pictures, arrest me. I dare you.

—Yang Zhong[1]

IN THE SPRING OF 2015, Shanghai-based artist Dai Jianyong posted an image that would land him in jail. On his Twitter, Instagram, and other social media accounts, he uploaded a picture of the newly appointed Chinese president Xi Jinping with his eyes closed so tightly they formed creases all around. The image went viral, and soon thereafter, Dai was brought in for questioning by the police. If the charges against him held—namely, "creating a disturbance"—he would face up to five years in prison.[2]

Why would a picture of Xi closing his eyes tightly be so offensive to the authorities? In Chinese, this sort of selfie image is known as a "chrysanthemum face," and the word "chrysanthemum" is slang for "anus." Dai popularized it with various photos of himself in different locales around the world, such as in a selfie in front of various Buddha sculptures and the Statue of Liberty. The face of Xi Jinping, transformed into the obscene face thanks to basic photoshopping, took a particular hold on Chinese-language social media. Dai even depicted it on a suitcase and a can of Coke. The mustache drew comparisons with Hitler, though their mustaches are not identical, and tied into *Xitele*, a play on words with "Xi" and "Hitler."[3]

Dai was not the first person in China to be arrested for meme-ready material. Two years prior, Xi Jinping built on the harmonious society policies of his predecessor, Hu Jintao, and the government began a crackdown on what they called rumors. According to a ruling by the Chinese supreme court, any person who was found to have posted a piece of libelous information that garnered more than five hundred shares and/or five thousand views could be in violation of the law.[4] The law was ostensibly part of a larger effort to curb the spread of dangerous misinformation and rumors.

Misinformation can have disastrous effects. In 2011, after the nuclear plant meltdown in Fukushima, Japan, a rumor began spreading on Chinese social media that the radiation would spread overseas and that iodized salt could help prevent radiation poisoning. This wasn't untrue, but in reality the radiation was less likely to cause much damage by the time it reached Chinese shores. Citizens rushed to stores in a panic, emptying aisles of their salt products, with the sort of violence and stampeding one might see in the United States on a major shopping day like Black Friday.[5] Researchers on Sina Weibo noted that phrases such as "iodized salt" and "nuclear radiation" were more likely to be censored in an effort to curb the rumors.[6]

Rumors like these can harm people—both because of the rush for supplies and because of the misinformation about effective treatments against radiation—and it's right for the government to want to prevent citizens from becoming swept up in the viral machine of the internet. At the same time, the definition of "rumor" has been used expansively, often to quash inconvenient truths that the government didn't want people to know. But with no official definition, the word's meaning is left to interpretation by officials, who can utilize this ambiguity as a vehicle of censorship. The law against "spreading rumors," approved by the National People's Congress, stipulated imprisonment of up to seven years for anyone who "fabricates or deliberately spreads on media, including on the Internet, false information regarding dangerous situations, the spread of diseases, disasters and police information, and who seriously disturb social order."[7]

The internet is difficult to control, and internet memes are even more so. Once an idea, an image, or a turn of phrase takes hold on the internet, it goes viral across networks in unpredictable ways. Traditional censorship methods in China had trouble curbing them, and the raucous online communities of the Chinese internet took advantage of opportunities to simply evade and remix to get a message out. The authorities adapted, supplementing their usual online censorship methods by focusing on the root of these memes: people themselves. Digital rights scholar Rebecca MacKinnon has explored this phenomenon, calling it *networked authoritarianism*. According to MacKinnon, the Chinese government is one of the leading innovators:

> In the networked authoritarian state, while one party remains in control, a wide range of conversations about the country's problems rage on websites and social networking services. The government follows online chatter, and sometimes people are even able to use the Internet to call attention to social problems or injustices, and even manage to have an impact on government policies. As a result, the average person with Internet or mobile access has a much greater sense of freedom—and may even feel like they have the ability to speak and be heard—in ways that weren't possible under classic authoritarianism. At the same time, in the networked authoritarian state there is no guarantee of individual rights and freedoms. People go to jail when the powers-that-be decide they are too much of a threat—and there's nothing anybody can do about it. Truly competitive, free and fair elections do not happen. The courts and the legal system are tools of the ruling party.[8]

It's difficult to control the internet, but it's much easier to control people's bodies. In 2012, the government instituted a requirement that all participants in online life register with their real names and identification cards, often with an associated phone number. SIM cards for mobile phones, once readily available for purchase on the streets, soon required a photo ID and address before one could use a viable data plan.[9] A number of memes blew up on social media ahead of the law's passage. Particularly popular were pictures of people with *x*'s on their mouths, representing their official silence.[10] The law passed, and it's now nearly impossible to simply set up a social media account in China without that account being connected in some way to your name and home. This paved the way for the laws regarding rumors, which in turn has paved the way for the country to develop an extensive social credit system, modeled in part on the American credit system, that ties social rewards and punishments to one's behavior online and offline.[11] By tying online identity to online activity, and online activity to real-world punishments, the country has created an environment where people have to actively make a decision: If this message I post goes viral, what will happen? Will I be able to get a job? Get a line of credit? Will I be seeing the inside of a prison cell? China is not the only country to consider implementing systems that track online activity and tie it to offline consequences, and we should expect to see patterns like this in many countries, including in democracies.

By 2013 China had seen its first string of people arrested for spreading rumors. One was a teenage boy named Yang Zhong, living in Gansu, a small province in China's northwest. A man had been found dead outside a karaoke club, and police ruled his death a suicide. But Yang spent time interviewing friends and relatives nearby and challenged the official account of the man's death. He posted to Sina Weibo: "You don't want the world to know what happened? What are you afraid of? I am not afraid of you. I took pictures, arrest me. I dare you." They dared, and Yang was detained for a week, officially for spreading rumors.[12]

After his release, which came thanks in part to public pressure, Yang posted a picture of himself flashing a peace sign while wearing a T-shirt that said "Make change" in English. The chief of police in the region soon was suspended. Apparently emboldened, Yang promised an interview afterward on Weibo, but the interview, which was supposed to be live-streamed, was canceled before it could start, and his Weibo account soon vanished.

Memes continue to float through China's social media sphere, unimpeded by strictures about content. GIFs of Xi Jinping depict him invariably as a clown, a pro wrestler, and a dragon, poking fun at the "Uncle Xi" image he carefully cultivates around the country, with an aim to solidify his reputation as a hard-line but providing leader. A particularly popular meme captures Xi's face and body stature in the form of Winnie the Pooh, a cartoon that is now regularly censored because of its potential use for mocking him.[13] Why one meme gets censored, another leads to arrest, and another is completely ignored is a question with a deliberately opaque answer. By keeping private internet companies and citizens in the dark about the exact location of the dividing line, the government can foster a culture of self-censorship. This form of censorship is the most effective, wherein costly enforcement mechanisms don't need to be deployed to keep people from spreading an uncomfortable truth. Instead, unsure of the consequences of speaking out online, many people are likely to never speak out at all.

A 2015 study of Chinese censorship led by Jason Q. Ng, a scholar from the University of Toronto's Citizen Lab, sheds light on the specific strategies behind these new forms of censorship. Ng found that, contrary to popular belief, there's actually a wide variety of political discussion online. Censorship is more likely to occur in group chats rather than private chats, as the former carries the risk of mobilizing people.[14] Scholar Steve Smith has pointed out the historic role that censorship—and easing restrictions on it—has played in Communist countries:

> For Communist regimes, rumor represented both a form of unauthorized speech (and thus a potential threat to social stability) and a useful insight into popular attitudes and mood. This ambivalence reflected the dilemma of the regimes, which on the one hand were "wary of allowing citizens to express uncensored opinions about matters of public import in public," and on the other were "extremely anxious to know what people were thinking."[15]

Without democratic institutions, for a government to understand what its people are thinking can be extremely difficult. But any meme spread on the internet has the potential to transform quite rapidly into a movement, as people are inspired and organize both online and in the streets. Up to this point, I've talked a lot about China's efforts to curb undesired language, memes, and ideas on the internet. The flip side is its open embrace of internet culture.

One day while logging on to Sina Weibo, I wanted to choose an emoji for a post I was making. Emoji are visual character sets that appear in line with text, like a little apple or banana or, most famously, a yellow smiley face. Today, emoji are a consistent and fixed set of picture images managed by the Unicode Consortium, but they were predated by custom emoji sets in Asian social media environments. On Weibo, for example, these characters can be selected through a quick drop-down menu, and they contain many of the familiar icons along with some Chinese-specific ones, like the Chinese word for broadcast, a phrase meaning "give strength," and a bouncing rabbit.

That's when I noticed an odd image: a llama standing next to the emoji for *jiong* (囧), an archaic Chinese character repurposed on the internet as a face (You can see it, right? You don't need to be able to read Chinese to spot it), and another pun, the "Spirit Horse" (神马), which sounds similar to the Chinese word for "what." On Weibo, you can hover your mouse over any given emoji to see its Chinese name, and when I hovered my mouse over the llama, I saw the telltale words: "grass mud horse." I was shocked. How could such a subversive symbol be available on Sina Weibo as an official character? I then turned my attention to WeChat, which has a number of sticker sets available. Sticker sets became popular in messaging apps as an augmentation of emoji. Rather than inline images, they take up a whole message, and they're frequently animated. Once again, I saw a llama, dancing, smiling, even cussing. Unlike the Weibo emoji, it didn't explicitly say "grass mud horse," but its meaning was easy enough to imagine. The emoji's official name was the Choco Milk Alpaca, and it was as grass mud horse as could be.

How did the grass mud horse, a symbol of internet freedom the world over, end up as an official image on multiple Chinese social media platforms? The answer is difficult to swallow, but exploring this question helps one understand the other prong of China's internet strategy, which is to embrace memes and, in so doing, embrace a new form of propaganda used by many governments. In traditional, preinternet propaganda, governments tried to distill a single notion of truth, one that ran counter to reality but nonetheless offered an alternative reality. In the world of broadcast, this alternative reality came from a single source and was disseminated through multiple media outlets, often state controlled and compliant with messaging instructions.

The internet changed that. In places traditionally controlled by state propaganda, like China, Russia, Azerbaijan, and Egypt, the internet allowed people, including activists, to create alternative narratives. In China, instead of quietly accepting the "harmonious society," they were able to sow new narratives and messages into the world and raise a middle finger to singular messages. What happened was an explosion of new stories, new narratives, new perspectives that flowered across the internet as people found a voice and a community, often for the first time. In that plurality came power, as we've seen so many times. But therein lay a weakness.

Shortly after the 2016 US election, Russian chess grandmaster and human rights activist Garry Kasparov wrote about new forms of propaganda. Speaking from the perspective of Russia, he noted that today's propaganda looks less like a singular message and more like a plurality of messages, a plurality so great that the sole point of it is to create cognitive exhaustion:

Information "overload" has led people to resort to their own methods of media filtering. Some people simply shut it all out, essentially starving themselves of important information and thus becoming easily manipulated voters. Others, struggling to verify the validity of the news they read, might pay attention only to the source, in an effort to conserve mental resources and avoid drowning in a sea of information.[16]

How does this technique manifest in a place like China? Recall that the country is rumored to be hiring hundreds of thousands of paid internet commentators, known as the Fifty Cent Party. Governments like Russia's and Azerbaijan's use similar methods, creating a virtual army of people ready to engage online. The popular perception of China's Fifty Cent Party is that they argue vociferously with people who might be promoting a message that the government disagrees with. But in many ways, this misses the point. Anyone who's ever tried to argue with a troll on the internet knows how difficult this can be. Trolls bring up multiple points, and at the first sign of disagreement, they double down on their perspective. Weaponizing this practice can help governments spread their message to online channels.

A study led by sociology professor Gary King at Harvard University showed more clearly the Fifty Cent Party's strategies. King and his team examined thousands of messages on Sina Weibo and WeChat, carefully selecting for terms and accounts that seemed to be in line with Chinese government messaging. In this plethora of messages, they realized that most paid commentators weren't trying to persuade anyone online or offer a counterargument. Instead, during key moments, like when an online action seemed to be gaining momentum to rally people to organize or when there was a major government event that people were likely to comment on and critique, the progovernment messages increased significantly. The researchers described this as "cheerleading for the state" using symbols of the current leadership or symbols from the history of the Chinese Communist Party.[17]

The goal is to create a system of distraction through a plethora of engaged narratives. And, as King and his colleagues observed, it's incredibly powerful: "Distraction is a clever and useful strategy in information control in that an argument in almost any human discussion is rarely an effective way to put an end to an opposing argument. Letting an argument die, or changing the subject, usually works much better than picking an argument and getting someone's back up (as new parents recognize fast)."[18]

Indeed, while the resources of the internet seem infinite, our attention spans are not. Most human beings can concentrate on only a few things at once, and we can devote extensive cognitive effort for a limited amount of time each day. Attention is central to how the internet operates, and meme-wielding activists understand this well as they push their causes and narratives. As we scroll through our feeds on the subway or bus, click on websites in the office, and listen to podcasts on the way home, we are making critical decisions about how and where we want to drive our attention. And the internet, with its overload of GIFs, images, videos, push notifications (the text alerts that pop up on your phone when you get a text message or app alert), and passionate tweets, regularly offers narratives that compete for our attention. Those who understand this learn how to create eye-catching, emotionally fulfilling media experiences that compel us to pay attention. Scholar Tim Wu has argued that this understanding has also created a new class of business people, called "attention merchants," those who understand that with attention comes money. As they perfect the ability to attract people's attention, they are able to sell better and more effective advertisements. This is not necessarily a bad thing, Wu noted, but it is something all of us need to be aware of, so we can decide how and when to pay attention.[19] I'd argue that attention activists have also entered this fray, and what we also have now are attention propagandists.

Smart governments trying to spread a message understand better than most that contemporary propaganda is a battle for attention and narrative. In 2015, a mysterious online group called On the Road to Rejuvenation Studio posted a video titled *How to Become a President*. In it, a cartoon version of Xi Jinping rises through the ranks of leadership in the Chinese Communist Party, leveling up like Donkey Kong. As the video explains, he rose meritocratically in a process entirely different from that of Western democracies but, the video hints, one supposedly much more stable and requiring less corruption. In another video, which went viral, Xi Jinping performs a rap, explaining how he's going to tackle government corruption at all levels and reduce levels of air pollution. No major outlet is able to firmly identify the studio's name and history, and it appears to have emerged solely for propaganda purposes.[20]

Memes create narratives, and narratives hold power in our minds. The more a meme sticks, the more likely the deeper narrative sticks in turn. A catchy song called "Xi Dada Loves Peng Mama" (Peng Liyuan is Xi's wife) caught hold of the Chinese internet, declaring the president's virility and leadership potential:

> China produced an Uncle Xi,
> He dares to fight the tigers.
> Not afraid of heaven, not afraid of earth,
> Dreamers all look to him![21]

These videos, embraced by and often commissioned by the party, are designed to reach young people, and they inspire a host of GIFs and remixes, often flattering. Some people mock the videos, but many embrace them. In the modern world of propaganda, it is much better to offer an alternative narrative or many narratives. Call it Streisand Effect jiu jitsu: rather than try to suppress attention for something you want censored (and accidentally trigger more attention), drive that attention somewhere else, anywhere, in all directions, till people latch on, lose interest, or get tired.[22]

Which brings us back to the grass mud horse. Why would Chinese social media platforms embrace such a profane and powerful symbol against internet censorship? Without being able to interview them directly, I can only speculate. But when we consider government media strategies, it's plausible to think of this embrace as co-opting, a way to defang the grass mud horse of its symbolic power. Because, devoid of its contextual usage among activists, the llama is just a llama, and its profane name comes across as puerile humor. The llama on official platforms isn't meant to embolden activists—they'll always figure out creative ways to challenge government policies; it's meant to strip the symbol of its potency by introducing it to nonpolitical people long before they get a hint of its political content. One of meme culture's greatest strengths—its ability to shape and remake images and imbue them with powerful symbology—is also one of its greatest weaknesses: so easily co-opted and transformed into something new, or so many new things that people become fatigued trying to learn the truth. And in the end, the very idea of truth is called into question.

FAKE, FAKE, FAKE, FAKE

Folkloric content can, of course, accurately reflect the
world, i.e., be true. But the frame doesn't begin and end
with veracity. It begins and ends with participation.

—Whitney Phillips[1]

THE WINTER DAY in 2016 was a relatively brisk one in Washington, DC, when
a gunman walked into Comet Pizza, a popular independent pizza joint, pulled
out a Colt AR-15 assault rifle, and opened fire. He fired three bullets but fortu-
nately didn't take any lives or injure any people. The gunman surrendered and
was taken into custody.[2] In the United States in 2015 alone, more than thirteen
thousand people died from gunfire, and more than twenty-five thousand were
injured.[3] In gun-related deaths and injuries per capita, the US greatly surpasses
any other wealthy nation. Shootings are often attributed to mental health issues,
frustrations at work, and a general culture of violence. This shooting was slightly
different: online meme culture played a strong role in the violence.

The gunman who entered Comet was not the only one who had paid a visit
to the pizza place. Over the course of a few weeks, multiple people had come
through the restaurant. A conspiracy theory had circulated on the web, starting
with posts on 4chan, Reddit, and Twitter and amplified by Infowars and other
right-wing news sites: Comet's basement was the central space for a sex ring involving children, and Hillary Clinton and Democratic Party money were supporting this criminal front.[4] The conspiracy took the catchy name of #Pizzagate—in
the American context, adding "-gate" to a word gives it the air of a criminal political conspiracy, in the vein of the break-in at the Watergate Hotel, where Richard
Nixon had sent staffers to break into Democratic Party offices and steal confi-
dential documents.[5] The Pizzagate gunman drove from North Carolina to, in

his words, "self-investigate" the online claims and memes. Disgusted by what he perceived to be moral decay and a lack of concern from local authorities, he took the law into his own hands. But by the time he was apprehended, he surrendered peacefully. Court documents noted that the man "found no evidence that under-age children were being harbored in the restaurant."[6]

In so many ways, Pizzagate reflected the evolution of a simple digital meme (in this case, a pizza parlor involved in criminal conspiracy) into a series of visual ones (people posted images and videos that purported to connect the dots in the conspiracy) and then into a performative one (people visit the parlor and share pictures and observations on a variety of websites). *BuzzFeed* reporter Craig Silverman found a 4chan thread that showed people actively trying to makes memes that connected Clinton with sex trafficking.[7] It was a meme that became a minor movement, part of a narrative of seeking justice and righting wrongs, and that movement nearly took people's lives.

Pizzagate also serves as an example of fully fabricated news that had major consequences offline. It resembles mass online-harassment campaigns, in which people organize against a single target and use both digital and physical methods to intimidate their targets, ranging from online verbal abuse and stalking to sending prank packages to a person's home. The most striking reality is this: there is absolutely no evidence of Comet Pizza being involved in any criminal conspiracy. Nevertheless, the claim rapidly circulated and amplified across a variety of channels.

Shortly after a heated election among what seemed to be an increasingly divided electorate, the problem of "fake news" entered popular American discourse. *BuzzFeed*'s Silverman, who coauthored the *Verification Handbook*, a guide to identifying and verifying misinformation on the internet, released a scathing story that identified teams of Macedonian teenagers fabricating news, often in support of right-wing causes, and circulating it online in the United States.[8] Other reporters identified individuals in places including Long Beach and Denver who spent their days gaming online news feeds to promote stories that were frequently painted in the most emotional, partisan ways possible.[9] The goal was less to spread propaganda and more to game the attention ecosystem and generate as much ad revenue as possible.

Soon, the term "fake news," originally meant to identify news that was fully fabricated, came to be used in a more partisan way. During the campaign, Hillary Clinton supporters noted the plethora of fake news about their candidate, such as stories that she was gravely ill. Trump supporters, on the other hand, utilized the fake news accusation for any claims that reflected poorly on the nominee, such as one that had to do with him lying about his taxes. Trump himself tweeted about "fake news," frequently placing the term in all caps. The phrase started to lose meaning: it could refer to news that was fully fabricated with the intent to deceive the public, to stories that got a few facts wrong and were accidentally shared, and to partisan content that someone simply disagreed with.

At Harvard's Shorenstein Center on Media, Politics, and Public Policy, Claire Wardle serves as research director at First Draft News, a coalition of organizations concerned about better online verification practices. She argued that we should think about distinguishing between misinformation—incorrect information circulating online—and disinformation—deliberately incorrect information shared with the intention to deceive.[10] These categories necessarily overlap, but I've found it helpful to think about how to distinguish intent.

Memes play a key role in the spread of both misinformation and disinformation. An online culture of remix and a suite of tools to enable it means that misinformation can take multiple forms. After Wardle spoke about the role of memes in misinformation ecosystems, she was tagged on Twitter with an image of herself where her skin was painted green, like the witch from *The Wizard of Oz* and *Wicked*. Someone else took that remixed image and slapped Pepe the Frog's face on top of Wardle's, making a parodic visual statement about her.[11] This was a simple example of real news—she had indeed spoken on television—but the image itself took on a false tone. Wardle's framework breaks down the motivations for sharing even further, using alliteration to make the point: people share online for *many* reasons—to punk, to provoke, to politicize, to profit, to polarize. "If we're serious about developing solutions to these problems," she writes, "we also need to think about who is creating these different types of content and why it is being created."[12]

It's tempting to think of fake news as a series of falsehoods. The very framing of this word, however, misses the broader point, because it orients you toward whether the claim is true or false. This is helpful, but it assumes that people share things online because they're 100 percent concerned about accuracy. By this logic, simply pointing out the inaccuracy will help stem the flow of falsehoods on the broader web. But people share, as I've explained, because of deeper political allegiances and viewpoints.

A critical report published by Alice Marwick and Rebecca Lewis at the technology think tank Data and Society asserts that meme making is part of a larger effort to manipulate the media into spreading alt-right and alt-right-affiliated views: "Taking advantage of the opportunity the internet presents for collaboration, communication, and peer production, these groups target vulnerabilities in the news media ecosystem to increase the visibility of and audience for their messages."[13] This involves a pipeline of news that moves from highly experimental social networks like 4chan and Reddit, onward to right-wing blogs and news sites, till they finally reach mainstream media. "For manipulators," notes the report, "it doesn't matter if the media is reporting on a story in order to debunk it or dismiss it; the important thing is getting it covered in the first place."

As I read this report, I was struck by the similarity of the media-manipulator pipeline to the activist meme-maker pipeline. Make a number of memes, relying on a high rate of remix and mashups, testing, and iterating on ideas over time. When something seems to stick, use sympathetic blogs and other influencers to drive attention. Over time, the media might be refined further, and a new narrative emerges that mainstream media covers. What works for Pepe works for famous cat memes works for the grass mud horse. Across the board, memes can fuse new narratives in society and influence behavior, and as Wardle and the Data and Society researchers have made clear, many of those narratives can themselves be highly destructive and manipulative.

What memes, among other social media phenomena, help fuel is the expansion of the Overton Window. This refers to the window of acceptable public discourse and was named after public policy analyst Joseph Overton. NYU professor Clay Shirky points out its implications in relation to the 2016 US presidential election:

> The Overton Window was imagined as a limit on public opinion, but in politics, it's the limit on what politicians will express in public. Politically acceptable discourse is limited by supply, not demand. The public is hungry for more than politicians are willing to discuss. This is especially important in the U.S., because our two-party system creates ideologically unstable parties by design.[14]

By exposing people to each other, and each other's ideas, memes are part of a broader phenomenon that expands the range of acceptable discourse, feeding a hungry public who wants to talk about issues that in previous eras might not have been discussed as openly. At times this can support progressive, antiauthoritarian actions. At times, this also means the expansion of false narratives and information. What's key to understanding the window is that these strategies are adaptations to the communications environment, where algorithms on such platforms as Facebook and YouTube float up content that is optimized for attention and emotion, and where broadcast media tunes in to platforms like Twitter for breaking news. By serving up content and information most conducive to users' ways of taking in information, many platforms reinforce divisions in society. Algorithms, which often reflect the biases of their makers, have a crucial role in this amplification, but private social networks, which don't use algorithms, show that much of what you see online is very much driven by people sharing, remixing, and sharing some more.

Early in Barack Obama's presidential career, a rumor started circulating in private email networks: Obama was a Muslim born in Kenya. He is neither of these things. Obama was raised as a Christian and attended the Trinity United Church of Christ. He was born to a father from Kenya but can claim as his birthplace Honolulu, Hawaii. But the rumor carried along an implicit argument: if he'd been born outside the US, per constitutional law, Obama might be ineligible to be president. In an article for the *Nation*, journalist Chris Hayes traced the path of this rumor, which came from an indeterminate part of the internet.[15] It started first with email chains and evolved into stories shared on Facebook and Twitter and into media articles and websites. Obama's political opponents, such as Donald Trump, played a key role in amplifying the rumor and bringing attention back to it. The memes were plenty: a picture of Obama in traditional Kenyan garb, taken at the time he visited his family in Kenya, was slapped onto collages of other images and text that reinforced the idea of foreign birth.

For people of color in the United States this internet trend—given the name "birtherism"—was a reminder of many moments when they encountered others who assumed they were born elsewhere. The journalist Touré wrote about the history of this phenomenon as some of the earliest rumors about Obama began circulating, and how birtherism fits into a long trajectory of cultural assumptions and mores:

During slavery, blacks who weren't on a plantation were subject to being checked for free papers—documentation that proved they were free and not an escapee. Many free blacks carried these free papers in their pocket at all times. This free paper check is echoed today in the repeated demand to see Obama's documentation as an American. Donald Trump and Rick Perry and the rest of the birther crew are virtually marching up to the White House, knocking on the door, and saying "Can you prove that you belong here? We're uncertain. We just want to check."[16]

Memes give voice to, reinforce, and amplify these things, but they frequently come from other aspects of culture. Memes arise within a broader environment of media, relationships, and culture that shape belief systems. They rarely come out of nowhere; even memes based on falsehoods contain within themselves a kernel of truth. In *Dreams from My Father*, Obama's seminal autobiography, he recounted a childhood spent in multicultural Hawaii, the Muslim-majority country of Indonesia, and, of course, rural Kenya.[17] This multicultural, multinational background is not synonymous with being foreign born—in fact, per US law, one can be born abroad and still be a US citizen by birth, so long as at least one parent is American. Presidential candidates John McCain, born in Panama, and Ted Cruz, born in Canada, enjoyed this right.[18] But for Obama, this evidence of foreignness appeared to be enough to facilitate a range of rumors: Obama is Muslim, Obama was raised in a madrassa (a training center for radical Islamic terrorists), Obama was born in Kenya.

Obama eventually released his birth certificate, which clearly demonstrated his birthplace in Hawaii. This should have ended any question as to his origins, but the flames of doubt were only fanned further: some believed an image of the birth certificate had been edited in Adobe Illustrator.[19] The very tools that allowed people to shape and remix were the same ones that led certain people to believe the image of the birth certification must itself be fake. Media figures continued to raise doubts about his birthplace, and for years, right-wing websites continued to raise questions. The matter was never fully settled by its premier pusher, Donald Trump, until 2016, when the presidential candidate declared: "President Barack Obama was born in the United States, period. Now, we all want to get back to making America strong and great again."[20] After years of pushing the question, Trump took no questions from reporters following his statement. Whether the birther trend was the result of misinformation, disinformation, or some combination of both is not clear. What is clear is that birtherism had the powerful effect of lifting the voices of those who sought to challenge the authenticity of Barack Obama's birthplace, while simultaneously feeding an overall culture of distrust around him.

What's to be done about fake news? As Claire Wardle has pointed out, there's a difference between fully fabricated news and news that's misleading and mistaken. The latter can be addressed with better newsroom practices, more checks from editorial teams, and help from online platforms. I've been part of efforts to encourage major platforms like Facebook and Google to flag incorrect content online through a series of signals that appear on their platforms.[21] Many groups are looking at how to develop artificial intelligence systems to automatically detect online misinformation. Each effort is a microcontribution to curbing what is a highly complex and multifaceted challenge, one that carries risks of amplifying misleading information while simultaneously inadvertently replicating systems of censorship pioneered by countries such as China in the face of "rumors."

But I bring up the birtherism example because of its origins: email chains. An open system, email can't be controlled in the same way a news-feed algorithm can. Today, a large number of rumors circulate via private chat networks on mobile messaging apps, WhatsApp and Telegram, for example, which are encrypted and therefore impossible to access from outside these communities. (Most but not all messaging apps are encrypted; for those that are not, companies and governments have ways to gain access to the messages within.) When people believe things and share them, regardless of attempts to dissuade them, they are engaging in confirmation bias—that is, finding facts and data that confirm their already existing beliefs.

Cultural researcher and ethnographer Whitney Phillips has noted that focusing on the very framework of "fake" versus "true" misses the point: people are more likely to share and engage with content online because they want to create and perform a political identity. Identity and community are at the heart of meme culture. Phillips has proposed that we think about fake news more as folkloric news—or "folk news"—to focus on motivations rather than accuracy.[22] It's not that content online can't be true or false; it's just that we're missing the bigger picture when we think just about factual accuracy. This is why I often find the framework of "fandoms"—what the University of Southern California media scholar Henry Jenkins defines as "the social structures and cultural practices created by the most passionately engaged consumers of mass media properties"—can be useful when thinking about how content is shared online.[23] The language of fandom emphasizes the social motivations for people to engage with others online and that savvy mass media producers work actively with their fan base. In this view, it's not facts that matter first; it's the social situation of the content being promoted. What matters more is that a combination of perceived facts, networks of reinforcement and encouragement, and visual and performative media combine to a totality that looks more like folklore or fandom than traditional journalism. Folklore and fandom tie in to more complex value systems that fact checking alone cannot solve for.

Nausicaa Renner at the *Columbia Journalism Review* noted that much of fake news gets attention through memes. In one simple example, Renner pointed out that people read the falsified articles on *Breitbart* less frequently than they viewed the images the site shared to accompany each article. Each image contained a simple array of statements and figures and pointed back to the article, and these images got way more traction than the articles themselves.[24] Even more concerning is that entirely new networks form around misinformation. This only makes the problem bigger. Echo chambers—networks that receive only specific sets of content—reinforce each other on the web and rarely do they receive exposure to potentially opposing views. In a study conducted by Yochai Benkler, Ethan Zuckerman, and others at Harvard University and the MIT Media Lab, the right wing in particular has effectively created an echo chamber of its own, isolated from even center-right communities.[25] When one is no longer exposed to opposing information, it can seem as if everyone agrees with you. The memes, the media, the entire story all seem to point in one direction.

What, then, is to be done about misinformation ecosystems and the memes that amplify them? What about contemporary propaganda and disinformation, which so readily takes the form of rumors? It can be tempting to add legal frameworks to address the problem of fabricated news and misinformation. But the risk of censorship presents a difficult challenge, as the examples of China and other countries demonstrate, when a government can define rumors to serve its own best interests while quashing genuinely false information that is demonstrably harmful to the general public. Legal frameworks can't address the deeper problem of belief systems and are difficult to enforce in the face of how rumors spread, often in a decentralized way and via private social media. In the worst case, legal frameworks can be designed to strengthen authoritarian governments and weaken democratic systems like the free press.

The early metaphor about the internet—as an information superhighway—has obscured this reality in many ways. Access to information is an important part of what makes the internet valuable for activists, journalists, researchers, and policy makers. But in so many ways, the internet serves more as an affirmation superhighway, a way to affirm political beliefs and identities. Memes play a key role in this problem, as they are more frequently emotive in nature, giving people a place to express themselves and their values. Sometimes this can help marginalized perspectives find voice and access; other times, this serves to marginalize viewpoints even further. Any attempts to circulate useful facts and figures can fail quickly, because networks can be so easily isolated online, and besides, the people making up those networks have different value systems that don't always accept the presentation of evidence.

This fracturing of the American public, with people increasingly disputing not just opinions but also facts, has a number of potential consequences. While broadcast media has hosted a number of systemic biases that shut out minority perspectives, its advantage has been in generating a singular national narrative, or at least a singular set of facts. In a world of social media and multiple platforms, neither of these things is possible, even while historically marginalized communities find ways to build around their causes. Without a common basis for reality, it can be difficult for citizens and lawmakers across the country to make reasonable policy decisions and recommendations. Neo-Nazi groups and others can use echo chambers to recruit violent actors into their belief systems. In addition, growing distrust in online information feeds a larger context of distrust in media and institutions. People with a sincere desire to research and learn from the internet can become discouraged and confused by the plethora of conflicting information. Chess grandmaster and political ambassador Garry Kasparov has pointed out that the long-term effect isn't to spread a single narrative; it's to spread multiple ones. And as trust drops in institutions, it doesn't go away entirely. Trust just moves elsewhere.

Writing about the "post-truth future," Chinese internet-culture researcher and ethnographer Christina Xu has pointed out that a drop in trust can have counterintuitive effects.[26] Knowing that institutions no longer have their interests at heart, people in China are now less convinced that the government is genuinely trying to curb harmful rumors. On the other hand, misinformation thrives in the Chinese context, and institutions can't be trusted to share accurate facts. In the long term, this means people turn to each other—whether through friend and family networks or value networks online—to get information and find kinship. In places like Turkey and Azerbaijan, increased distrust in both the internet and established institutions means people don't go on the internet at all; governments aim to generate a culture of belief that the internet is an untrustworthy space, so they decide not to access it. In China, where internet usage is high, any potential activism is offset by a fractured public and increasing distrust in other people and institutions.

Before the internet, the goal of propaganda was simple: tell a single story, dominate the media environment, and repeat the information until people either believe it or succumb to at least agreeing in public life. The central power of traditional propaganda is also its weakness: any attempt to break this single story is a threat to the system. Controlling the media environment is a costly endeavor. Memes, as a powerful tool for generating new narratives, are well suited to challenging this form of propaganda. It is nearly impossible for a single story to take hold, because forms of narrative resistance are so easy to come by. Rather than resist the internet's ability to create a story, today's propaganda takes advantage of it by creating too much information. Contemporary disinformation attempts to do at least two things: (1) overwhelm people with a series of conflicting and confusing narratives such that they give up trying to make sense of it all, and (2) string along those who do sincerely believe the story, and recruit them in amplifying the disinformation.

Using the narrative-building capacity of the internet is increasingly an online strategy for regimes and agents of disinformation hoping to control the conversation. In addition to controlling it overtly—methods like jailing or harassing "offenders"—states now can also wield memes to generate an alternative discussion and shift the narrative online. Researching social media–based propaganda in Russia, journalist Adrian Chen has found that at least one paid agency, the Internet Research Agency, exists that generates memes, blog posts, and comments that either favor the government or challenge and mock any posts that seek to resist these narratives. The agency uses all the tools that activists have had at their disposal, like Photoshop and video editing tools, to test and disseminate messages online. They are rewarded for their efforts monetarily.[27] As special counsel for the US Department of Justice Robert Mueller charged, some of these efforts sought to influence the outcome of the 2016 US presidential election.[28]

And here, ultimately, is one risk of the environment of misinformation and disinformation: on the one hand, any sincere form of activism can be deemed fake and therefore libelous or outright criminal by the powers that be. On the other hand, governments and anyone with a social and political message can embrace the power of memes and social media rather than resist it. Regardless, the outcome appears to be predictable each time: decreased trust in media, institutions, and other people more generally, combined with decreased usefulness of the internet in helping spread an activist message. The internet's greatest power is also its greatest weakness, and the human brain's capacity to make sense of competing stories is susceptible to being easily overwhelmed and confused.

Challenging this new landscape of misinformation and disinformation won't be easy, and there are precious few examples to give us reason for optimism. A 2017 report by Claire Wardle and internet researcher Hossein Derakshan for the Council of Europe argued that combating misinformation and disinformation will require understanding how and why these types of media resonate.

> We need to fight rumours and conspiracy with engaging and powerful narratives that leverage the same techniques as dis-information. [Some] effective strategies for dis-information include: provoking an emotional response, repetition, a strong visual aspect and a powerful narrative. If we remember the powerful, ritualistic aspects to information seeking and consumption, the importance of integrating these elements into our solutions is obvious.[29]

And as it turns out, effective activism might require strategies that leap forth from the internet and enter the physical world, and that command attention and narrative in ways that cut across different forms of media and make themselves impossible to ignore, just as activism has always aimed to do. And maybe, just maybe, there's a way to talk about how the narrative power of the world's internet memes can be brought to bear on the increasingly complex challenges that face our world.

CHAPTER 6

· · · · · · · ·

A CONTEST OF MEMES

Let them in! Let them in!

—Multiple attributions

WHEN THE INTERNET FIRST CAME ALONG, it was marketed as a remarkable tool for leveling the playing field and disrupting traditional media powers. As with any new communications technology, however, understanding how it actually interacts with existing structures of power has taken some time. In that regard, the tools of memetic communication are a little bit like jiujitsu—a martial art that allows physically smaller people to take down much larger opponents. But jiujitsu is only effective if your opponent doesn't know your tricks. What happens when a much larger, stronger person also learns jiujitsu?

We have entered a new world of memetic contention, one where meme culture has become as much a tool for those in power as it has for those seeking to challenge it. Movements of hate have embraced this culture as much as movements of justice. What remains clear is that internet culture and offline culture are intertwined—internet culture is, in fact, culture, and what happens online influences culture at large in both subtle and compelling ways. And as memes and other actions expand the conversation space, they shift culture for some, while hardening culture for others. In a world where more people have a media vehicle by which to express their views, social movements must navigate a world of dissensus. How they negotiate this contention is one of the vital questions of the twenty-first century.

WHERE THE WIND BLOWS

But when you carry a life in you, what she breathes, eats and
drinks are all your responsibility, and then you feel the fear.

—Chai Jing[1]

SOME DAYS THE AIR IS THICK IN BEIJING, the sort of thick that makes you squint your eyes to double-check what's in front of you. The air tastes to me like metal or sour eggs, maybe a mixture of both, and over a few days I can develop a phlegmatic cough. In ancient times the city was known for its fierce summer sandstorms, but in 2008, as the city prepared to host the Summer Olympics, researchers found it to be the most polluted site of the games ever.[2] In China's capital city, gleaming white buildings turn brown over time, and a cake of grime lines the outside of major buildings. The city is not the most polluted in the world—that honor goes to Zabol, Iran—but it's arguably one of the most famous for its pollution.[3]

China has made sweeping efforts to curb pollution in its most affected and populous cities. This includes such major cities as Beijing, Shanghai, and Tianjin, but it also includes cities lesser known outside the country, like Chongqing, Chengdu, and Guangzhou.[4] As part of its commitment to the 2016 Paris climate accord, the government has worked to decrease its dependency on coal—the leading cause of pollution in its major cities—and increase its investment in renewable energy, like wind and solar farms, with a goal of having some 20 percent of its energy come from renewables by 2030.[5] The country is also transitioning its industrial base from one of pure production to include more creative industries, thus limiting its dependence on an industry that causes air pollution in the first place.

The day-to-day reality of smog is visible in the widespread use of smog-repellent face masks, air filters for cars and buildings, and a general practice of checking the daily smog index, like checking the weather forecast. Chinese-made phones, such as Xiaomi, Meizu, and Huawei, all offer local smog statistics on their weather apps. In addition to the temperature, citizens can check for PM2.5 ("PM" for particulate matter) levels. PM2.5 is the most harmful part of air pollution because it is small enough to travel into the lungs, causing symptoms like coughs, sore throat, and sneezing. Over time, with extended exposure to these particles, people are at risk of developing bronchitis and even lung cancer.[6] World Health Organization guidelines suggest an annual average of 10 micrograms or fewer of PM2.5 per cubic meter as a safe level for breathing—in Beijing, the level has reached as high as 212 micrograms.[7] Particulate matter is both dangerous and powerful, and citizens take precautions on bad smog days to limit their exposure by staying indoors when they can or by wearing special masks. Those with financial resources and access can afford air filters for their cars and homes.

In 2011, despite the thick air that people breathed in each day, many citizens had no reference point for determining what clean air is. The city government restricted any data collected about the air and pushed a narrative that the hazy atmosphere was officially fog or, at worst, mild pollution.[8] State media outlets were forbidden to publish anything about the smog events. The city government's story was effective: as someone who's grown up seeing polluted days in Los Angeles and foggy days in San Francisco, I immediately could tell the difference. But I had also relied on professional weather forecasters telling me to expect a foggy—or smoggy—day. In Beijing, when I took taxis, entered restaurants, and chatted with people casually while waiting for the bus, they commented on the fog rather than the smog.

The fog-smog narrative is a classic form of disinformation driven, in this case, by a state actor. Disinformation campaigns have existed since time immemorial; they are a way to sweep away inconvenient truths and construct in their place an alternative "truth." What happened in China between 2009, when pollution started becoming too serious to write off as sandstorms or fog, and 2014, when the government released its first official decree against pollution, sparking a nationwide push for clean air and clean water? Taking a closer look can help us understand what battling disinformation in the twenty-first century looks like and how the memetic culture of the internet bleeds into the physical world.

In 2008, the US Embassy in China started a Twitter account called Beijing Air (@beijingair).[9] It had a simple goal: publish data about the air in the city, collected directly from the embassy grounds. The embassy was technically on US soil, and therefore its staff could safely collect and disseminate the data. But the impact was limited: with Twitter being blocked and the data communicated primarily in English, the site largely reached a Western audience and only a limited Chinese one. Even when a site like Twitter is blocked in China, it's not impossible to tap into it. Many foreigners, accustomed to accessing popular social networks—Twitter, Facebook, Instagram, YouTube—find an entry point through a VPN, or virtual private network, which creates a simple way to encrypt data from blocked sites and allow it to tunnel through the block. Chinese citizens can do the same. The cost of a VPN is fairly negligible on an average Western salary—no more than fifty dollars per month, and more frequently only ten dollars per month—but this cost can be prohibitive on the low end of a local salary.[10]

The system of internet censorship and incentives in China can be powerfully effective, discouraging use of certain sites while encouraging use of others. There are ways to work around this system. But we have to start thinking of memes as part of the old cat-and-mouse game of evading censorship. Indeed, environmental activism in China has a long history, driven by NGOs, going back to the mid-1990s and has encountered both censorship and resistance from the government.[11] In mid-2000, the Chinese government set up an environmental complaint system to accommodate requests for change.[12] In a similar way, as memes adapt to a traditional censorship environment, governments develop a new strategy. In China this has taken the form of disinformation and distraction narratives, which take the power of memes and the internet's general ability to generate new narratives and perspectives and apply that to a narrative of the government's own choosing. Governmental authorities then impose stiff penalties on those whose virality is too successful.

In 2011, antipollution advocates in China had a new tool at their disposal: the iTunes App Store. At the time, iPhones were financially out of reach to most Chinese consumers, and censorship was not applied extensively to what apps were made available on the App Store. A few activists developed apps, like

DirtyBeijing, that took data from the Beijing Air feed and visualized that in clear and simple language.[13] These apps contained a simple feature: take a screenshot and share it to Sina Weibo. And share people did. They began posting the photos of the day, explaining what PM2.5 was, and using the data, they could state whether the air in, say, Beijing was dangerous.

At the same time, another meme emerged on the Chinese internet. People simply began posting photos of the air around them. Some people posted from high-rises, others from down on the ground looking up into the sun. Others posted pictures of themselves wearing masks, and others the walls of their buildings, which showed clear signs of pollution. This collective action helped establish clear patterns of pollution across the country and within different cities, making clear that air pollution wasn't an isolated incident on a given day, nor that only one person questioned the idea that the haziness was fog.

A number of activists also distributed low-cost air sensors. This was a crucial strategy to countering the idea that Beijing Air was dispensing biased data. According to Ellery Biddle, editor of *Advocacy Voices*, the sensors played an important role in helping people collect data for themselves. Because these sensors were do-it-yourself, people could not only collect the data but could also talk about it with friends and share it online.[14] Projects like artist Xiaowei Wang's Float Beijing used kites with sensors that would collect data in the skies and drew on a long kite-flying tradition in China.[15] Another project, Clarity, was a keychain-sized sensor that collected data in a highly distributed fashion.[16]

During this time, filmmaker and journalist Chai Jing released online *Under the Dome*, a groundbreaking documentary about air pollution in the country. Running at more than an hour, it went surprisingly viral, with 150 million views on Chinese social media.[17] When a long video goes viral, I usually watch, as it suggests that it's struck a nerve, causing people to sit and pay attention. In the film, Chai talks about how she became pregnant and learned that her child had a tumor: "I'd never felt afraid of pollution before, and never wore a mask no matter where. But when you carry a life in you, what she breathes, eats and drinks are all your responsibility, and then you feel the fear."[18]

China's environmental minister praised the documentary for its honesty and impact, but the film was censored after a few days.[19] Even then it was too late. So much of meme culture depends on the strength of people's video-editing skills, and they were able to cut and paste images and clips, thus disseminating short bits of video and memes or share the entire video file directly.[20] People started conversations online about pollution.

Over time, international pressure grew as Western journalists also began writing about the pollution situation. Journalist Mark MacKinnon, in the Canadian *Globe and Mail*, captured the sentiment of many journalists at the time who were living and writing in Beijing and other polluted Chinese cities. The US embassy's assertions, he wrote, "that the air usually wobbled between 'unhealthy,' 'very unhealthy' and 'hazardous,'" was "being seized upon by anxious Chinese Internet users and even some domestic media outlets as proof that air pollution was far worse than their government was telling them." Yet, MacKinnon continued, state-run media said the pollution in Beijing the day he was writing was "moderate" and urged people to "open the windows and inhale the fresh autumn air."[21]

Activists in China also studied messaging strategies from the international environmental rights movement.[22] Even though the Chinese government seeks to influence international journalists living in the country, they can't fully control the narratives being produced. Sina Weibo gave journalists abroad an opportunity via social media to see the growing conversation. For example, the site Tea Leaf Nation covered online phenomena like *China Air Daily*, an online publication that would collate citizens' documentation of air pollution around the country.[23] These in turn created a pipeline of articles about pollution and Chinese citizens' growing discontent and sparked further action from middle-class Chinese, who are more likely to travel (and therefore see what blue skies look like) and have greater economic and political muscle within the country.[24]

As I hope this book is making clear, memes always exist in a broader media environment, and in fact political memes take their strength from this fact. Different types of media have different audiences and impacts, and internet memes play one role in the bigger picture. While people posted photos, selfies, and GIFs to discuss the impacts of pollution on their lives, the number of news articles, broadcasts, documentaries, and international conversations increased. "The most effective use of social media for social transformation occurs," MIT professor Sasha Costanza-Chock writes, "when it is coordinated with print and broadcast strategies, as well as with real-world actions."[25] Specific to the situation in China, Ellery Biddle emphasized that overcoming the misinformation about pollution was a "distributed project," where multiple people took data, shared feelings and photos, and generally had a chance to connect dots.[26] There was no one message, no one form of media, no one person who effected the change in the face of tremendous disinformation efforts—the multiplicity was critical.

It's also critical to understand how memes are part of a larger effort to find a narrative that works. In a diverse media environment under a democracy, finding the right narrative becomes a matter of driving attention: if the narrative catches on, it catches on with all the other media outlets, and from there, it might help drive policy decisions, voting patterns, town hall conversations, and other events. In a more authoritarian context, where media outlets are subject to more centralized control, narrative plays two roles. First, it can determine how quickly any conversation is censored or at least discouraged. Second, narrative can influence whether the international community pays attention and what type of pressure they exert.

The story of the blind lawyer activist Chen Guangcheng is a good example here. When people tried to talk about a highly sensitive topic—the illegal detention of a human rights lawyer—they faced direct censorship. But memes, in their roundabout way, helped keep his face before the public and stories about him alive. And in that they served their second function, which is to gain international attention. Because the memes were so catchy, and because they were visually striking and told interesting and even funny stories, they tapped into media outlets' need for novelty. Stories on multiple niche sites in China captured the original CGC (Chen Guangcheng) memes, and from there larger and international media outlets picked up more stories.

Chinese government and politics researchers Elizabeth Plantan and Chris Cairns at Cornell University analyzed the conversation about pollution and why it seemed to grow despite government attempts to censor it. Plantan and Cairns didn't focus specifically on memes, but their insights elucidate the broader context in which the memes operated. As people posted pictures, data visualizations, and selfies, a number of narratives about pollution emerged.[27] One narrative focused on climate change, which, while compelling, is often too abstract for many people. Another sought to blame the government for neglect. This was a big no-no, and many leading activists chose not to go down this path. The narrative that worked? Public health and its impacts. Indeed, in many of the early memes, people noted the bad coughs and hacking they experienced, but they didn't assign blame per se on the government. Harvard researcher Natalie Gyenes told me that in the American context, public-health explanations frequently avoid some of the overt politicization that other topics face.[28] People care about their health, they want to live longer, and they're keen to follow trusted sources to ensure they can be healthy. In the Chinese context, discussions about public health can similarly avoid overt politicization, even if they hew closely to a sensitive topic like pollution. As Plantan and Cairns observed, public health provided a pretext for action without directly blaming the national government.

As pressure mounted from within (among citizens, advocates, NGOs, and journalists) and without (among foreign governments and media outlets), the Chinese national government made a pledge to respond. In 2012, Beijing's environmental agency began placing PM2.5 measurements in its calculations and set monitoring standards across dozens of cities.[29] The standards they set allowed them to say that they were taking action and to direct public pressure to other organizations as needed. It also improved their appearance in the international community, thus helping improve their foreign policy aims and continuing their efforts to attract tourists (and tourist dollars).[30] What was the effect? Over time, I noticed the narrative about the air shifted from "fog" to "smog," eased along by open data initiatives, memes, and media that aimed to surface the truth about air quality. As the government took hold of the narrative, they were able to point at local malfeasance and corruption rather than governmental neglect, overt censorship, and manipulation of data.

A small memetic case study can help illustrate this macro conversation. In 2013, thousands of dead pigs washed up on the shores near Shanghai.[31] This glittering city that was once controlled by Western colonial powers is China's economic powerhouse and host to some of the wealthiest and most educated people in the world. Shanghainese children consistently outperform the world overall in math and science.[32] Imagine seeing pigs washing up on the streets of Manhattan, and you can get a good idea of the shock this sent through residents of the city.

Like cats, pigs are animals ripe for memeing. They have funny, expressive faces, rotund bodies, and distinctive noses and tails, and they show up frequently in cartoons. They are also a key figure in *Angry Birds*, the popular video game that swept the world in the 2010s. In the game, players direct different birds and catapult them into obstacles in an attempt to destroy green piglike creatures. Artist Crazy Crab, who sparked the sunglasses memes for Chen Guangcheng, had had a long, creative journey with the pigs and frequently used them to represent the Communist Party in his cartoons. He had an opportunity to transform these pigs into Angry Pigs leaping from the banks of the Pudong River and taking over the skyline.

Other artists and meme makers contributed clever remixes. At the time *Life of Pi*, a film depicting a young man living on a raft with a tiger, was one of the most popular in China. Posters for *Life of Pig* emerged, with the tiger replaced by a pig, and the raft floating alongside Shanghai. People posted the pig emoji multiple times, making creative designs with the pig and water emoji. Coming amid years of conversation about air pollution, the memes also tapped into deeper wellsprings and conversations about public health. The Ministry of Agriculture stepped in, investigating the incident in Shanghai while also pointing blame upstream from Shanghai, in Zhejiang. At the same time the government suppressed a planned protest, while news stories pointed to the government's heroic efforts and, instead of censoring stories about pigs, used them as an opportunity to tell a story about cleaning house and making Shanghai a better, more civilized place. All the while, the underlying causes of the environmental disaster—poor government incentives for small farmers—were not addressed publicly.[33]

To understand how change operates in China is to understand how a responsive authoritarian state uses public opinion to shape its own power. Paradoxically, this yields conditions that enable a certain range of collective action, so long as the change is deemed gradual enough by the powers that be.[34] In a democracy, when people advocate an issue they believe in and they find success, a new institution can typically be built, with its own internal and external accountability mechanisms. In a responsive authoritarian state, that process is much more opaque. Without accountability mechanisms, institutions can say one thing, "We're working in your best interests," while doing another, thus exacerbating the existing problem and laying blame on smaller organizations and local governments. Focusing on health and the impacts of pollution remains an acceptable narrative, one with roots in early meme culture and discussions about pollution. At the same time, a conversation about the deeper roots needed for change remains as elusive as ever, readily censored or ignored. The response to pollution almost certainly represents progress—people can now be well informed before stepping out the door—but questions remain about whether it's truly enough.

In China, in a matter of a few years, a remarkable new culture has emerged. Now when I visit, people openly talk about air quality in different cities. "Smog" and "fog" are different concepts, and people can talk about the health effects of the former. They wear masks, check the air quality, make efforts to advocate for clean air and water (within certain limits), and see their doctor. Today, Chinese-made phones feature pollution data on their interfaces. Baked into the weather app, they forecast the temperature, whether it will rain or snow, and whether you should wear an air mask or plan to stay indoors. Air filters are sold openly in markets in Beijing for both cars and homes, and people regularly post selfies wearing air masks. When Facebook founder Mark Zuckerberg posted a picture of himself taking a friendly jog in Beijing, Chinese netizens poked fun at his thinking that jogging would be a good idea, especially without a mask on.[35]

At the same time, this narrative allows the government to stay in control, even while pollution envelops the country's major cities. Clean air is now effectively a commodity akin to clean water, as air filters remain in vastly unequal supply, affordable only to the middle and upper classes, leaving many people and their children vulnerable to the bad air and unable to work on particularly difficult days. The national government continues to try to restrict alternative sources of information, pushing only official statistics and even insisting at times that fog is still the core issue and detaining people for "rumor mongering" about particularly bad air.[36] Even given all this, it's easier today than ever before to talk about the air, the water, the need for the basics of clean and healthy living. The culture has shifted, even as the ability to speak deeply about the underlying issues remains restricted, even as air pollution has measurably worsened over the years.[37]

What's remarkable is how, in a country where trust in institutions is low but censorship and misinformation are high, a critical mass of people recognized that they were being tricked by government data about pollution. To me, it's not coincidental that this particular form of memetic advocacy involved something we can see before our eyes as well as the distribution of physical sensors and independent data. Recall how the gunman at Comet Pizza came to the conclusion that no illegal activities were happening there only after he saw (or didn't see) them. Recall how easy it was for people to dismiss the accuracy of Obama's birth certificate, because it was impossible for most to see it with their own eyes. Recall how many people felt the need to go to Ferguson to see the protests with their own eyes.

The physical has power that overcomes even the most vigorous misinformation efforts, even the most compelling countermessaging, and as memes go physical and enter protests, gathering spaces, and civic centers, people send signals about what they're willing to stand for. You can deny an image online or a statistic as false, but seeing people with your own eyes showing up for something they believe in is much more difficult to turn away. In an authoritarian environment, this can create unique opportunities for change, even within a limited scope, as people find roundabout ways to make space for conversation despite government opposition. In a freer media environment, it takes the form of warm bodies on the streets.

THE STATE OF AFFAIRS

Traditional media didn't cover us until it was so evident on
social media that they could not close their eyes anymore.

—Gisela Pérez de Acha[1]

FUE EL ESTADO. These words, Spanish for "It was the state," were painted on
the corner of Mexico City's Plaza de la Constitución (Constitution Square) using thirty liters of paint. The street art was both a physical declaration and a
digital one; photographed from above, it was designed for maximal impact on
social media. This action occurred during a megamarch organized by parents
of the Ayotzinapa 43, a group of students who had gone missing under mysterious, likely violent, circumstances. #RexisteMX, the group responsible for
what it called a "monumental painting," stated that the image went viral and
had joined a chorus of hashtags that sought to place responsibility for the disappearances on the Mexican government.[2] The group's name—a portmanteau of
resiste and *existe*—was coined before the disappearance of the students, and its
activism extends to both the internet and in person, including utilizing drones to
spray-paint the city.[3]

Like modern-day Rome or Xi'an, Mexico City rests atop an ancient city, that
of Tenochtitlan, the capital of the Aztec empire. The Zócalo, the popular name
for Constitution Square, lies at the heart of the ancient capital, whose buildings
were replaced by the Spanish after they established a new empire. Like any public square, it has long served as a point of contention. At the height of the 1968
student movement for greater democratic rights, it held five hundred thousand
protesters gathered outside the nearby Presidential Palace. The party in power,
the Institutional Revolutionary Party, even held its own counterprotests in the

same square. The movement was soon quashed by government tanks in another public square, Tlatelolco Plaza.[4]

From the National Mall in Washington, DC, to Victoria Park in Hong Kong, public spaces for gathering offer great opportunities for cities to foster a common culture and set of principles and to encourage commerce and leisure. The Spanish word *plaza* extends back to the ancient Greek *plateia* (πλατεῖα), reflecting in many ways the ancientness of this concept. But they are also sites of contention and protest. Symbolic sites like the Zócalo, Tiananmen Square, and the National Mall represent the heart of a government and as such can attract symbolic acts of resistance. And just as different physical public spaces contain different politics, so do different digital ones. Today, most of our digital public spaces are in fact owned by private corporations, which make decisions about how and where content appears. Some, like Chinese platforms, are under the strong hand of the state, while others, like Facebook and Google, retain ostensible independence from states but increasingly face regulation on the one hand and propagandistic attacks on the other.

The internet, the newest public square, where governments, media, private corporations, and average citizens all collide in conversation, carries with it these same tensions and opportunities for symbolic action. It is no accident that some of the most famous networked movements, from the Arab Spring in Egypt to Occupy Wall Street in New York, have combined internet activism with physical occupation of a symbolic public space. During the Arab Spring, protesters took over Tahrir Square in Cairo, and during Occupy, protesters claimed Zuccotti Park, a private park in the Wall Street district, as their own. Just as the Zócalo contains layers of pre-Hispanic, colonial, and modern history, so does the internet add another layer of contention in the history of human society. Its intersections with physical space extend notions of public spaces, crossing borders and boundaries to create new sites of resistance, and new sites of response to that resistance.

Around 2015, I noticed that signs started appearing in various US cities asking if people had seen the "Ayotzinapa 43," forty-three young Mexican students.[5] On Valencia Street in San Francisco, for example, some two thousand miles from Mexico City, I walked past a large mural depicting the forty-three faces on a giant sign saying "Ayotzinapa Have You Seen Them?" In San Jose and Los Angeles, small signs with the students' faces, like missing-persons posters, began to appear. The missing had come not from down the street but from a village in another country. Yet these young men's faces and names had somehow made their way up north, to some of the wealthiest cities in the United States.

They were from the district of Guerrero, Mexico, and attended a rural teachers college known as Escuela Normal Rural Raúl Isidro Burgos, in Ayotzinapa. Based in a largely rural community, the college is known for training leftist activists.[6] I have never been to these small towns, and until a few years ago, I had never heard of them.

On September 26, 2014, the young men planned to commandeer buses to go to Mexico City, where a 1968 student massacre was going to be commemorated in Tlatelolco Plaza.[7] In Mexico such protests can end violently, with either the police, drug gangs, or both working in concert disrupting the protests through violence and, at times, killing people. The forty-three men from Ayotzinapa never returned. Along their journey to Mexico City, they appear to have been stopped by local police. Sometime after that, as a number of articles have speculated, they may have been handed over to a brutal drug gang known for disappearances and assassinations of their enemies and of people who get in the way. As this book goes to press, most of the men have not been found, and they are officially considered missing rather than killed.

Disappearances like this are common in Mexico, and they have a long history. Indeed, the students' very bus ride was intended to commemorate the murder of hundreds of people in the Tlatelolco district of Mexico City in 1968, a detail that would help propel the story of their disappearance into international discourse. Human Rights Watch has documented more than 250 known incidents in Mexico, noting that kidnappings and enforced disappearances can be conducted by a variety of actors—police, gangs, the military—and could number hundreds of thousands more.[8] (A scathing 2017 report from ProPublica outlined the level of violence one village suffered at the hands of a drug cartel, which razed the area and disappeared many of those living there.[9]) There is even a Spanish word, *desaparecidos*, to describe those who have been disappeared, a practice not just in Mexico but in the Philippines and many Latin American countries.[10] Typically, the disappeared are poor and vulnerable, likely to be forgotten by society at large after being taken away. Most are never found again, and only their families and friends remember their stories.

Such disappearances are a strategy that spurs fear among affected communities. Like a warning shot, taking away a visible minority is intended to keep the majority silent about potential injustices they might witness. And unlike murder, a disappearance creates a special type of fear, a lack of closure. It never quite goes away; there can be no funeral, no memorial, no plaque in commemoration, because those who have been taken away might still be alive, however slim the chances. The victims' families are kept in a permanent state of waiting.

In the documentary *They Took Them Alive*, Mayra, the aunt of one of the missing forty-three, reflects on the pain:

> A missing person, as long as they haven't turned up dead, is still missing. With death comes resignation. But this doesn't let you live. We have hope that we'll find them. Because if we give up or say, "They must be dead by now," it's like killing them ourselves.[11]

The nation as a whole usually stays silent after such incidents, but with the Ayotzinapa 43, protests broke out in Guerrero. They grew fiercer as people took to social media, using hashtags like #Ayotzinapa to broadcast their actions. When Mexico's attorney general declared that he was tired (*"ya me cansé"*) of the push for investigation, people on social media created #YaMeCanse to express their outrage. The hashtag also expresses that citizens are tired of a lack of action from their government. They even called for President Peña Nieto's resignation, with #DemandoTuRenunciaEPN (I Demand Your Resignation, EPN), which trended globally.[12] The protests and consequent awareness rippled through Mexico, causing nationwide outrage about what had happened. #TodosSomosAyotzinapa (We Are All Ayotzinapa) broke out and then expanded to the Spanish-speaking world (mostly Latin America), as people everywhere watched the protests through Twitter, YouTube, Facebook, and Instagram. The men may have disappeared, but those who survived them were determined to generate visibility for them. The names, faces, and ages of the young men who vanished and pictures of protesters holding enlarged photos of their loves ones were posted on an Instagram account, @ayotzinapavive (Ayotzinapa lives).[13]

As journalist Julie Schwietert Collazo explained to me in an interview, "Literal physical depiction of people is an important practice" in Mexico.[14] Physical photos are common in Mexican culture, whether in subways, where people ask for help in locating disappeared people, or on church bulletin boards in rural areas, which show photos of a husband and wife to-be. The Instagram account and physical protests functioned in a similar way, while being public in digital space. These public mementos could receive hearts and comments. These posts function as digital tombstones, a gathering place for many people, friends, families, and concerned observers, to leave kind words and memories about each individual.

Just as important, these photos could be downloaded. They could be shared. People could post and repost them, and they used hashtags to create visibility for these students. And as with anything that becomes sufficiently popular on the internet, it soon sparked remixes. #IllustradoresConAyotzinapa (Illustrators with Ayotzinapa), a team of illustrators from Mexico City, invited illustrators from across Mexico and the Mexican diaspora each to depict a single individual who had disappeared.[15] These forty-three illustrators each provided a new portrait, inspired by the individual's picture and what they knew about him, and they posted these to Tumblr. The names and pictures began circulating once more, this time imbued with a color and aesthetic designed for a social media space.

Online, people started another action: reciting the names of these individuals. These recitations took the form of tweets and YouTube videos in which the people assembled would recite the names while the faces of the missing men scrolled by. These montages have been viewed millions of times, and each view amplifies a name that might have otherwise disappeared. The dance collective Semillas (Seeds) composed a song and dance routine that they published online in the form of a documentary. The troupe's name draws on the famous activist phrase "They tried to bury us, but they didn't know we were seeds."[16] Others sang *corridos*, a traditional Mexican song form that shares news and stories. These *corridos* were posted on YouTube, where they reached Mexicans in the diaspora.[17] In dance videos, performers twirl, jump, and pose, and at the climax, they scream out a number and a name of the disappeared, in succession, until all forty-three are named. The recitation of names lasts a few minutes, and the full weight of the name is a reminder of an individual now lost and who may not ever return. Within this simple gesture there is so much emotional power. In the stories of Chen Guangcheng and Trayvon Martin, those who were disappeared or died were single individuals. In the story of Ayotzinapa, they were many, and the response rippled forth from a small town, out to Mexico City, from there to the Spanish-speaking world, and then to the world at large. Their portraits, riding on hashtags and online actions, went viral in a way that is rare even today, drawing attention to a rural community overlooked by the global community.

In her book *Globalization and Its Discontents*, the social theorist Saskia Sassen noted that globalization seems to be uneven in its effects.[18] *National Geographic* defines globalization thus: "Globalization is the connection of different parts of the world. Globalization results in the expansion of international cultural, economic, and political activities. As people, ideas, knowledge, and goods move more easily around the globe, the experiences of people around the world become more similar."[19] A globalized corporation like McDonald's, for instance, provides similar services whether in the United States, China, or South Africa. A McDonald's customer can use a global credit-card system such as Visa or MasterCard to make a transaction. And the music played in the fast-food restaurant is probably a globally recognizable musician—Shakira, Taylor Swift, or Kanye West.

But in major cities, globalization seems to be moving much faster than in rural areas. Cities like Paris, London, Beijing, Dubai, and New York resemble each other more than they do their rural neighbors. Not only do their economic opportunities differ substantially, but so do their cultures and values. In Paris, you can find a cute café, a nice bookstore, a McDonald's, and a hip bar, and, except for language, these institutions will function similarly to those same or similar establishments in another major city, like Buenos Aires, thousands of miles away. But when you drive just a few hundred miles east of many major cities, the story is different: big box stores and low-cost food in the United States, and in developing countries, often limited electricity and internet infrastructure. Mainstream media, centered in cities, largely ignores the stories of rural communities. Thanks to the internet and a concerted offline effort, the stories of forty-three students from a rural Mexican community spread to the urban center, throughout Latin America, and globally.

When the names and faces of the Ayotzinapa 43 started going viral, they entered a technological context that included nearly 45 percent of Mexico's population on the internet, a population with loved ones who likely spanned the globe.[20] Networks were much denser and interconnected thanks to a student movement that started in 2012 and 2013 called #YoSoy132 (I Am 132), which laid the groundwork for the new generation of networked activist communities.[21] Moreover, the

Mexican diaspora played a key role in helping the story of the forty-three reach international media through protests, writing, and other actions.[22]

At the same time, the opposition had become more sophisticated to the workings of the digital plaza and how trending topic algorithms helped Mexican activists amplify their messages to media and the broader world. A network of bots spread disinformation and confusion on some of the movement's core hashtags. Mexican lawyer and activist Gisela Pérez de Acha noted to me in an interview that this flood of incorrect or simply distracting information made it difficult for people to find each other and disseminate information on key hashtags, including #YaMeCanse.[23] She explained that activists found ways to work around the obstacle, including adding numbers to their hashtags, like #YaMeCanse2 and #YaMeCanse3. The bots kept up, and they were a "huge setback." As blogger Alberto Escorcia said in *Wired* magazine, activists created novel slogans and messages to keep content fresh and make clear to Twitter's algorithm that they were not bots.[24]

Twitter bots and other artificial intelligence mechanisms that automatically generate content like photos and videos are increasingly a challenge around the world.[25] Similar to the paid propagandists of the Fifty Cent Party in China, human and machine "cyber troops"—as they're called by the University of Oxford's Computational Propaganda Project—now appear in many online spheres.[26] In Uganda and Kenya, where people so effectively used Twitter to generate new narratives, cyber troops have emerged in apparent efforts to sway elections and harass people.[27] Unlike activists, bots in particular never tire, and they can produce nearly infinite variations. As technological innovations progress, we should expect to see more of these techniques.

Key in this regard were the physical actions the families of the forty-three took, which helped people build these real connections. They gathered regularly in Mexico City to protest. A year after the disappearance, the families of the forty-three young men of Ayotzinapa traveled from Iguala to different cities in the United States. They called their project Caravana 43, and they launched accounts on social media. The families divided their touring group by region, with subgroups of families visiting different parts of the United States, and they used the hashtag #caravana43 to post pictures of their gatherings. They spoke out at rallies and protests, all the while carrying signs about their sons and nephews. Some of these signs were photos, and others were illustrations downloaded from the internet. Attendees took pictures of the signs and recirculated them on-line, and in this way, the different caravans across the United States were united through a single hashtag and a dedicated social media presence. As those images circulated, so did remixes, such as the number forty-three in a heart and other forms of poster art.[28]

Is it fair to say that murals are internet memes? That dance can be a meme? As concretely physical as any art object one can imagine, it seems the answer would be no, murals and dance can't be memes. But many murals contain the hashtag #Ayotzinapa43, and they reference illustrations and photos of the faces circulating on the internet. And as Caravana 43 arrived in Austin, Chicago, and the UN headquarters in New York, and in other cities, the members were greeted with cheers, solidarity, and, yes, murals. They took pictures of themselves, held up their signs for the cameras, and posted the images. These strategies were designed for virality, for getting attention, for making sure the world would not forget.

Making visible the faces and names of the dead and disappeared is a strikingly common strategy around the world. In 2014, when more than two hundred girls in rural Nigeria were taken away by Boko Haram, their mothers marched in the streets carrying photos of their daughters. Their chants eventually took the form of #BringBackOurGirls, a hashtag that circulated in international circles, reaching as far as the Obama White House.[29] And #BlackLivesMatter activists have used the hashtag #SayHerName to emphasize the names and lived realities of women killed or abused by police officers.[30] Recall, too, how the Chen Guangcheng selfie memes sought to replicate the symbolism of Chen's sunglasses, drawing attention both to him as an individual and to the larger systemic oppressions he aimed to fight against.

The viral strategy of calling to mind the names and faces of the dead and disappeared draws from a long history of using photos to highlight missing people. In the United States, for instance, milk cartons have long been used to show a picture of children who've gone missing. Throughout Germany, *stolpersteine*, "stumbling stones," with people's names on them remind visitors where someone who died in the Holocaust once lived. In the ancient Mediterranean world, making a death mask captured a deceased person's likeness, keeping their image alive. Pictures and photos call to mind the specificity of a person, the humanity in a face and a name. If a disappearance makes families feel as if their loved ones are in a permanent state of purgatory, photos keep that person alive, and the network now has a way to amplify that person's image across continents and contexts.

"The most powerful element of the digital narrative about Ayotzinapa 43 was the brutality of the government," noted Alejandro Gómez Escorcia.[31] Escorcia manages the social media presence for the Museo Nacional de Arte (National Museum of Art) in Mexico City, where he has helped organize workshops about memes. "The image of men without faces was terrible and left a very deep imprint in the social memory [of Mexicans]." In Mexico, he noted, memes are everywhere, exploring a wide variety of social issues, from feminism to science and sports: "What thing can keep us together? The memes, as a cultural code, have the power to show the common, the consensus, the similarity. Also the memes are powerful when we show the different and the unmentioned."[32]

Virality is often discussed as a passive action: "These pictures went viral." It's easy to imagine pictures, like actual genetic viruses, being picked up and floating around the internet, finding new hosts for their bodies. But as Henry Jenkins, Sam Ford, and Joshua Green have argued in their book *Spreadable Media*, it's often more helpful to think of them as active media that people share for a variety of reasons.[33] When something goes viral, it goes viral because people actively choose to share them, to remix them, to place them in their social media feeds, and by so doing, place them in the social media feeds of other people. And with the story of Ayotzinapa, people also had to translate these names and stories and make sure they could be understood by English speakers in order for the stories to reach a global audience.

In 2017, protesters gathered for the third anniversary of the disappearance of the Ayotzinapa 43, and while evidence of gaps in the government's story builds, the young men seemed no closer to being found.[34] That the story of Ayotzinapa has not gone away is a reflection of their families' state of suspension, and they and supporters continue to protest and signal that they have not forgotten. There has also been an important shift: the Ayotzinapa 43 have become a symbol of something much larger. Writing in *CounterPunch*, journalist Laura Carlsen noted that

> Mexicans from all over the country felt something snap when they heard of the students abducted and disappeared in the city of Iguala. They responded with demonstrations that reached hundreds of thousands strong in late 2014. Their

slogan—it was the state—changed the way people think about the Mexican government, its relationship to organized crime and the war on drugs that has taken more than 140,000 lives in the past nine years.[35]

When something becomes a symbol, it references something much larger than what it directly denotes. In *Global Injustice Symbols*, author Thomas Olesen notes that Nelson Mandela has become more than a man; he symbolizes democracy, resilience, human rights, and even reconciliation.[36] In other words, a movement's symbols stand for the values of the movement (think rainbow flag) and for a culturally specific narrative (think marriage equality). Both of these aspects of a symbol generate power for a movement, and in an interconnected era, this power is increasingly global. It's what helped propel the names and faces of students in a rural Mexican village to the heart of a global US city. And that in turn propels action: people on the streets making themselves impossible to ignore.

In the same way, the forty-three are invoked in larger narratives and stories about state violence and disappearances and their link to the drug war. That students disappeared while aiming to attend a protest about an incident decades earlier, in 1968, helped transform their disappearance into a symbol with a much longer history. Journalists and activists could draw links between then and now and craft a narrative that helped people see historical and geographic patterns as interconnected rather than isolated incidents. It's this ability to create patterns in observations and writing that makes the difference between a meme as an attention-getter for a single incident and a meme as laying the groundwork for a broader conversation that includes national media, government agencies, international media, citizens, and civil society.[37]

Also important was the sight of parents marching bravely across the United States and Mexico to raise the possibility of change, even if that change seems an impossible goal. "It was . . . a way for Mexicans in Mexico to feel like this wasn't just another footnote in international news," Collazo noted in our interview. "All of these calls for international contributions were particularly important for people in Ayotzinapa and people in more rural communities to see what's happening, and furthermore, to see that people care enough about it to take time to render their own drawings."[38]

Drawing lines, making connections—recall how powerful memes can be in a distributed space, helping people find each other across geographies and affirm each other's beliefs. This same sense of networkedness also helps fuel narratives, as it opens the door for multiple people to contribute pieces to that narrative, to repeat and iterate on symbolism, to amplify across different networks. This is the project of making and shaping culture. What's crucial is having a rich network of bloggers, journalists, policy makers, activists, and others who can take the seeds of a larger story and grow them into something longer lasting. And by understanding this dynamic, we can understand where and how memes can be effective, even in the face of great challenges.

Disappearances continue in Mexico, and the true fate of the Ayotzinapa 43 may never be fully known. A few weeks after Mexico elected a new president who promised to start a Truth Commission for the Ayotzinapa 43, the students' classmates graduated without them present.[39] Creative media alone cannot change a long-running problem in a matter of years. Legal and cultural change can take generations, especially in the face of powerful opposition. It moves along slower than we can imagine. But what art and media do, online and offline, is create an archive of cultural memory, a record of conversations and subtle shifts that have transpired, making forgetting an impossibility and all but ensuring future conversations can ensue. Schwietert Collazo says:

> Even if the government hasn't taken any responsibility—and it hasn't—even if the families of the 43 haven't had any relief, I think it's still really crucial that these creative products remain in existence and that they remain accessible online by the people as documentation of what happened and the response to it, not just something that people noticed and then carried about their lives. Somewhere there exists this archive that there was this groundswell of outrage, and it can remain accessible for people to look at and listen to and read as part of the overall accounting of this particular chapter in the history of Mexico.[40]

And art, more than an archive of history, can break through a noisy environment and become impossible to ignore in the present. Pérez de Acha told me that "traditional media didn't cover us until it was so evident on social media that they could not close their eyes anymore. We need visual and strong messages and things that just get through your soul and you just understand it without reading five hundred pages of legal analysis. I think art is a very powerful tool of change."[41]

POWER PLAY

The image had the capacity to convert something
abstract, distant and complex into something con-
crete, proximate and simple.

—Lin Prøitz[1]

CULTURE SHIFTS, CULTURE CHANGES, culture is informed by much deeper
processes than the internet, but the internet also informs culture. Memes come
from deep wellsprings in society, and as more of society comes online, more
memes of contention and disagreement appear. In addition to opposing their
governments, meme makers find opposition among their peers, in both digital
and physical space. The work of building and shaping culture is one role that
meme makers play, and the tools they have at hand continue to multiply.

Writing about her work in immigration justice in the United States, activist
Favianna Rodriguez describes the role of the arts in social and political movements: "We should also ask ourselves, 'What are the valuable contributions
artists can make in the idea space?' Artists don't think like policy folks. They
don't think like organizers. And this is a good thing. They think big, visionary ideas. We can't necessarily claim that reading a novel or watching a sci-fi
movie . . . will move people to action, but the experience expands our imagina-
tions and creates a climate where we can be visionary."[2] Reflecting on the fact
that cultural change operates in longer terms than policy, law, and other areas
of activism, Rodriguez continues:

> When is the right moment to inject culture into a political movement? Think
> about culture as rain readying the crops. You go to the theater, watch sports or
> listen to music, and culture just happens to you. You're not expecting to debate

the merits of a political message when you listen to music or read a book. You're more open to how culture is going to transform you, so you walk into it with an open heart.[3]

Memes float through our technological spaces, and they surprise us, opening our hearts and transforming us, even in small ways. When memes grow and multiply, they send a signal about society. And as those signals enter the physical world, they reflect the changes that have been occurring all along. New technologies enable three factors that facilitate meme culture: rapid and easy production; quicker, broader distribution; and a place for makers and consumers to find each other. In the digital context, computers and mobile phones enable creation, while stronger broadband networks provide a means for distribution. The internet and more specifically social platforms and user forums help people create community across a global scale.

The first memes in a given culture are often text based because of limited bandwidth and access to technology. Text-based memes have taken the form of Usenet groups, IRC chats, and Twitter trending topics. As bandwidth increases and access to photo-editing technology increases, more image memes appear, which float around on image-based sites such as Reddit, Tumblr, Facebook, and Twitter. Video-editing technology and smartphone cameras then allow for more video memes, which appear on some of the aforementioned networks and also on video-specific platforms like Vine and YouTube.

We're now increasingly at a new stage involving physical objects. While people make object memes on their computers, there needs to be a way to actualize a digital file in the physical world. For many protest signs, that involves simply printing out the item at home or at a local print shop (of course, many protest signs involve good old markers and pens). For hats and totes, that means outsourcing to a production house, which has routinized core processes for a certain range of objects. The mode of discovery can rely on social networks, but it can also rely on online shops such as Etsy and eBay and aggregators such as Google Shopping and Amazon, which make it easy to find the object memes. And not being digital, physical objects need a physical mode of distribution. In the United States, this means shipping services such as the postal service, UPS, and FedEx, all of which can transport an item from one side of the country to the next in a day, and packaging services like Shyp or in-house packaging at sites like Teespring, which reduce the labor and logistics for someone who just wants to get a T-shirt out into the world.

The overall effect is clear: object memes are now the next wave of activist meme culture to reach scale, and as they mix with online and offline culture, they extend the impact of the internet into physical space and culture. In an interview, activist and organizer Jeronimo Saldaña told me that his inspiration for making a Make America Mexico Again hat came first from seeing a digital remix on his Facebook feed, then thinking he could do that himself. Encouraged by friends, he figured out the logistics of making the hat, focusing on ethically sourced materials, and getting it out into the world.

> Now I'm seeing the importance of taking my online community and sharing with them as part of the work I do on the ground. We take what we're doing with online hashtags and online friendships and move things and make sure we talk to other folks about it. Everybody discusses things that happen online. Everybody discusses Trump's tweets, whether or not they have Twitter. These digital technologies influence you even if you don't have access to the internet.[4]

Indeed, ahead of the 2017 Women's March, object memes had already been emerging. In Hong Kong, there were yellow umbrellas, umbrella stickers, and origami. In the Movement for Black Lives, there were hashtag shirts and signs referencing #BlackLivesMatter, #ICantBreathe, #SayHerName, and others. Up and down the Americas, Ayotzinapa student photos appeared on placards, banners, and murals. And in the 2016 US election campaigns the most obvious were Nasty Woman T-shirts, hats, and tote bags, some of which came from the campaign but most of which seemed to come from dozens, perhaps hundreds, of makers with different designs, ideas, and variations. On the Right were the Deplorables T-shirts, hats, and tote bags.

As meme culture spills into the physical world, it becomes more difficult to say that something happening on the internet is just on the internet when in fact it could be shaping culture in ways that are not immediately apparent until, over time, we see it emerge in a protest, a violent rally, a political gathering. Artificial intelligence technologies, capable of creating and distributing content rapidly, will almost certainly be the next phase of this progression, though we should also expect new artificial intelligence methods to become better at sussing out these creations. And today, we see this contest of memes playing out as much on the streets as on the phones, and its effects ripple into policy and power.

A week after the inauguration of Donald Trump, I stood among thousands of people in Boston's Copley Square who were gathered to protest the new administration's immigration policy. I weaved my way with friends through the dense crowd, which seemed to coalesce in two major areas: a drum circle in the fountain (left dry in the winter), where people were dancing and swaying and chanting, and at the steps of Trinity Church. Every now and then people would grab the megaphone and lead the group in a chant. All around me people were holding up signs, shouting, singing, and taking photos to share online. It was just a week since the Women's March, and people seemed to be carrying the very same signs they had used in the march while others had created new ones.

A few miles away, at Logan International Airport, a parallel group gathered with great urgency. They, among others in international airports around the country, were chanting messages like "Let them in! Let them in!" Lawyers from the American Civil Liberties Union (ACLU) stationed themselves at the airport so they could immediately advise newcomers on their rights. Video from other airports across the country showed throngs of people in an unprecedented wave of airport-based protest, taking over escalators and crowding exit terminals with music, dance, chants, signs, sit-ins, and other actions, all of them live-streamed and shared to social media.

Just hours before, Trump had signed an executive order that declared that all immigrants from seven countries be barred from entering the country for ninety days.[5] While ostensibly the block was intended to reduce terrorism, most mainstream media outlets widely interpreted this as a ban on Muslims, as all the banned countries were majority-Muslim nations (and, curiously, none of the recent foreign terrorist acts in the United States had been committed by people from these countries[6]). Indeed, the executive order was ultimately struck down by two federal courts, with the help of strong advocacy from immigration lawyers and the ACLU. Judge Derrick K. Watson of the Federal District Court in Honolulu noted the potential bias of the ban, stating the executive order was "issued with a purpose to disfavor a particular religion, in spite of its stated, religiously neutral purpose."[7] The ban seemed to be a fulfillment of Trump's promise, early in the campaign, for "a total and complete shutdown of Muslims entering the United States until our country's representatives can figure out what is going on."[8]

As I circled through the crowd and documented signs and creative actions, I saw two older hijabis take the megaphone. One woman shouted, "I love this country!" as the crowd cheered. When the music resumed, she danced along, as did many others. The urgency and uncertainty of the moment—that actual refugees and immigrants were stopped in their tracks at the airport—was matched only by the urgency of the crowd. Throughout much of the country, anti–Muslim ban marches also took place. Among those marching elsewhere was Marcus Benigno, director of communications and media advocacy at the ACLU Southern California. He works at the Los Angeles chapter but was in San Francisco at the time, and he coordinated efforts to get the word out about places for protests. Benigno explained his work:

> What Twitter did in that moment is . . . [create] a clear organizing and mobilizing effort. Despite the stay that we were able to get, much of the pressure on these federal judges was driven by media frenzy and images of people and their outrage. So I think, yes, on the one hand lawyers could have done it, but we couldn't have won, couldn't have had collected those stories had we not used social [media]. That's just the basic utility of getting the word out, using social [media] to connect with people who were directly impacted.[9]

Benigno also noted the importance of the framing of the executive order as a "Muslim ban," a narrative that took hold in the news media and in general conversation, even if the order was carefully worded not to include references to Muslims per se. When then White House press secretary Sean Spicer denied it as such, his denial reinforced the framing: people began talking about whether or not it was a Muslim ban.

In 2004, linguist and cognitive scientist George Lakoff popularized the concept of framing in politics. A frame is a conceptual lens that affects how one looks at something. Compare the framing of a "Muslim ban" versus a "travel ban"—one makes explicit that religion is a factor while the other puts the focus on the logistics of travel. Writing after the election of Donald Trump, Lakoff described one of Trump's skills as "preemptive framing," in other words, setting the terms of the conversation, often simply by using Twitter.[10] Regarding the Muslim ban,

Trump arguably lost the framing conversation, and this can be attributed to the swift actions of Benigno and other activists.

Back in Boston, a few signs in particular stayed with me. "Refugees Welcome" many said. Others declared that immigrants were welcome here. One, in Chinese, said that Chinese Americans welcomed immigrants from other countries. And another sign showed a drawing of a young boy turned face down and wearing blue shorts and a red shirt. I recognized him immediately: his name was Alan Kurdi, and he was a Syrian refugee who had been denied legal entry into the United States along with his family. I paused for a moment because I knew how far his image had traveled, from the Turkish coast in 2015 to Boston in 2017.

In June 2015, Kurdi and his mother set off from Kobani, Syria, as part of the long journey to Europe that many Syrian refugees undertook.[11] The Kurdi family ultimately hoped to reach Canada, where they had family members willing to sponsor them.[12] Ravaged by a civil war since 2011, Syria's living conditions grew increasingly worse, triggering a wave of millions of Syrians traveling through Turkey, across the Mediterranean Sea into Greece, and then walking, swimming, biking, and catching rides upward through the Balkans and into the Schengen Zone. By the time the Kurdi family left Syria, the refugee crisis, as it came to be called, was the largest such crisis since World War II.[13] He himself would never make it past Turkey, but his image would go global in a way that shifted the global conversation about refugees.

When Kurdi's body washed ashore on the coast of Bodrum, Turkey, photojournalist Nilüfer Demir from Doğan News Agency took a number of photographs.[14] While images of refugees had already entered media discourse in Europe, this image went viral in a particularly impactful way. Researcher Francesco D'Orazio, a vice president of product and research at Pulsar Social and a lead researcher at Visual Social Media Lab, relied on special image recognition algorithms to track the spread of the photo in its many manifestations, making for a unique case study of visual culture. He found that the photo spread first among people and media in Turkey and the broader Middle East region. It then caught the attention of Liz Sly, a *Washington Post* bureau chief based in Beirut with a broad reach among the Western journalism community. From there, it reached the entire world, though it held particular resonance in Europe, where the refugee crisis had its most immediate impact.

In a special report by the Visual Social Media Lab, D'Orazio writes about the significance of this moment:

> At this point in time, almost five hours after the photos have been published online and three hours after they appeared on Twitter first, the Turkish press is the only one officially covering the story, no international news organizations are covering it. And in the void left by the media Twitter has managed to amplify the story to a global audience. But it hasn't simply seeded the story globally. Twitter acted as a decentralized catalyst that has delivered the story to a highly relevant group of people (journalists, activists, politicians, aid workers interested in the region). . . .
>
> This doesn't mean that journalists are not getting involved in this process. In fact, they are leading and engineering the viral spread of the images, but they are posting their content on Twitter exclusively and independently from their publications.[15]

The role of journalists in our memetic ecosystem has grown tighter over the years. Where once internet culture might have been an odd outlier, it is now part and parcel with much of society. This reflects an interaction between the popular culture of the internet and the power of broadcast media, and it continues not just as a text-based conversation but also a conversation that includes images, videos, and memes. Memetic activists understand this, as do digital propagandists, as do authoritarian governments that seek to dampen a message's spread by targeting journalists.

In the moment it was certainly surprising to see how quickly the image of Alan Kurdi spread. This image, of all images, depicted no overt violence or suggestion of the war that he and his family were fleeing. It didn't show his face, nor did it show his family members. He looked as if he was sleeping peacefully, and perhaps that's why, in so many cases, an image that goes viral is one that causes cognitive dissonance. Seeing a young boy, no more than five years old, lying dead on a beach was emotionally overwhelming to so many people around the world. For many in the West, the beach connotes play and sandcastles for children, not this.

Pulsar Social could detect the spread of images across the internet based on their color and shape. This allowed it to detect a photo of a sand drawing made to look like Kurdi, and to see a variety of cartoons and paintings made of him.

While the original image had gone viral, it sparked a wide variety of memes, many of which commented on Europe's neglect of refugees' needs, while others, like the sign I saw in Boston, simply reproduced the image. Some of the most poignant ones depicted Kurdi still alive, arriving in Europe to a warm welcome. The image drove attention to the refugee crisis in a new way, sparking a series of discussions in media and among policy circles about how best to receive refugees, who had been entering Europe for months before the Kurdi image appeared. It helps to understand the context: the most recent wave of refugees was triggered by the war in Syria, but many refugees come from Pakistan, Iran, Yemen, Nigeria, and South Sudan and other countries that face not necessarily war but economic crises and devastating poverty. The refugee crisis reminds us that globalization affects not just the internet, with ideas and media circulating the world, but also people who must pack up and leave. The crisis is a reminder of our interconnectedness, and the internet amplifies the images, stories, and responses to those stories that the crisis engenders.

Over time, the Visual Social Media Lab noticed that discourse in European media shifted shortly after the Kurdi image went viral, a process they documented into a groundbreaking rapid response report that tracked and analyzed the image through an interdisciplinary lens.[16] Instead of *migrants*, a word referring to anyone who seeks to move to another country, media began talking about *refugees*, a word referring to someone who moves out of fear of war or violence in their home country. This legal and verbal distinction matters because, per the United Nation's 1951 Refugee Convention, refugees and people rendered stateless are due special protections, given the vulnerabilities they face.[17]

Coincidentally, just a few hours before Kurdi's death, the hashtag #Refugees Welcome went viral in the United Kingdom, eased along by celebrities and media who reposted images of people holding up signs saying "Refugees Welcome."[18] Many in the UK and Europe were concerned about the difficult process of receiving refugees and the historic implications of rejecting them (in the 1940s, for example, the United States had quotas for the number of Jewish refugees it would receive; many of those refused entry would ultimately be killed in the Holocaust.[19]) The simple hashtag took off, resonating among a number of Europeans, both in English and in their mother tongues.

Stickers and memes saying "Refugees Welcome" began to emerge. People were invited to place these stickers on their homes and businesses, to send a signal to refugees that they would be safe there. The most popular stickers depicted a family crossing the street. I recognized it immediately from John Hood's designs of street signs in Southern California that depicted a family running to cross the highway.[20] In that one, the image combined with the phrase #RefugeesWelcome, a new iconography was born, which drew from depictions of immigrants entering the United States. "Refugees Welcome" also transformed into a series of decentralized organizing groups in Amsterdam, Berlin, Budapest, and other cities. Gathering in Facebook groups, they coordinated donations of resources: food and clothing, visits to common arrival zones (these typically were train stations), protests, and other forms of assistance. Many other ad hoc groups emerged, some to provide direct assistance in refugee camps, others to support refugees en route, and others to provide support and services in the city. As part of my work as director of product at Meedan, for instance, I worked with The Space in Berlin, which coordinated art making, music, community dinners, and other activities for refugees and newcomers to the city, while helping them integrate with the broader community.

As Visual Social Media Lab researcher Lin Prøitz noticed, many people in Europe were moved to participate specifically because of images they had seen, including the one of Alan Kurdi. Interviewing a focus group of people over the course of many months in both Oslo, Norway, and Sheffield, England, she found that the images stayed in their minds and caused an emotional stir that propelled them to action. And in working together, they were able to share those emotions:

> The assemblages of the many young volunteers and the collective actions were a response based on a collective shared story, "past the politics, past the scapegoating of refugees." The image had the capacity to convert something abstract, distant and complex into something concrete, proximate and simple, which had affective significance.[21]

The global spread of the image helped them form networks with other people, and also important was that the clarity of the image created a focal point for them, turning what until then was a diffuse and unfamiliar issue into one with a name, a clear reference point, and collective emotional energy behind it.

But supporters of refugees were not the only ones to see these images, nor was the Alan Kurdi image the only one to go viral. Also common were photos of mass waves of dark-skinned refugees, which emphasized faceless masses, and images of incidents of violence, which emphasized isolated occurrences. Even innocuous-seeming images, like those of refugees carrying cell phones, triggered a series of questions about whether they were truly refugees—after all, how could they afford a cell phone if they were really that needy? These images, too, stirred emotion and sparked the emergence of movements. As media scholar Ray Drainville argued, manipulated imagery about refugees even played a role in the Brexit Leave campaign.[22]

In *The Journey*, an hour-long, six-part documentary in which American filmmaker Matthew Cassel follows a family of refugees on their journey from Syria to Sweden, one such person is Edwin. He leads efforts in the Netherlands for a group called Pegida, which aims to prevent more refugees from arriving in Europe. Like Refugees Welcome, but with a decidedly different mission, Pegida has multiple chapters throughout the continent, and has a distributed leadership structure. Edwin references photos of refugees crossing Hungary and says he wants them to assimilate and fears the cultural changes they are about to bring.[23]

Meme theorist Ryan Milner has argued that, when it comes to politics, meme culture mixes pop culture and political issues, and social and political issues are negotiated and debated. "More arguments can happen in more ways because of the connection between pop, media, and politics," he says. "Appreciating the value of pop savvy mediated commentary means appreciating the role of participatory media in political engagement."[24] The Kurdi image, which quickly reached popular status due to its virality, entered the field of memetic contention.

In counternarratives promoted by sites like *Breitbart*, blogs, and even politicians, the Kurdi image was called into question, and some raised the notion that it was perhaps a cleverly stage-managed attempt to depict refugees in a positive light.[25] The image was remixed into much darker ones, showing ISIS sneaking into Europe cloaked amid the waves of refugees. Rather than a narrative of welcoming refugees, a narrative emerged that they were coming to Europe to transform European countries into Islamic ones. A few signs and memes remixed "Refugees Welcome" into "Rapefugees Welcome," referencing reports of incidents where refugees attacked white European women. Memes in right-wing circles show pictures of refugee tents in the middle of Paris and Brussels, suggesting that the cities have crumbled since the mass arrival of refugees and that the United States could be next.

As memes, images, and videos circulate throughout the internet, they appear as-is in people's feeds, frequently disconnected from the origin of the images and deeper story. The images gain meaning from the way they are remixed and framed, from one's existing framework of the world, and from any other context, like the person sending it and any commentary they add. The potential of images circulating online is that they can so easily be memed into messages that amplify these images and draw attention to critical social issues. The risk of images circulating online is that they can so easily be memed into messages that amplify a countermessage. Depending on your point of view and political persuasion, you'll find a certain range of memes reassuring, helping you find like-minded souls. For another range of memes, you'll find points of contention.

This pattern happens with every major social and political meme. When Donald Trump popularized his Make America Great Again hat, activists created the remixes "Make America Mexico Again," "Make Racists Afraid Again," and others to challenge the original symbolism. When racial justice activists transformed the image of a hoodie into a symbol of justice for Trayvon Martin, pranksters and others began a performative meme in which they lay flat on the ground with a hoodie, a bag of Skittles, and an Arizona Tea can, and created the hashtag #Trayvoning. In Hong Kong, for every yellow ribbon, there seems to be one in blue, a color that emerged out of support for the police.

These narratives and counternarratives can have lasting effects as they influence media and legislation. In a world of remixing and mashups, there is rarely stasis in our media, and so frequently, when one group generates a meme that resonates widely, a group in opposition can generate a remix that enters the discourse. Sometimes this means challenging the auspices of power. Other times, this means reinforcing power along racial, economic, gender, and other lines. This lack of stability in meme culture migrates upward into media and political discourse, and it shapes culture, sometimes amplifying long-standing divisions. This is especially true with a meme like #RefugeesWelcome, which has spread internationally but taken different forms, depending on the specific legal, political, or cultural context it operates in.

Culture takes complex turns of contention in the face of extraordinary events like a global refugee crisis and waves of immigration (although this will soon no longer be extraordinary, as we should expect the rate of refugees to increase in the face of conflict and climate change). That images and rhetoric cross the oceans should no longer be a surprise: the internet connects the world in unique ways that were difficult to achieve before. At the same time, the internet also divides, sharpening divisions and stances on what different corners of society believe are acceptable reasons to migrate to a country. Even as culture changes, culture hardens, and power soon follows. This tension is no more clear than in the global dialogue about immigration and refugees and the range of policies and perspectives put forth. Despite warnings from human rights organizations, the European Union eventually made a deal with Turkey to prevent boats from leaving its coasts, thus effectively shutting down a key path of migration, and in the United States, policies to reduce immigration have only continued to grow, including increased detentions and separating parents and children at the border.[26] Individual cities, states, and nations may have more open policies, but the overall trend seems to be toward closing borders or making them so terrifying as to dissuade would-be refugees.

That societies fragment into disagreement is an ancient story, and power plays a major role here in determining who eventually wins. One of the central questions of twenty-first-century political communications is the role of the internet in this story. I think back to the notion of *digital dissensus*, which scholar Penny Andrews described so well. Today's world is one of dissensus, full of tension and dissent. The internet has indeed brought the world together, and the internet has amplified narratives and perspectives that have not traditionally existed in mainstream media. The removal of traditional gatekeepers has limited the ability to maintain singular media narratives. This has allowed the marginalized to tell their stories in new ways. It has also allowed the powerful to fracture, distract, and suppress dissent in the general public. Those aligned with hatred and bigotry are finding new ways to build media power and organize. Algorithms and platform designs seem to be exacerbating the challenges. Real human suffering continues apace amid this broad dissensus.

What is clear is that all these groups are learning the new modes and methods of social influence that the internet affords, and memes are playing a key role in this regard. What is less clear is whether unified media action and narrative building by anyone who does not completely control internet platforms can be possible anymore. In contexts such as this, the marginalized lose a key path to power—the ability to build and amplify their narratives—while those with access to legal, military, and financial power can muscle in their agendas. This contest of memes is an ongoing one.

Which then begs several questions: Where do political memes come from and why is there such a broad range of views? Why do some resonate more than others? Why do they take hold in some groups and offend others, compelling people to create countermemes and narratives? And what effect do they have in the long term? These questions must be asked of any new, influential medium, whether it be the printing press or the evolution of film. When it comes to the internet, these questions are still unanswered, and the history of the internet in politics, protest, and power is still being written by scholars, technologists, journalists, activists, and anyone else who's made a contribution to the web.

To try to find answers, I want to take a step back from politics and get to the core of culture. Let's go back to meme fundamentals: fuzzy creatures.

CHAPTER 7

. . . .

FIELDS

Think about culture as rain readying the crops. You go to the theater, watch sports or listen to music, and culture just happens to you. . . . You're more open to how culture is going to transform you, so you walk into it with an open heart.

—Favianna Rodriguez[1]

THE DESIRE TO SHARE, REMIX, AND REPURPOSE has a long history in human society. Thinking of memes as *enabled* by technology helps us see the patterns and waves of meme culture as part of a continuum of how culture works more broadly. The spillover of meme culture in the physical world, whether objects contain memes or become memes in themselves, goes both ways: the world around us informs the memes that we create and share online.

Meme-wielding movements need to ask what political memes excel at, namely, creating symbols, slogans, and narratives through an often unpredictable culture of iteration and co-creation. All major movements in history have relied on media strategies to generate momentum, but they must also consider other levers of influence for driving long-term change, including politics, law, research, markets, direct action, and other forms of power outside the scope of this book. At the same time, these efforts in turn must draw emotive, attentional, and narrative power from media.

There are many things we can compare memes to. Like mirrors, memes reflect, amplify, and distort culture. Like street art, they are tools to reshape and react to our digital gathering places. When we look to the future of memes, we should also look to the past. Like seeds, they contain within them the potential for shaping change, but only if given the right conditions.

THE RISE OF THE GOAT

Our approach to freedom need not be identical but it must be intersectional and inclusive. It must extend beyond ourselves.

—Janet Mock[1]

IN 2013, SOME THIRTY THOUSAND GOATS went missing in Uganda. The goats were intended as a government project for local farmers.[2] Goats play a key role in Ugandan society, providing a source of milk and food. Goat meat, uncommon in the West, is a popular dish with rice and *posho*, a light grits-like meal made with flour and a little bit of collard greens. That thirty thousand goats went missing was no accident—people took it as a sign of government malfeasance and corruption, part of a longer stream of mishaps. The Ugandan humor site Urban Legend Kampala poked fun at this issue, as the goats were ultimately located. In a post on the site, goats were shown hanging out with Vice President Edward Ssekandi, who posed with the Obama family at the White House. They also started a hashtag trend, #WhereAreTheGoats, which got a decent uptake among social media users.[3]

The technique of using animal memes as political commentary was familiar to me—after all, it had emerged with cats and llamas—but the idea of goats was a new one. Having grown up primarily in urban areas, I rarely interacted with goats in daily life, seeing them mostly in petting zoos alongside sheep and horses. But after spending a few months in Kampala, I recognized the humor immediately. In Uganda's capital city and throughout much of the country, goats wander freely through people's yards and villages. They are part of daily life in much the same way cats and dogs are in many Western and Asian cities. Indeed, dogs are far less common and cats rarely seen, as the latter are frequently perceived as pests rather than pets.

"Chicken and goat humor reflects a larger culture of animal rearing in Uganda," noted Peter Kakoma, humorist and Urban Legend Kampala co-founder. His description was an entry for a world map of animal memes that the Civic Beat, the global research collective I cofounded, helped curate with the Museum of the Moving Image in New York in 2015.[4] And, as we would soon learn, Uganda's internet is not alone in its love affair with goats.

The idea of the map was simple: we invited internet culture scholars, writers, and observers to contribute an animal meme that best represented the internet culture of their country. The map was part of a larger show called *How Cats Took Over the Internet*, curated by Jason Eppink, which examined the history of cat humor, videos, and memes in internet culture. The world animal meme map was meant to show the diversity of animal meme cultures throughout the world, with more than a dozen contributions from people looking at internet cultures in places as diverse as Tajikistan, Mexico, Bangladesh, Brazil, Cambodia, and Syria. Creatures like donkeys, llamas, dogs, and, of course, cats made appearances, but one creature in particular seemed to emerge again and again: goats.

Contributor Zara Rahman, a writer for *Global Voices* and a human rights researcher at the Engine Room, shared the Goats of Bangladesh, a popular Bangladeshi Facebook group that personifies goats talking about daily life, from dating challenges to politics to, of course, puns.[5] In one image a goat appears despondent, reflecting on the challenges of life:

> It's just there are so many goats out there, you know? So many goats I know I may never meet or see in my life. So many goats I could have made a connection with. So many goats that could help me. So many goats that could understand.[6]

Modeled after the popular blog *Humans of New York*, the Goats of Bangladesh, as Rahman notes, reflects the importance of goats in daily life in the country, where they roam freely through the streets alongside people.

Zipping over to Brazil, goat humor seems to be popular in many rural areas, including the northeast of the country. As internet culture writer Bia Granja explained, "A number of animals including goats, pigs, and capybaras have become popular subjects of online humor in Brazil." Granja, who founded YouPix, an internet culture site and event with thousands of attendees in São Paulo, has made a living exploring Brazil's internet culture. O Bode Gaiato (The Wag Goat) takes the form of a goat head on a baby's body, and it reflects a certain puerile humor. As an image macro (an image with bits of text placed on it), O Bode Gaiato complains about having to wash the dishes, about being told what to do, about maybe never being able to date again. And it popularized the phrase *"Armaria, nãm,"* slang for *"Ave Maria, não,"* which means "Holy Mary, no."

And let's not overlook what's happening in the West. University of Southern California media researcher Kate Miltner contributed an entry about goat humor in the United Kingdom to the map. While many people's first impression of the UK is the teeming metropolis of London, it is largely a pastoral country, as Miltner noted. She recounted the rise of goat memes and humor over the years, with a popular goat video game, fainting goat videos, and image macros. With goats in Uganda, Bangladesh, Brazil, and the UK making their way around the internet, a clear trend in our map emerged: goats, far more than cats, seemed to be the world's internet darling. Could this really be true? To be clear, we didn't do statistical analysis or deep data analysis, nor did the map cover all corners of the world. But the thought experiment was interesting. Maybe goats at least deserve their rightful place alongside cats in the meme pantheon.

To understand why goat images and references on the internet seem to be on the rise, it helps to step back, way back, to some thirty thousand years ago. In the south of France, the Grotte Chauvet-Pont d'Arc is one of the best preserved sites of prehistoric art. A master archive of life at the time, it shows sophisticated techniques for media creation and depictions of space, line, and movement. It is also filled with animals: bears, cave lions, rhinoceroses, bison, and aurochs (a type of cattle that is now extinct).[7] Look closely at some of the photos and you can see, for instance, heads and tails in apparent motion. The filmmaker and cave painting researcher Marc Azéma has suggested that these depictions were an early form of cinema, showing sequence as in a comic strip and even, perhaps, showing motion under flickering lights.[8]

Writing in *Nautilus* magazine, journalist Zach Zorich vividly describes the experience of seeing the animals before him:

> Paleolithic art may have been spiritual—prayers for a successful hunt—or maybe they related specific events—the time when a pride of lions hunted a large rhinoceros. Or perhaps it was like modern-day art, and fulfilled a variety

of roles that aren't easily put into categories. Even though the images were mostly of animals, what the art conveyed to me was humanness.[9]

When I read stories like this, I think about the contemporary fascination with animal GIFs and images. If the peoples of the Grotte culture depicted rhino heads rising and falling and bison flicking their tails, the peoples of the internet show pug tails wagging and cats jumping up and down. I think about Eadweard Muybridge, whose photos of horses and ostriches in motion are sometimes credited with being a precursor to animation and, yes, GIFs.[10] We humans have always depicted animals, and, more significant, we've depicted the animals important to our lives. In the Victorian era, those were horses; in prehistoric France, they were aurochs and cave lions (cats, arguably!); and today, they compose a wild menagerie.

Now fast-forward to the early days of the internet, when cats (seemingly) took it over. The internet's first users were primarily two groups of people: academics, who wanted to share research papers with each other, and the military, who wanted to improve communications and intelligence sharing. Most of these folks were in the West, especially the United States. Indeed, some of the earliest infrastructure of the internet was laid on US soil, relying first on the existing network of telephone wires before more sophisticated fiber-optic cables were laid. Accessing the internet required a computer with a modem, and few computers at the time had modems built in.

While images like "the cloud" and "cyberspace" pervade the popular imagination of internet users, these images obscure the reality of the internet, which is that it's a very physical structure. "The information superhighway" is a dated metaphor that obscures the ways people use the internet for affirmation and other emotional benefits, but the comparison with a road system is apt for the actual physical structure of the internet. The highway system in the United States, as in much of the world, is a system of tiered roads. There are the big highways that connect major cities on opposite ends of the country and contain eight lanes and sometimes even more. There are supplementary highways with fewer lanes and less traffic. And branching off of those highways are surface streets, some as skinny as a single lane with little room for parking. Farther still, you'll find dirt roads, and even farther still, there are no roads, just a path carved out by cars over time. We are living in a time of an increasingly diversified internet, which is increasingly connecting the world, if unevenly in pace. The process is slow and steady, and as new groups come online and formulate new networks, new voices are heard.

The emergence of new communities online is as much a story of the physical reality of the internet as it is about the digital interactions they have. In *Tubes*, author Andrew Blum describes the physical structure of the internet, from the wires underneath us to the major routing towers and the massive cables that slink along the bottom of the ocean: "Undersea cables link people—in rich nations, first—but the earth itself always stands in the way. To determine the route of an undersea cable requires navigating a maze of economics, geopolitics, and topography."[11] While internet technology is more sophisticated, it is, in many ways, the same range of infrastructure as what makes telephones and the telegraph work: lots and lots of cables, and a way to transmit and interpret data sent along those cables.[12]

Okay, so what does this have to do with cats and goats? The point here is that the earliest infrastructure for the internet emerged in urban areas in Western countries, frequently accessible to people from middle-class backgrounds and doing information work. It's these countries where cats are more likely to be kept as pets. Indeed, the very idea of keeping an animal as a pet, that is, as a companion animal rather than a work or support animal, is a relatively new idea in history, and it's not a universal idea among the world's cultures. Throughout most of history, cats were kept for their functional purpose in hunting rodents, and the same could be said of dogs, most of whom have been bred with specific purposes in mind, like hunting, keeping guard, and scavenging for rabbits.

Over time, the internet began to extend to other parts of the world. Submarine optic cables were laid across the world, connecting coastal cities, like Singapore, Caracas, and Chennai.[13] In turn, countries connected their cities, towns, and villages to these cables. Sometimes, as in rural Uganda, this connectivity comes first in the form of massive towers dotting the landscape. Other times, it requires digging up road and laying cable to connect an urban village in China. Frequently it's a bit of both, and even more frequently people's first experiences of the internet come via mobile phone rather than a computer, and their lives and livelihoods can appear very different indeed from middle-class America.

In understanding this gradual process of connecting the world, we can understand why goats have emerged as a major animal meme. As rural societies come online in the Global South and more high-income countries, they bring their values, their lives, and their perspectives with them. For a middle-class American sitting at home with a broadband connection, that means a few photos of their cats doing silly things. For a Brazilian or Bangladeshi in a rural part of the country, the animals around them are far more likely to be goats than cats. Naturally, then, memes and humor about goats rather than cats are more likely to resonate with them.

Okay, but why goats in particular? Rural societies throughout the world have cows, chickens, and pigs, among other creatures. And the answer, I think, comes easily when you get to know goats a bit more. They are silly creatures, jumping sideways, sticking out their tongues, poking around the house, and climbing things. They resemble cats and dogs in many ways. Chickens, while funny, don't have such expressive faces, and cows are too big. Pigs would be solid candidates, as they are naturally curious and expressive animals, but they rarely enjoy the same freedoms as goats, as they're frequently kept in pens.

The world animal meme map was in many ways an evolution of a map of Chinese memes that the Civic Beat developed for the Asian Art Museum in 2015.[14] In that map we placed different political and fun memes, to show that these memes were situated in specific societies and events. "Memes are mirrors," noted internet culture researcher Latoya Peterson in a panel I organized at the Personal Democracy Forum at New York University.[15] At a panel I organized at the Victoria and Albert Museum in London, Kate Miltner compared them to "a funhouse mirror of society."[16] Mirrors are an apt metaphor because mirrors reflect, amplify, and distort. But to work, mirrors need something to stand in front of them. That something is the lived, embodied experience of day-to-day life that internet culture taps into.

And indeed, a meander through the world's memes shows a broad diversity of lives and lifestyles. In Tajikistan, says University of Toronto researcher Alex Sodiqov, donkey memes populate the internet, drawing on a long history of donkey, or *khar*, humor long predating the internet. In Peru, notes journalist Juan Arellano, llama humor reflects Andean culture, where llamas are both beasts of burden and quite silly. A llama sticking its head out, saying, *"Ola k ase"* (a deliberately misspelled version of *"Hola, que hace?"* or "Hey, what's up?"), bounces around much of the Spanish-speaking world. In Saudi Arabia, people post photos of themselves kissing their camels.[17] In China and Japan, cats still meander about, as they do in much of the world.

However, not all internet cultures turn to animals for their memes. Duke University scholar Negar Mottahedeh points out that in Iran, animal memes in general have not resonated; rather, she notes, the color green has been a more important meme, as a color of resistance and reform. In Syria, memes are used in all sides of the armed conflict to share views and spread misinformation and propaganda, as internet scholar Donnatella della Ratta, who has long engaged with Syria and Syria's internet, describes.

The meme map, which has since been shown at the Institute for the Future in the San Francisco Bay Area and at the Victoria and Albert Museum, grows over time thanks to additional contributors. One day I hope the map will include even greater detail about specific regions of countries and not just countries as a whole. I'm also interested in mapping how memes spread transnationally, as so many of them influence each other in both subtle and overt ways. The map, along with this book, is an exercise in cultural specificity, in looking at the details of a given culture for what they are and trying to describe them through the lens of the culture.

While taking an ostensibly silly approach, the meme map also proposes a serious question: How can discussions of internet culture be grounded in the specificity of lived experiences? Going back to the questions of memes and countermemes, it might seem natural to ask if memes are causing new problems in society. Are they polarizing us? To a certain extent, that might be true: memes help people find like-minded souls, and it can be easier to work with those who reinforce our views rather than challenge them. This phenomenon suggests that the internet creates isolated communities. But the idea of echo chambers presupposes that being around like-minded people is necessarily a bad thing. In fact, as journalist Emily Parker argues, it can be incredibly useful for movement organizers to develop cogent strategies and build up their core team.[18] In my own observation, having a place for affirmation and comfort is a critical aspect of activism, and echo chambers can do just that, especially for marginalized communities.

To a certain extent I find it more useful to think of memes as signals and signs of deep-seated beliefs in society. As Farida Vis, Manchester Metropolitan University professor and founder of the Visual Social Media Lab, said on a panel I organized at the International Journalism Festival, people are frequently caught up with how images online are racist rather than with racism itself.[19] Indeed, there is a natural human tendency to blame the new kid on the block—in this case, memes and internet culture—for the deep-seated views, values, and problems that a society faces. This tendency ignores the broader environment, from blogs and newspapers to radio and television to churches and schools and family dinner conversations, that shapes our worldview. It is this worldview that we bring to the internet, and it is this worldview that is challenged and reinforced by what we find online.

Which brings me back to cats and goats, back to Refugees Welcome, to Black Lives Matter and Blue Lives Matter, to yellow ribbons and blue ribbons, to Pepe the Frog and the grass mud horse. As the world's internet population diversifies globally, we should expect more animals, more global perspectives, more rural perspectives, more right-wing perspectives, more artificial intelligence agents and agents of government. As I write this book, less than half of the world is online, and the remainder come from widely different backgrounds. The perspectives people bring to the internet are grounded in the societies from which they arise, and meme cultures reflect, amplify, and distort values in culturally specific ways. The rise of the goat is a sign of many things to come, and the new meme menagerie in general is a useful metaphor for where political meme culture needs to go next and the limits of its influence.

Looking to the future of political meme culture requires looking to the future of politics and contention as a whole. The greatest challenges today are global in scope: irreversible climate change; armed conflict and the refugees fleeing it; heteropatriarchal violence against women, trans people, gays and lesbians; vast income inequality; rising ethnosupremacy and xenophobia reinforced by state violence; the prison industrial complex; the disintegration of trust in media and civic institutions; the erosion of democratic rights and structures; the returning threat of nuclear conflict and ongoing conflicts around the world. These issues and many others have long, complex histories that will be difficult to disentangle and dismantle.

On the other hand, the greatest opportunity humanity faces is through globalism and intersectionality. The issues today are deeply interconnected and intersectional, reaching across borders. Early signs of this can be seen in the Dakota Access Pipeline controversy. In 2016, when Dakota Access, a subsidiary of Energy Transfer Partners, was planning to build an oil pipeline through Sioux tribal lands, Native American organizers gathered at Standing Rock in South Dakota to protest, citing treaty rights.[20] As journalist Jacqueline Keeler observed, the network building around #NotYourMascot, the movement against the use of Native American culture in sports mascotry, had laid the groundwork for this action, which coalesced around the hashtag #NoDAPL, or No to the Dakota Access Pipeline.[21] The movement gained greater attention as climate change organizers also took up the cause, and #NoDAPL went national and even international, highlighting the pipeline's potential damage to the environment along with the specific dangers it posed to Native Americans living in the area.

In 2015, activists in Argentina launched #NiUnaMenos, or Not One Less, to call attention to an epidemic of femicide in the country.[22] Protests organized under this hashtag included chants, T-shirts, and comics that brought to light specific issues. The word "femicide," coined and popularized in 1976 by sociologist Diana Russell, was meant to highlight that women are frequently targeted for killing because of their gender, part of a larger phenomenon of gender-based violence that includes domestic abuse, rape, and sexual harassment in the workplace.[23] The hashtag swept much of Latin America, where violence against women has reached historic highs, and movements began coalescing in Mexico, Peru, and even across the Atlantic, in Spain. The 2017 US Women's March organizers cited the actions of Not One Less as their inspiration in light of the openly misogynistic remarks of Donald Trump.

In all these movements, activists have made efforts to center the voices of those most marginalized, such as transgender women of color, Muslims, and undocumented immigrants. In the United States, the Women's March has helped organize and amplify specific memetic actions for these communities, such as #IStandWithLinda, in support of Muslim and Palestinian American activist Linda Sarsour, who was attacked online by right-wing groups, and #DefendDACA, a series of actions around the country in defense of the Deferred Action for Childhood Arrivals (DACA) bill, which provides certain benefits to undocumented youth who grew up in the United States. Speaking at the march, organizer Janet Mock captured some of these themes:

> Our approach to freedom need not be identical but it must be intersectional and inclusive. It must extend beyond ourselves. I know with surpassing certainty that my liberation is directly linked to the liberation of the undocumented trans Latina yearning for refuge. The disabled student seeking unequivocal access. The sex worker fighting to make her living safely.[24]

I highlight these brief examples not to say they are perfectly inclusive. As Jacqueline Keeler told me in an interview, Native American voices and issues of Native American sovereignty in the United States were frequently sidelined in the broader discussions about Standing Rock.[25] The Women's March was widely critiqued early on as a movement centered on white American women, although its leadership has diversified significantly since its early days. Nor does this globalism support only progressive, antiauthoritarian movements. The transatlantic spread of Pepe memes in white nationalist communities in Europe, the United States, and even China speaks to emerging networks and values in a seemingly paradoxical transnational push for nationalism.

Rather, I want to identify an emergent trend occurring as I write this book: people are learning from each other globally and intersectionally. Again, this is nothing new: Martin Luther King Jr. famously studied the work of Mahatma Gandhi and the principles and strategies of nonviolence to bring about social change. And once again, we are building new communities, affirming each other, driving attention, and generating new narratives for the twenty-first century, helped along by the internet. Sometimes, this includes rhetorical and symbolic strategies, as when the rainbow flag gains new stripes in support of communities of color. Other times it means generating global solidarity networks and learning substantive strategies, like how to handle tear gas or how to safely occupy a public space, and how to use one's privilege to amplify the voices of those frequently underheard. The internet has made us more visible to each other than ever before and gives us a pathway to share and communicate. Crossing borders and boundaries and reaching past the traditional confines of the nation-state is all the more necessary given how complex and interconnected the challenges we face can be.

In today's world, memes are the seeds from which social movements grow, but to flower, they must find their homes in the fertile ground of minds and cultures. This notion of seeds—*guazi* in China, *semillas* in Mexico—pops up so frequently across activist meme cultures. The idea that something as mighty as a forest of giant redwoods can come from a single tiny seed is a powerful one. But to give it true substantive power, we need to understand how to nurture these seeds.

SIGNS AND SEEDS

They tried to bury us. They didn't know
we were seeds.

—Multiple attributions[1]

BEAUTIFUL SWASTIKAS ADORN the walls and cushions in the two-hundred-year-old Zhiyun Temple of Lijiang, China. Shortly before I finished this book, I hiked up to the temple, whose Chinese name translates to "pointing to the clouds" and which gleams gold from afar. It was erected as the largest Tibetan temple in the region. . The word *swastika* is a Sanskrit word meaning auspiciousness, and in English it is sometimes referred to as a crooked cross, with hooked arms that can point clockwise or counterclockwise. Swastikas are endemic to Buddhist, Hindu, and Jain iconographies, and, by extension, much of Asian culture from South to Southeast to East Asia.

I am personally most familiar with the Buddhist manifestations of this: many depictions of the Buddha that I've seen place a swastika in middle of his chest, reflecting the peace in his heart, and in other traditions, they represent the holiness of his footprints. I see swastikas regularly in my travels through East and Southeast Asia, at Zen, Pure Land, and Tibetan Buddhist temples in China, Korea, and Hong Kong. They adorn meditation cushions, banners, and walls, dangling in the sky for well wishes and peace. The swastika likely originated in India, symbolizing for Hindus divinity and creation. Its bent arms reflect intuition over purely rational intellect.[2] For Jains, the four arms stand for the four forms of rebirth.[3] During the South Asian holiday of Diwali, people place swastikas on their doorsteps to send good wishes to those entering the home.[4] The symbol was even used by the Ancient Greeks and in much of Eastern Europe, with the world's oldest-known swastika pattern housed in Ukraine.[5]

In temples in the United States, swastikas appear much less frequently because of their strong associations with Nazism. Indeed, at the start of 2017, I began seeing swastikas in the United States in physical space in public places, and they gave me chills of fear rather than a feeling of peace. The first one I saw was etched subtly in a parking lot, where, if a car was parked, I would never have seen it. It looked like I could have just rubbed it off easily and that someone drew it as a dare. Another swastika I saw was more permanent, scrawled into drying cement and set to dry. I even walked into a subway station in a busy American city and saw posters and walls covered in swastikas and other white supremacist symbols. At a violent white supremacist rally in Charlottesville, Virginia, people carried flags with the swastika on them, an action that US Holocaust Memorial Museum director Sara J. Bloomfield said should be "a warning to all of us."[6]

Online, images of swastikas began going viral; frequently they had been scrawled on walls and windows, in shops and alleyways. One particularly memorable pair was spray-painted on a small building and came with a remixed phrase—"Make America White Again"—as if to hammer home the point explicitly that swastikas represent a particularly violent strain of white supremacy.[7] Some folks posted humorous ideas for getting rid of them, like turning them into a Windows 95 logo or boxes, but the trend was clear: swastikas were on the rise.[8] These icons began emerging in the context of a sharp increase in hate crimes and hate speech, both online and offline, that flourished in the aftermath of the 2016 US presidential election, continuing a years-long trend documented by numerous civil rights organizations, such as the Southern Poverty Law Center.[9]

The swastika contains so much potent symbolism because of its historic use in the European conflict of World War II. In the 1920s, the National Socialist Party in Germany needed a symbol for their movement, which was quickly rising to power after World War I in the midst of great social and cultural discontent. The swastika had already been in popular use throughout Europe and the Middle East, where it also symbolized luck and hope per the traditional Asian meaning, and a number of political parties referenced it. Archeologist Heinrich Schliemann helped popularize it in the modern age after trips to Greece, Tibet, and Turkey, showing its long history. Seeking to tell a story that tied Germany to the ancient Aryans, the National Socialist Party repurposed the swastika for their movement and remixed it with clean, bold graphic design. It likely was meant to counter the iconic hammer and sickle of Communism, which had already grown to be internationally influential.[10]

In the German language, "National Socialist" is *Nationalsozialist*, and was abbreviated simply to *Nazi*. The swastika soon became permanently associated with the Nazi Party. Adolf Hitler, long before he ascended to lead Germany, wrote in his autobiography *Mein Kampf* (My Struggle) that the flag's bold iconography was deliberate after a number of iterations:

> I myself, meanwhile, after innumerable attempts, had laid down a final form; a flag with a red background, a white disk, and a black swastika in the middle. After long trials I also found a definite proportion between the size of the flag and the size of the white disk, as well as the shape and thickness of the swastika.[11]

He gave thundering speeches under the banner of this flag, and the party's military goose-stepped in its wake as they sought to make the country glorious once more. Filmmaker Leni Riefenstahl famously captured this iconography in *Triumph of the Will*, which opens and closes with stunning imagery of the swastika and throughout captures the symbol fluttering in the wind. Through innovative uses of media led by minister of propaganda Joseph Goebbels, the Nazis generated a new narrative about making Germany a strong, powerful country again united by an Aryan bloodline and ridding the country of Jews, Roma people, homosexuals, disabled people, and others deemed undesirable. Within a few decades, men and women wearing swastikas on their uniforms, flying swastika flags, and operating swastika-adorned military vehicles would plan and carry out the Holocaust, an industrialized genocide at a scale never before seen in the world. Though genocide had been practiced long before the Holocaust, it was the Holocaust that spurred Polish Jewish lawyer Raphael Lemkin to coin a word for the specific atrocity.[12]

How can a symbol stand for such contrasting views, for love, peace, and nirvana on the one hand, and for hate, genocide, and destruction on the other? Traveling frequently between continents as I do, I am always struck by the elaborate meaning behind this one symbol and the complex stir of emotions I feel when I see it. A symbol more than ten thousand years old, it has morphed and been remixed over the millennia, a glacial meme taken up by countless cultures and traditions.

The basic shape can be found in ancient Roman homes, and likely was handed along the cultural trade route of the Silk Road. It appears in Native American traditions, independently of the Asian practices, where it also has a holy connotation. It receives different treatments and materials, sometimes plastic, wood, metal, or fabric, sometimes black, brown, gleaming gold. The swastika is a meme that precedes the internet, its changes measured in centuries rather than seconds, shifting and adapting with each new culture that takes it on, remixes it, and shares it.

Since time immemorial, the symbols, slogans, performances, and narratives of movements have been subject to remix and repurposing as the movements grow and change. They are imbued with meaning and intent by the cultural and political context from which they arise, and they connect people to larger community identities. Many developed movements emblazon their physical infrastructure with symbols, whether that's meditation cushions or concentration camps, and those symbols in turn stand in for the story and identity that the movement has created. Performative actions—the *sieg heil* in Nazism and *mudra*, or hand positions, in Buddhism—help us embody the values for which we stand (literally) and send a clear signal to others in a crowd. We chant in unison, we adorn our homes with photos and images of what we care about. No symbol, no action, no narrative is an island; it gains power through the way it's applied and a community's force of will and commitment of resources behind that application.

We live in a time of rapid change and uncertainty, and as we look to history, we see that it's during times of great tumult that new symbols and narratives take hold in society. They do not happen automatically but rather through a long series of iterations that cross media and creators, often through remix and reclamation of existing practices. In 1958, as the specter of the Cold War cast a shadow of global nuclear annihilation on the world, British designer Gerald Holtom designed the peace sign, which he initially placed on pins.[13] The sign was quickly adopted as a global symbol for nuclear disarmament, appearing on flags, signs, buildings, and, now, in emoji: ☮. In the United States, protesters riffed on poet Allen Ginsberg's call for "masses of flowers," and the Flower Power movement began to resist the draft and the Vietnam War. People repurposed the V for victory hand gesture from World War II, with their index and middle fingers held up, to symbolize peace: ✌.[14]

During the civil rights movement in the United States, the songs "We Shall Overcome" and "Keep Your Eyes on the Prize" echoed throughout marches and churches, sung by black and mixed communities. Both of these songs, so memorable and still sung today, are remixes. In 1900, the Reverend Charles Albert Tindley, born the son of slaves, wrote "I'll Overcome Some Day" as a gospel song, which eventually transformed into the iconic "We Shall Overcome."[15]

The American folk song "Gospel Plow" had been popular before the movement, with a refrain:

> When my way gets dark as night
> I know the Lord will be my light
> Keep your hand on the plow
> Hold on hold on[16]

From that explicitly religious imagery came a different refrain, one focused on the fight for equality. It built on the original song's meaning but with an explicit reference to the civil rights–era practice of Freedom Rides, taking buses to join civil rights activists in other states. This refrain, embedded within the larger song, accompanied people for decades, giving them spirit, emotion, and strength:

> I'm gonna board that big greyhound
> Carry the love from town to town
> Keep your eyes on the prize
> Hold on hold on[17]

In the late nineteenth and early twentieth centuries, and then again during the American civil rights movement, another set of symbols took hold on the national stage: the regalia of the Ku Klux Klan.[18] Dressed in white, Klan members don a conical hood that covers the face except for two holes for the eyes. It's a chilling image that evokes holy robes in Western religious traditions, such as the white robes of bishops and clerics in Christian churches. The hood most notably resembles those of penitents from Europe. Unlike the swastika, it's not clear that the Klan robes came directly from these traditions, but the resemblance is difficult to deny. The religious symbology fit the titles they gave themselves: grand wizard, knights, priests. But the holiness was but a dark euphemism. Under these hoods Klan members began a decades-long practice of domestic terror, targeting black and minority communities for violence, including lynchings, and, in their most iconic act of intimidation, burning a cross outside a person's home. Their name derives from the Greek *kuklos* (κύκλος), or circle, for the circled cross they burn, a message of fear co-opted from West African traditions and combined with Christian symbolism.[19]

Political meme culture in the twenty-first century reflects only the latest iteration of this long process of building the media of movements and contesting competing values. Since the time humans have been making art and media, we've been making remixes and mashups, building culture on top of culture and fusing it with culture. Indeed, the desire to share, remix, and repurpose has long precedents in human society. Rather than think of memes as fully unique to the twenty-first century, it's more helpful to remember that people have been generating the media, slogans, and performances for their movements for all of recorded history, and they've frequently been borrowing from, co-opting, and challenging opposition groups at the same time.

Thinking of memes as *enabled* by technology helps us see the patterns and waves of meme culture as aspects of culture more broadly, indeed of humanity itself. It is now much easier to create new media and disseminate them across geographies and among like-minded people, but these practices have long occurred. The spillover of digital meme culture into the physical world, where objects contain memes and become memes in themselves, means that the traditional divide we want to create between internet culture and culture at large is not a useful one. This framing also helps us understand what political memes excel at; namely, giving us symbols, slogans, and narratives. They shouldn't be confused with political, military, legal, or mass media power, each of which has its effects on movements. Nor should we ignore whether and how to understand the technological structure of the internet as a system with biases and benefits that movements and groups in power utilize to drive attention and narrative.

All major movements in history have relied on media to build community, drive attention, foster narratives, and nudge culture forward or backward. That memes play a role in twenty-first-century expression should be seen as a given by now, a theme I explored in chapter 1 with the rise of cat memes. In this book I have explored four different modes of media influence: fostering networks of affirmation and affiliation through play (chapter 2), generating and driving attention through media charisma (chapter 3), shaping and testing narratives with a culture of experimentation and iteration (chapter 4), and shifting culture in the physical world, often subtly at first and in the face of memetic contention (chapter 6). I devoted time to how opposition groups and governments also use memes, whether to sow confusion or tamp down dissenting views (chapter 5). These explorations rely on a number of theoretical frameworks and stories that look at deeper points. Each movement case study I presented contained all these modes of influence, and entire books could be written about them. My intent with this book is not to make a comprehensive analysis or detailed history but rather suggest some key roles that memes play in contemporary movements.

At this point I find myself with more questions than answers. Movements, by definition, are never still, and all the movements for social change I've written about in this book have faced tremendous challenges and undergone significant transformations over the years that I've been observing them. Platforms have come and gone while the global political situation remains in significant flux.

When I look at a social change meme, these are some of the questions I ask:

Is this an internet meme? If so, what manifestations does it take? These are basic questions, but not all digital phenomena are memes, and not all internet memes are restricted to the internet. In my simple, functional definition, I think of internet memes as digital objects that are remixed, transformed, and shared both in digital and physical space in a community. This is especially true for social change memes, which I define as memes that play a role in advocacy or expression of a social issue or policy change. When working with students, I like to do a mapping exercise. We start with a meme-sparking event, such as a gaffe from a politician or a tragedy like a political disappearance or police shooting. We then map manifestations that emerge, such as hashtags and image macros, and we trace those to look at videos, T-shirts, GIFs, chants, and other online and offline forms of expression. This is a way of emphasizing that media does not magically "go viral" but rather undergoes a process of remix and transformation separate from simply sharing broadly. What's important is making sure that what we're looking at is indeed a meme, and for me, that distinguishing factor frequently is the aspect of remix and transformation, which makes memes, well, meme-y.

What do these memes suggest about the culture they come from? Memes are like mirrors, reflecting, amplifying, and distorting culture. Just because people are paying attention and hearing the narratives you are generating doesn't mean they come to the same conclusions. Human belief has a much deeper core, influenced by cultural upbringing, family conversations, religious background, and other factors. Focusing on memes as causing something like ethnonationalism or protest misses the complex interaction of factors that make a movement grow and evolve. And, indeed, even as a meme spreads in one community, it can encounter fierce resistance from another; the charisma of memes often relies on first having a core belief system that agrees with the substance of the meme itself. I'll complicate the mirror analogy in a little bit, but what I like about it is that a hall of mirrors ends up magnifying and distorting existing cultural patterns; memes can be consequential in shaping culture, building off of what's already there. Applying cultural analysis to memetic practices can help us see some of the deeper patterns they participate in.

What are the formal qualities of the meme that make it effective? Whether it's an animal meme, a selfie meme, a performative meme, or other form of meme, memes take forms that help them resonate in a particular culture. The laughing, dancing llama that embodies the grass mud horse draws from the animal's expressive face, which looks mischievous and rebellious. The Hands Up Don't Shoot selfie meme draws from the strong cultural connotations of placing one's hands up in front of the police. At the same time, the hands-up gesture is a broadly visible one in a large crowd when performed together. The umbrella logo of the Umbrella Movement took its defining form when mashed up with the bright yellow of the ribbons that have long stood for voting rights, both in Hong Kong and globally.

It can be easy to dismiss memes as trivial media objects. Comparing the formal qualities of, say, goat memes to cow memes (something I've done!) sometimes feels silly. But they are worth the same analysis and scrutiny that a painting in a museum or film in a festival deserves. Looking at the range of forms a meme takes helps us understand how and why it's resonated in culture. Perhaps we should also be thinking about meme historical contexts, and we should make sure to think about multimedia manifestations, how hashtags, hats, and hand gestures all interact to form a larger meme culture.

What networks, organizations, and institutions are helping drive memes forward or reduce their influence? What are the politics and structures of the digital plazas in which they circulate? In other words, what kind of "teeth" do meme makers have access to? Some of the most powerful movement-related memes didn't just happen—they were the result of dedicated activists with a savvy media strategy and connections to politics. Today, effective media strategies must be participatory, and the idea that they somehow spontaneously "happen" should be dispelled; instead, people more frequently perfect their media strategies over time, iterating on and testing them intentionally with new ideas and mashups, until something sticks. Strengthening this ecosystem—with more diverse journalists in the newsroom, with more progressive people in legal and political systems, with more intentional and thoughtful platforms—can help strengthen the influence of memes in society as a whole.

The converse is also true: weaken this ecosystem, and you can reduce the power of memes. This is evident in Hong Kong, where Umbrella Movement organizers have been jailed and therefore made ineligible to run for office, and in mainland China, where the government controls not just the press but also the social networks, flagging content that goes viral. In the case of authoritarian governments, memes reflect the work of highly digitally literate bodies that seek to leverage the power of memes to spread a unified message or create enough confusion to tamp down attention on a message they don't like. Shifts in infrastructure, such as changes in algorithms, regulation on internet service providers, and installation of surveillance and tracking mechanisms can all dampen the effectiveness of memes and the internet in general as a tool for activists to achieve social influence. Legal mechanisms and physical intimidation can then exact control on people's bodies and sources of income.

What story are these memes driving attention toward? And what counterstory (or stories) are opposition groups developing to contest it? That many memes require so much context means that people are likely to find each other through in-group humor and conversations, and in more repressive environments, they can protect themselves from undue scrutiny. Platforms like Facebook, Twitter, and WeChat are designed to grab our attention with notifications, algorithms, and interactions. Digital meme culture frequently plugs into an ad-based ecosystem to drive attention to issues, and this ecosystem frequently rewards novel and emotive content. As this ecosystem changes, we should also expect memetic strategies to change over time, and we should expect activists and groups in power to devote more time to shaping the ecosystem of technology, not just responding to it.

This attention lays the groundwork for narrative building and cultural shifts that movements require to be successful. Attention to the Ayotzinapa 43 bolstered the larger narrative of government corruption and neglect in Mexico.

Attention to #NotYourMascot bolstered the networks and narratives of Native American agency that helped eventually shape the story of mascotry in American sports culture and, to an extent, the protests at Standing Rock. The ability to drive attention is a way to say, "This. Pay attention to this." From there, communities can test, iterate, and amplify specific narratives that take hold within their groups, with outside activist and advocacy groups, and with the broader world.

At the same time, with that attention can come significant dangers, as the world turns its eyes toward a specific event or movement. As anyone who's waded in a trending topic can attest, the crush of people commenting on an issue isn't always pretty. The narrative capacity of memes in particular can be a matter of concern: the easy ability to create and test different memes means that governments can create multiple narratives, thereby spreading alternative narratives or exhausting people about the source of truth and trust. Opposition groups can remix an existing narrative for their own purposes and transform that into a larger counterstory.

I WANT TO GO BACK to this idea of memes as mirrors, an analogy I once fully embraced but now feel needs complicating. The idea of a mirror loses some of the potential of memes, which contain within them the possibility of fostering larger cultural shifts. When I see a policy maker invoke a phrase like "black lives matter," when I see a data visualization of air pollution in a mobile app, I see the outgrowth of the seeds of meme culture planted many years ago that opened up acceptable discourse. Asking questions and suggesting ways to understand this process has been the focus of this book, which adopts a cultural and media studies perspective to examine what is often perceived as a highly technical space and to help us think beyond the digital to the broader media ecosystem and the physical world.

Media strategies, of course, are not enough. They are just one component of social change, which is a long and difficult process that requires a wide variety of disciplines, including law, policy, research, technology, and business, each of which contributes to the success of a movement or hinders its progress. Legal scholar Lawrence Lessig's framework of four types of constraints of human behavior—law, social norms, markets, and architecture—are all realities that the memes of movements must contend with.[20]

Jeff Chang, cofounder of the Bay Area–based arts and activism organization Culture Strike, has argued that before legal change, there must be cultural change.[21] The alt-right concept of meme magic reflects an implicit understanding that memes play an important role in shifting culture and discourse. Cultural organizers increasingly turn to and leverage meme culture in their work. Legal and cultural change work in conjunction with each other, and sometimes legal change precedes the deeper changes that society needs to undergo to accept a new norm. But the principle is there: culture influences people and people influence life. If we want a more just and equitable society, we need to develop a culture of justice and equity in our own communities first. If we want to spread hate, we grow that hate within our own communities and bring that hate to the larger world.

In the introduction to this book I describe the sunflower seed spray-painted on a wall in Beijing. The sunflower seed, or *guazi*, is a common snack in China, and it had become a symbol in 2011 of Ai Weiwei, whose art installation at the Tate Modern consisted of tens of thousands of porcelain sunflower seeds. When Ai was disappeared, supporters posted sunflower seeds all over the world—on social media, in the streets, on T-shirts—as a veiled but potent symbol of the artist and what he stood for.

I see the seeds of activism everywhere: the Semillas dance group in Mexico emerged in response to Ayotzinapa, citing the oft-repeated phrase "They tried to bury us, but they didn't know we were seeds!" The chant, in English, can also be heard at Black Lives Matter protests in the United States. Its origins are murky, but it appears to have come from a couplet by queer Greek activist and poet Dinos Christianopoulos:

what didn't you do to bury me
but you forgot that I was a seed[22]

How did Christianopoulos's poetry resonate so far and wide as it did? In some ways, it became a meme of its own. As digital ethnographer Alexandra Boutopoulou has noted, the poet had faced criticism from his literary community. "The essence of the couplet," she explained to me, "lies within its very power to put down roots and bloom worldwide, especially when its creator had barely ever left the Greek borders."[23] Like a meme, Christianopoulos's words floated far from their origin and sprouted in very different cultural contexts.

Just as a garden can have both weeds and flowers, seeds can help society or cause significant harm as they sprout. Speaking at the US Holocaust Memorial Museum, media scholar Susan Benesch outlined stages of genocide, noting that crimes against humanity do not suddenly happen; they grow slowly over time. About speech acts that lead to genocide (emphasis mine), she says:

> First, speech is understood in context. . . . This model takes into account the relationship between speech and other pre-genocidal dynamics, such as the typical lack of alternative media outlets. It recognizes that speech is dangerous because of where and when it is made—it is like a seed that will sprout only in the right soil. *Therefore the model must describe the soil.*[24]

Immigrant rights activist Favianna Rodriguez discussed this metaphor (see chapter 6) when talking about cultural change, taking time for it to be fostered and nourished. The effects of media may look inconsequential in the moment, but all media, including memes, contain within themselves the power to shift culture and norms.

Following the seed metaphor through is helpful: a seed is small, its potential hidden within a shell, and it can grow to great power only under the right circumstances—"the soil," in Benesch's words. This is also when the seed is the most vulnerable, either due to overt violence or to being overwhelmed by other seeds. It requires nurturing and care and a fertile environment. Nor is a seed a beginning; it is part of a continuum of trees and other plants that spread multiple seeds everywhere, in the hope that a few eventually stick. Seeds must be carried by wind, animals, and others to achieve their greatest impact. And even once the forest is built, we cannot take for granted that it will always be so; we must water and maintain what we have, while being ever watchful of the new seeds taking root. New seeds might spread a weed or predatory plant that hurts our movements, or they might reflect an evolution and necessary progress.

The tiny media actions we take online—sharing memes, taking selfies, gathering in the streets—are the seeds of social change. I see them when people raise their hands and chant "Hands up, don't shoot" to counter a white supremacist rally in the United States, when protesters and common citizens lift their umbrellas in Hong Kong outside the halls of government, when stickers appear throughout Europe declaring "Refugees Welcome." I see how Blue Lives Matter chants spark Blue Lives Matter bills, how blue ribbons and red ribbons counter and confuse the yellow ribbons of Hong Kong's democracy movement, how Refugees Welcome marches in turn face oppositional stories about the dangers of refugees and further strictures on the borders of the European Union.

I see seeds that people tried to bury in the portraits of forty-three disappeared young men from rural Mexico, their faces painted on murals throughout California and the American Southwest, on Tumblr, Twitter, and Instagram, and carried along to protests in Mexico City and New York City alike. They join the seeds of the other dead and disappeared, spoken out with #SayHerName for African American women, shared with #BringBackOurGirls from Nigeria, borne on sunglasses for a blind lawyer-activist in China.

There are seeds in pink knitted hats sewn and scattered through the streets of the United States and the feeds of social media, and seeds in red baseball caps at Donald Trump rallies, and seeds in the Pepe the Frog shields carried to violent clashes with "antifa" (antifascist activists) on the streets of Berkeley and Charlottesville. I see #UgandaIsNotSpain every time I see more African journalists representing African issues in the global media and challenging long-held narratives about the continent. And I see meme communities going slowly underground in China in the face of government opposition, even while some, like the memes against pollution, have flowered in a difficult environment. I see new global communities coming online and forming the seeds of representation of worlds and cultures.

Memes are the media through which we test and iterate and envision and contest the type of society we want to live in. They may seem inconsequential, but they contain within them a world-changing, movement-building capacity if provided the right soil and the right care. Without that, they wither away into obscurity. I can see them growing, some terrifying in their violence, others reassuring in their inclusion, and I can see tremendous efforts to stamp them out. Look at the seeds. Look at the soil. See the conditions in which they grow. It's there that we get a hint of the mighty forests of our times, with all the goats, the cats, the llamas, the dogs, the frogs, the crabs, and every creature under the sun grazing within them.

ACKNOWLEDGMENTS

THIS BOOK BEGAN, arguably, when I picked up a camera one day and started photographing the cats in my house. They lay around lazily, as cats do, and they didn't seem to mind when I poked my lens in their faces and at their paws and snapped away. This was in the early days of the internet, long before iPhones and Wi-Fi and mobile LTE and all the affordances of connectivity that make the digital and physical feel more seamless today. I eventually found a way to upload them and share them with friends. So, my feline friends, I owe to you my first bout of inspiration, and may your kitty cat souls rest in paws.

In the early days of internet culture, before the concept of retweeting was baked into our technology, there was the concept of the "hat tip," a way to thank someone for referring you to something cool. I like the concept because it acknowledges our interconnectedness, and indeed, I owe hat tips to more people than I can possibly count. I am first of all grateful to the movements and their members, who have welcomed me as an observer, and to those who've graciously spent time sitting for an interview. Any errors I've made in representing a movement's history or values are mine and mine alone.

For the day-to-day grind of writing this book, I owe thanks to the Memes to Movements Brain Trust, a dedicated group of friends and trusted colleagues who provided critical feedback when it mattered most: Denise Cheng, Samantha Culp, Natalie Gyenes, Daniel Mwesigwa, Kira Simon-Kennedy, Ben Valentine, and Marley-Vincent Lindsey. To the staff at Beacon Press, especially my editor, Rakia Clark, and her assistant, Ayla Zuraw-Friedland; and to my agent, Rayhané Sanders, who emailed me one day and asked if I'd ever thought about the impossible. There are risks to writing such a global book, especially in taking the care necessary to cover movements from such different places, and I am forever grateful to their eyes, ears, and advice over the past few years.

I owe special thanks to the people who encouraged me in the early days: to Hrag Vartanian at *Hyperallergic*, who commissioned the first piece I ever wrote about memes in social movements and nurtured my emergent voice, and to ROFLCon and, by extension, the Center for Civic Media community, especially Ethan Zuckerman, Tim Hwang, and Christina Xu, and to Laine Nooney and Laura Portwood-Stacer, who invited me to write more. To Micah Sifry and Jessica McKenzie for opening the door for credibility in the civic tech community. To Jonathan Munar, who liked the idea of a column on art and social media. To the Civic Beat community, my cofounder Jason Li (who made the beautiful illustrations you see in this book), and to @Platea and the incredible steering committee: Aaron Chen, Jonny Gray, Ingrid Murnane, Christi Nielsen, Jennifer Ng, Joanie San Chirico, and Courtney Bryan. So many of our early experiments informed this book.

To the 88 Bar community, especially Tricia Wang and Jason Li (yep, same Jason above), who encourage me to write regularly about Chinese meme culture. To Ai Weiwei and his studio, in both Beijing and Berlin. To the Arts, Culture, and Technology Meetup community, with a special shout-out to founder Julia Kaganskiy. To China Residencies and Lijiang Studio, for giving me space to think and breathe.

To the communities of the Berkman Klein Center for Internet and Society and the Nieman Foundation for Journalism at Harvard University, where I broke bread with and debated some of the finest social movement thinkers, researchers, and journalists I've had the good fortune to meet. And to Sasha Anawalt, who called me out of the blue to invite me to apply for the University of Southern California's Annenberg Getty Arts Fellowship program, a fellowship that broadened my perspective about arts writing and its potential impact on the world. To the Art Center College of Design community, who taught me how to engage with the world and its media. To Farida Vis, Simon Faulkner, and all the amazing crew at the Visual Social Media Lab, who taught me the new ways of seeing.

To Meedan, with whom I've had the most incredible experience doing journalism and humanitarian response work, which have expanded my horizons about the importance of translation, verification, and the global impacts of journalism and social media, with a touch of Egyptian, American, and Brazilian humor. That's Ed Bice, Chris Blow, Tom Trewinnard, Karim Ratib, Abir Kopty,

Caio Almeida, Dima Saber, Daniela Feitosa, Wafaa Heikal, Nora Younis, Benjamin Foote, Clarissa Xavier, Alexandre Amoedo Amorim, Xiaowei Wang, Anas Qtiesh, Abdul Rehman Khawar, Pat Motte, and Mohammad El-Sawy.

To those who pushed me intellectually to think about networked culture, creativity, and social justice in deeper ways: Kendra Albert, Angela Mictlanxochitl Anderson, Zara Arshad, Kenneth Bailey, Fergus Bell, Marcus Benigno, Shelley Bernstein, Ellery Biddle, Alexandra Boutopoulou, Jay Brown, Anne Burdick, Babirye Leilah Burns, Orianna Cacchione, Natalie Cadranel, Matt Carroll, Christiana Chae, Kenyatta Cheese, Pheona Chen, Denise Cheng, Elizabeth Chin, Jan Chipchase, Sasha Costanza-Chock, Kate Coyer, Crazy Crab, Kiri Dalena, Noha Daoud, Sean Donahue, Ray Drainville, Tengal Drilon, M Eifler, Alicia Eler, Dina el Hawary, Jason Eppink, Merv Espina, Susan Etlinger, Phoebe France, Kingwa Fu, Dr. Goddess, Kian Goh, Veken Gueyikian, Anika Gupta, Jeffrey Hall, Dawn Haney, Anita Hawkins, Anne Henochowicz, Barry Hoggard, André Holthe, Grace Jung, Mark Kaigwa, Rachel Kalmar, Masato Kajimoto, Jacqueline Keeler, Miru Kim, Sean Kolodji, Anne Kruger, Olympia Lambert, Noemi Lardizabal-Dado, Alex Leavitt, Jennifer 8. Lee, Henry Wei Leung, Rebecca Lewis, Anqi Li, David Li, Silvia Lindtner, Katherine Lo, Katie Loncke, Jenny Ma, Cayden Mak, Divya Manian, Ma Yongfeng, Mao Ju, Alice Marwick, Marc Mayer, Brendan McGetrick, Joanne McNeil, Gemma Mendoza, Ruth Miller, Kate Miltner, Anne Elizabeth Moore, Negar Mottahedeh, Emily D. Parker, Latoya Peterson, Oliver Platz, Hong Qu, Zara Rahman, Donnatella della Ratta, Regina Rini, Alessandro Rolandi, Erwin Romulo, Edward Sanderson, Dorothy Santos, Connie Moon Sehat, Clay Shirky, Caroline Sinders, Joshua Stearns, Arden Stern, Tom Standage, Clive Thompson, Lokman Tsui, Zeynep Tufekci, Jane Uymatiao, Vasilis Vasaitis, Samuel Wade, James Wagner, Claire Wardle, Jeffrey Wasserstrom, Sara M. Watson, Rosten Woo, Phyllis Yao, Jillian York, Jen Yu, Francesca Zimmer-Santos, and Aaron Zinman.

To those who offered me their homes and spaces as I did my writing in all these parts of the world, I thank you for your couches, your food, your desks, your friendly pets. To the ones I haven't listed here, this is my fault and one of the consequences of the steady advance of age, and I hope you know I owe you drinks for life and hugs and so much more. And to my family, for their unconditional love and support and trying their best to understand what it is I do for a living. I'm still, as of press time, officially figuring it out.

NOTES

INTRODUCTION: HANDS UP, UMBRELLAS UP

1. Julie Bosman and Joseph Goldstein, "Timeline for a Body: 4 Hours in the Middle of a Ferguson Street," *New York Times*, Aug. 23, 2014, https://www.nytimes.com/2014/08/24/us/michael-brown-a-bodys-timeline-4-hours-on-a-ferguson-street.html.

2. Andrew Kling (@AndrewAKling), "#HongKong, thanks for the umbrella idea—turns out we needed them. #FergusonOctober #Ferguson," 1:08 p.m., Oct. 10, 2014, Twitter, https://twitter.com/AndrewAKling/status/520667210038001664.

3. Jigme (@JigmeUgen), "Solidarity from #HongKong's #UmbrellaRevolution- #ICant Breathe stay strong sister @rosetangy #BlackLivesMatter #umhk," 8:49 p.m., Dec. 17, 2014, Twitter, https://twitter.com/JigmeUgen/status/541816712967233536.

4. A *selfie*, considered the Oxford Dictionaries Word of the Year in 2013, is a self-portrait taken with a phone with the intent of being shared to social media. A *hashtag*, a word or phrase preceded by a hash sign (#), is a clickable, searchable term on social media. Posting with a hashtag makes your words findable by others using it. Hashtags started on Twitter as a way to organize conversations online amid a sea of other, potentially unrelated conversations, especially for conferences. They've since evolved as cultural objects, used frequently to express emotions, like #nope. In the context of a social movement, hashtags in many ways have started to look more like chants or symbols. Called out and repeated on the streets, on posters and in social media, hashtags makes community members visible to each other.

5. Daniel Victor, "Black Activists Arrested in Ferguson Protests," *New York Times*, Aug. 10, 2015; John Eligon, "The Quiet Casualties of the Movement for Black Lives," *New York Times*, Mar. 28, 2018, https://www.nytimes.com/2018/03/28/insider/black-lives-matter-stress.html; Taylor Crumpton, "Ferguson Protestor Edward Crawford Found Dead," *Teen Vogue*, May 6, 2017, http://www.teenvogue.com/story/ferguson-protestor-edward-crawford-dead; Jackie Zammuto, "You Captured Policed Abuse on Video. Now What?," WITNESS Media Lab, https://lab.witness.org/you-captured-police-abuse-on-video-now-what, accessed August 14, 2018.

6. Collier Meyerson, "The Case Against 'Blue Lives Matter' Bills," *Nation*, May 23, 2017, https://www.thenation.com/article/case-blue-lives-matter-bills.

7. Dara Lind, "Nazi Slogans and Violence at a Right-Wing March in Charlottesville on Friday Night," *Vox*, Aug. 12, 2017, https://www.vox.com/2017/8/12/16138132/charlottesville-rally-brawl-nazi.

8. Joyce Ng, "Youngest Lawmaker Vows to Quit Hong Kong's Legco Aged Just 32 If He Wins Second Term," *South China Morning Post*, Oct. 9, 2016, http://www.scmp.com/news/hong-kong/politics/article/2026513/nathan-law-says-he-will-remain-hong-kongs-legco-only-two.

9. Eli Meixler, "There May Be a Hidden Agenda in Hong Kong's Ruling to Spare Joshua Wong from Prison," *Time*, Feb. 7, 2018, http://time.com/5136748/hong-kong-joshua-wong-appeal.

10. Lizzie Dearden, "Hong Kong Protests: A Guide to Yellow Ribbons, Blue Ribbons and All the Other Colours," *Independent*, Oct. 5, 2014, http://www.independent.co.uk/news/world/asia/hong-kong-protests-a-guide-to-yellow-ribbons-blue-ribbons-and-all-the-other-colours-9775324.html.

11. Kiersten Schmidt and Sarah Almukhtar, "Where Protests Are Happening on Inauguration Day," *New York Times*, Jan. 19, 2017, https://www.nytimes.com/interactive/2017/01/17/us/inauguration-protests.html.

12. "Sister Marches," Women's March, https://www.womensmarch.com/sisters, accessed Aug. 1, 2017.

13. Kaveh Waddell, "The Exhausting Work of Tallying America's Largest Protest," *Atlantic*, Jan. 23, 2017, https://www.theatlantic.com/technology/archive/2017/01/womens-march-protest-count/514166.

14. "Krista Suh's '09 'Sea of Pink,' *Barnard College News*, Jan. 23, 2017, https://barnard.edu/news/krista-suhs-09-sea-pink.

15. "Transcript: Donald Trump's Taped Comments About Women," *New York Times*, Oct. 8, 2016, https://www.nytimes.com/2016/10/08/us/donald-trump-tape-transcript.html.

16. czg123, "The Crazy Nastyass Honey Badger (original narration by Randall)," Jan. 18, 2011, https://www.youtube.com/watch?v=4r7wHMg5Yjg.

17. Know Your Meme contributors, "Nope," Know Your Meme, http://knowyourmeme.com/memes/nope, accessed Aug. 1, 2017.

18. Know Your Meme contributors, "Longcat," Know Your Meme, http://knowyourmeme.com/memes/longcat, accessed Aug. 1, 2017.

19. An Xiao, "@Platea: Art in the Web 2.0 Ethos," *Art21*, June 25, 2009, http://magazine.art21.org/2009/06/25/platea-art-in-the-web-20-ethos; An Xiao, "Always Social: Social Media Art (2004–2008), Part One," *Hyperallergic*, June 14, 2010, http://hyperallergic.com/6644/social-media-art-pt-1.

20. Will Cary, "1stfans Twitter Art Feed Artist for January 2009: An Xiao," Brooklyn Museum, Dec. 23, 2008, https://www.brooklynmuseum.org/community/blogosphere/2008/12/23/1stfans-twitter-art-feed-artist-for-january-2009-an-xiao.

21. Ai Weiwei, *Ai Weiwei's Blog: Writings, Interviews, and Digital Rants, 2006–2009* (Cambridge, MA: MIT Press, 2011).

22. An Xiao, "Translating Ai Weiwei: Bringing Chinese Social Media Art to the English Twittersphere, Part 1," *Art 21 Magazine*, Dec. 2, 2010, http://magazine.art21.org/2010/12/02/art-2-1-translating-ai-weiwei-bringing-chinese-social-media-art-to-the-english-twittersphere-part-1.

23. Ai Weiwei (@aiww), "说出你的名字" 活动已截止, 参与者请确认你的姓名, 电话, 地址三项信息发送至, zm.liwu@gmail.com, 感谢每一位参与者!," 9:21 a.m., June 13, 2010, Twitter, https://twitter.com/aiww/status/16081994632.

24. James Fallows, "Arab Spring, Chinese Winter," *Atlantic*, Sept. 2011, https://www.theatlantic.com/magazine/archive/2011/09/arab-spring-chinese-winter/308601.

25. Sarah E. Bond, "Erasing the Face of History," *New York Times*, May 14, 2011, https://www.nytimes.com/2011/05/15/opinion/15bond.html.

26. An Xiao Mina, Global Lulzes Panel, ROFLCon 2012, May 22, 2012, https://www.youtube.com/watch?v=RDDi4Dj-EQI.

27. Kyle Chayka, "Today's New York Protest for Ai Weiwei [UPDATE]," *Hyperallergic*, Apr. 17, 2011, http://hyperallergic.com/22926/nyc-ai-protest; Abby d'Arcy Hughes, "Ai Weiwei Arrest Protests at Chinese Embassies Worldwide," *Guardian*, Apr. 17, 2011, https://www.theguardian.com/artanddesign/2011/apr/17/ai-weiwei-protests-1001-chairs.

28. "Chinese Artist Makes 'Fairytale' Come True for 1001 Visitors," *Deusche Welle*, June 13, 2007, http://www.dw.com/en/chinese-artist-makes-fairytale-come-true-for-1001-visitors /a-2607967.

29. Mark Liberman, "Flash Graffiti," *Language Log*, May 4, 2011, http://languagelog .ldc.upenn.edu/nll/?p=3125.

30. Adam Martin, "Why China Released Ai Weiwei," *Atlantic*, June 2011, https://www .theatlantic.com/international/archive/2011/06/why-china-released-ai-weiwei/352060/.

31. "Chinese Artist Ai Weiwei Returns to Twitter," *BBC News*, Aug. 7, 2011, http://www .bbc.com/news/world-asia-pacific-14435204; Marco Werman, "Ai Weiwei's 'WeiweiCam' Goes Dark," *The World*, PRI, Apr. 5, 2012, https://www.pri.org/stories/2012-04-05/ai-weiweis -weiweicam-goes-dark.

32. Bernhard Zand, "Ai Weiwei's New Life in Europe," *Spiegel Online*, Aug. 13, 2015, http://www.spiegel.de/international/world/artist-ai-weiwei-has-left-china-for-germany-a -1047793.html.

CHAPTER 1: THE REVOLUTION OF THE CAT

1. Lewis Carroll, *Alice's Adventures in Wonderland*, 1865, online at Project Gutenberg, http://www.gutenberg.org/files/11/11-h/11-h.htm, accessed May 3, 2018.

2. Jan Hoole, "Ancient DNA reveals how cats conquered the world," *The Conversation*, June 19, 2017, http://theconversation.com/ancient-dna-reveals-how-cats-conquered-the -world-79584; James Suzman, "How Neolithic Farming Sowed the Seeds of Modern Inequality 10,000 Years Ago," *Guardian*, Dec. 5, 2017, https://www.theguardian.com/inequality/2017 /dec/05/how-neolithic-farming-sowed-the-seeds-of-modern-inequality-10000-years-ago.

3. Donald Engels, *Classical Cats: The Rise and Fall of the Sacred Cat* (London: Routledge, 1999).

4. Ibid.

5. Miwako Tezuka, *Life of Cats: Selections from the Hiraki Ukiyo-e Collection* (New York: Japan Society, 2015).

6. Gabrielle Loisel, "The Devil in Disguise: The Cat in the West," *Toast*, May 12, 2014, http://the-toast.net/2014/05/12/devil-disguise-cat-west.

7. Abigail Tucker, "The Spooky History of How Cats Bewitched Us," *Washington Post*, Oct. 31, 2016, https://www.washingtonpost.com/news/animalia/wp/2016/10/31/the-spooky -history-of-how-cats-bewitched-us.

8. Michelle Dean, "The Secret History of Monopoly Tokens," *Flavorwire*, Sept. 11, 2013, http://flavorwire.com/414355/the-secret-history-of-monopoly-tokens.

9. Daniel Engber, "Why Are Dogs Popular in Books, and Cats Popular on the Inter-net?," *Slate*, Apr. 5, 2013, http://www.slate.com/articles/arts/books/2013/04/why_are_dogs _popular_in_books_and_cats_popular.

10. "Balto," Centralpark.com, https://www.centralpark.com/things-to-do/attractions /balto/, accessed Sept. 4, 2017; Richard Alleyne, "The Legend of Greyfriars Bobby Really Is a Myth," *Telegraph*, Aug. 3, 2011, https://www.telegraph.co.uk/news/uknews/8679341/The -legend-of-Greyfriars-Bobby-really-is-a-myth.html.

11. Know Your Meme contributors, "Happy Cat," Know Your Meme, http://knowyour meme.com/memes/happy-cat, accessed Sept. 4, 2017.

12. Ibid.

13. Know Your Meme contributors, "Grumpy Cat," Know Your Meme, Sept. 23, 2012, http://knowyourmeme.com/memes/grumpy-cat; Know Your Meme contributors, "Lil Bub," Know Your Meme, Aug. 17, 2012, http://knowyourmeme.com/memes/lil-bub.

14. Jon Brodkin, "Internet Defense League Creates 'Cat Signal' to Save Web from Next SOPA," *Ars Technica*, July 19, 2012, https://arstechnica.com/tech-policy/2012/07/internet -defense-league-creates-cat-signal-to-save-web-from-next-sopa.

15. Limor Shifman, *Memes in Digital Culture* (Cambridge, MA: MIT Press, 2013).

16. An Xiao Mina, "Memes and Visuals Come to the Fore," NiemanLab, http://www
.niemanlab.org/2017/12/memes-and-visuals-come-to-the-fore/, accessed May 3, 2018.

17. "Kate Miltner Writes LOLCats Dissertation for the London School of Economics,"
Huffington Post, May 10, 2012, http://www.huffingtonpost.com/2012/05/10/lolcats-dissertation
-london-school-of-economics_n_1506292.html.

18. Kate Miltner, "'There's No Place for Lulz on LOLCats': The Role of Genre, Gender,
and Group Identity in the Interpretation and Enjoyment of an Internet Meme," *First Monday*
19, no. 8 (Aug. 4, 2014), https://firstmonday.org/ojs/index.php/fm/article/view/5391/4103.

19. Deborah A. Prentice, "Pluralistic Ignorance," in *Encyclopedia of Social Psychology*, ed.
Roy F. Baumeister and Kathleen D. Vohs (Los Angeles: Sage, 2007).

20. Zeynep Tufekci, "Capabilities of Movements and Affordances of Digital Media: Par-
adoxes of Empowerment," Dmlcentral, Jan. 9, 2014, https://dmlcentral.net/capabilities-of
-movements-and-affordances-of-digital-media-paradoxes-of-empowerment.

21. Zeynep Tufekci, "Is the Internet Good or Bad? Yes," *Matter*, Feb. 12, 2014, https://
medium.com/matter/is-the-internet-good-or-bad-yes-76d9913c6011.

22. Tom Standage, *Writing on the Wall: Social Media—The First 2,000 Years* (New York:
Bloomsbury, 2013).

23. Jennifer A. Kingson, "'How Cats Took Over the Internet' at the Museum of the
Moving Image," *New York Times*, Aug. 6, 2015, https://www.nytimes.com/2015/08/07/arts
/design/how-cats-took-over-the-internet-at-the-museum-of-the-moving-image.html.

24. Mark Memmott, "The Iron Is Out, a Cat Is in as 'Monopoly' Changes Game
Pieces," *The Two-Way*, National Public Radio, Feb. 6, 2013, http://www.npr.org/sections/the
two-way/2013/02/06/171265745/the-iron-is-out-a-cat-is-in-as-monopoly-changes-game-pieces.

25. Engber, "Why Are Dogs Popular in Books, and Cats Popular on the Internet?"

26. Liat Clark, "Google's Artificial Brain Learns to Find Cat Videos," *Wired UK*, June
26, 2012, https://www.wired.com/2012/06/google-x-neural-network.

27. Ben Quinn, "Fur Flies as #CatsAgainstBrexit Stirs Up EU Debate," *Guardian*, June
20, 2016, https://www.theguardian.com/technology/2016/jun/21/fur-flies-as-cats-against
-brexit-stir-up-eu-debate.

28. Vyacheslav Polonski, "How #CatsAgainstBrexit Could've Saved the EU," Oxford
Internet Institute, Aug. 5, 2016, https://www.oii.ox.ac.uk/blog/how-catsagainstbrexit-couldve
-saved-the-eu.

29. "EU Referendum: The Result in Maps and Charts," *BBC News*, June 24, 2016,
http://www.bbc.com/news/uk-politics-36616028.

30. Clay Shirky, *Cognitive Surplus: How Technology Makes Consumers into Collaborators*
(London: Penguin, 2011).

31. Clay Shirky, *Here Comes Everybody: The Power of Organizing Without Organizations*
(New York: Penguin, 2009), 24.

32. Pew Research Center, "Internet/Broadband Fact Sheet," Feb. 5, 2018, http://www
.pewinternet.org/fact-sheet/internet-broadband/, accessed May 1, 2018.

CHAPTER 2: ALL ABOUT THE FEELS

1. Ethan Zuckerman, "Cute Cats to the Rescue? Participatory Media and Political Expression," in *From Voice to Influence: Understanding Citizenship in the Digital Age*, ed. Danielle
Allen and Jennifer S. Light (Chicago: University of Chicago Press, 2015), 134.

CHAPTER 2.1: HOIST HIGH THE PROFILE PICTURE

1. "Jill Biden" (@JillBidenVeep), "Joe is running . . . #MarriageEquality #LoveWins
#SCOTUS," 7:25 a.m., June 26, 2015, https://twitter.com/jillbidenveep/status/614439317
558181889, accessed Sept. 4, 2017.

2. Bill Chappell, "Supreme Court Declares Same-Sex Marriage Legal In All 50 States," *The Two-Way*, NPR, June 26, 2015, https://www.npr.org/sections/thetwo-way/2015/06/26 /417717613/supreme-court-rules-all-states-must-allow-same-sex-marriages.

3. Steve Friess, "The First Openly Gay Person to Win an Election in America Was Not Harvey Milk," *Bloomberg*, Dec. 11, 2015, https://www.bloomberg.com/news/features/2015-12 -11/the-first-openly-gay-person-to-win-an-election-in-america-was-not-harvey-milk.

4. Paola Antonelli, "MoMA Acquires the Rainbow Flag," *Inside/Out: A MoMA/MoMA PS1 Blog*, June 17, 2015, https://www.moma.org/explore/inside_out/2015/06/17/moma -acquires-the-rainbow-flag.

5. "The Stonewall Riots (June 28, 1969)," *A Brief History of Civil Rights in the United States*, Georgetown Law Library, http://guides.ll.georgetown.edu/c.php?g=592919&p =4182235.

6. David Fleischer, "Behind the Numbers of Prop. 8," *Los Angeles Times*, Aug. 3, 2010, http://articles.latimes.com/2010/aug/03/opinion/la-oe-fleisher-gay-marriage-20100803.

7. Jesse McKinley and Kirk Johnson, "Mormons Tipped Scale in Ban on Gay Marriage," *New York Times*, Nov. 14, 2008, http://www.nytimes.com/2008/11/15/us/politics /15marriage.html.

8. Zoe Fox, "The Digital Smackdown: Obama 2008 vs. Obama 2012," *Mashable*, Sept. 23, 2012, http://mashable.com/2012/09/23/obama-digitial-comparison.

9. *Adweek* staff, "Mapping Facebook's Growth Over Time," *Adweek*, Aug. 19, 2008, http://www.adweek.com/digital/mapping-facebooks-growth-over-time.

10. Laura Latzko, "NOH8: Strike a Pose," *Echo Magazine*, Mar. 12, 2015, http://echomag .com/noh8.

11. "'No H8 Day' in West Hollywood Marks Campaign's Anniversary," NOH8 Campaign, Dec. 13, 2009, http://www.noh8campaign.com/article/no-h8-day-in-west-hollywood -marks-campaigns-anniversary.

12. Brosnan Rhodes, personal interview, Jan. 4, 2017.

13. Adam Liptak, "Q. and A.: A Decisive Moment on Gay Marriage," *New York Times*, Mar. 25, 2013, https://www.nytimes.com/2013/03/26/us/background-on-same-sex-marriage -case-at-supreme-court.html.

14. Hayley Miller, "Picture Equality: Use HRC's App to Go Red for Marriage Equality," Human Rights Campaign website, Apr. 17, 2015, https://www.hrc.org/blog/picture-equality -use-hrcs-app-to-go-red-for-marriage-equality; "Marriage at the U.S. Supreme Court: A Transformative Moment for Equality," Human Rights Campaign, http://assets.hrc.org/files /assets/resources/SupremeCourt_Accomplishments-FINAL_1.pdf, accessed Sept. 4, 2017.

15. Emily Pierce, "Coons Is Red in the Face Over Gay Marriage," *Roll Call*, Mar. 27, 2013, http://www.rollcall.com/news/hoh/chris-coons-is-red-in-the-face-over-gay-marriage; Chad Griffin, "Hillary Clinton Joins Fight for Marriage Equality," Human Rights Campaign website, Mar. 18, 2013, https://www.hrc.org/blog/hillary-clinton-joins-fight-for-marriage -equality.

16. Sean Kolodji, "Red, Pink, and the Prop 8 Blues: The Overwhelming Online Support for Marriage Equality," *Civic Beat Reader*, May 3, 2013, http://reader.thecivicbeat.com/2013 /05/red-pink-and-the-prop-8-blues-the-overwhelming-online-support-for-marriage -equality.

17. Human Rights Campaign staff, "One Year Out: The Little Red Logo That Transformed the Marriage Equality Narrative," Mar. 25, 2014, https://www.hrc.org/blog/one-year -out-the-little-red-logo-that-transformed-the-marriage-equality-nar.

18. Mary Rowe, "Micro-Affirmations & Micro-Inequities," *Journal of the International Ombudsman Association* 1, no. (Mar. 2008), http://ombud.mit.edu/sites/default/files /documents/micro-affirm-ineq.pdf; Tanzina Vega, "Students See Many Slights as Racial 'Microaggressions,'" *New York Times*, Mar. 21, 2014, https://www.nytimes.com/2014/03 /22/us/as-diversity-increases-slights-get-subtler-but-still-sting.html.

19. "Jill Biden" (@JillBidenVeep), "Joe is running . . . #MarriageEquality #LoveWins #SCOTUS."

20. Samantha Murphy, "You Can Put a Rainbow Filter over Your Facebook Profile in One Click," *Mashable*, June 26, 2015, http://mashable.com/2015/06/26/facebook-pride -rainbow-filter.

CHAPTER 2.2: BEHOLD, THE LLAMAS

1. Skippybentley, "Grass-Mud Horse Cartoon and Rap (Cao Ni Ma)," YouTube, Mar. 12, 2009, https://www.youtube.com/watch?v=3D2eh4xehc4.

2. Pingp, "The Great Firewall of China: Background," Torfox: A Stanford Project, June 1, 2011, https://cs.stanford.edu/people/eroberts/cs181/projects/2010–11/FreedomOf InformationChina/the-great-firewall-of-china-background/index.html.

3. For the sake of explaining the puns, I have used the diacritical marks of pinyin roman-ization to do so. However, as they do not generally have meaning to nonspeakers of Manda-rin, throughout this book I will only use standard pinyin and Chinese characters.

4. Joseph Kahn, "China Makes Commitment to Social Harmony," *New York Times*, Oct. 12, 2006, http://www.nytimes.com/2006/10/12/world/asia/12china.html.

5. Hongmei Li, "Parody and Resistance on the Chinese Internet," in *Online Society in China: Creating, Celebrating and Instrumentalizing the Online Carnival*, ed. David Kurt Herold and Peter Marolt (London: Routledge, 2011).

6. Michael Wines, "A Dirty Pun Tweaks China's Online Censors," *New York Times*, Mar. 11, 2009, http://www.nytimes.com/2009/03/12/world/asia/12beast.html.

7. "Music Video: The Song of the Grass Mud Horse (草泥马之歌)," *China Digital Times*, posted Feb. 8, 2009, http://chinadigitaltimes.net/2009/02/music-video-the-song-of-the -grass-dirt-horse.

8. Skippybentley, "Grass-Mud Horse Cartoon and Rap (Cao Ni Ma)."

9. Know Your Meme, "Baidu 10 Mythical Creatures," http://knowyourmeme.com /memes/baidu-10-mythical-creatures-grass-mud-horse.

10. Steven Millward, "China Now Has 731 Million Internet Users, 95% Access from Their Phones," *Tech in Asia*, Jan. 22, 2017, https://www.techinasia.com/china-731-million -internet-users-end-2016.

11. Tricia Wang, "Talking to Strangers: Chinese Youth and Social Media," PhD diss., University of California, San Diego, http://triciawang.com/storage/ Dissertation_Tricia _Wang_021014.pdf, accessed Feb. 14, 2014.

12. An Xiao Mina, "90 Years of Chinese Communism: A Multimedia Celebration," *Change Observer*, Aug. 23, 2011, http://designobserver.com/feature/90-years-of-chinese -communism-a-multimedia-celebration/29628.

13. Ibid.

14. Li Hui and Megha Rajagopalan, "At Sina Weibo's Censorship Hub, China's Little Brothers Cleanse Online Chatter," Reuters, Sept. 11, 2013,http://www.reuters.com/article /us-china-internet/at-sina-weibos-censorship-hub-chinas-little-brothers-cleanse-online -chatter-idUSBRE98A18Z20130912.

15. Zuckerman, "Cute Cats to the Rescue?"

16. Jason Q. Ng and Pierre F. Landry, "The Political Hierarchy of Censorship: An Analysis of Keyword Blocking of CCP Officials' Names on Sina Weibo Before and After the 2012 National Congress (S)election," Eleventh Chinese Internet Research Conference, 2013, https://papers.ssrn.com/sol3/papers.cfm?abstract_id=2267367.

CHAPTER 3: AHEM, ATTENTION PLEASE

1. Alexis C. Madrigal, "Chinese Paper Takes Down Story on Great Firewall's Creator," *Atlantic*, Feb. 21, 2011, https://www.theatlantic.com/technology/archive/2011/02/chinese -paper-takes-down-story-on-great-firewalls-creator/71517.

CHAPTER 3.1: FROM SPAIN TO UGANDA AND BACK AGAIN

1. José E. Mosquera, "España no es Uganda," *El Mundo*, http://www.elmundo.com/portal/opinion/columnistas/espania_no_es_uganda.php, accessed Aug. 2, 2017.

2. Ibid.

3. Rosebell Kagumire, "#UgandaisnotSpain," YouTube, June 11, 2012, https://www.youtube.com/watch?v=5cfS5KSGA5I.

4. Samuel Ouga (@Ougasam), "On GPS . . .," 3:24 p.m., June 18, 2012, Twitter, https://twitter.com/Ougasam/status/214846061859184640.

5. Chris Wolf (@Christine Wolf), "Agreed . . . #UgandaIsNotSpain," 11:00 a.m., June 17, 2012, Twitter, https://twitter.com/ChristineWolf/status/214417237690421249.

6. The Professor is in (@WilGafney), "#Spain . . . #UgandaIsNotSpain," 11:03 a.m., June 17, 2012, Twitter, https://twitter.com/WilGafney/status/214418024348913664.

7. Jackee Batanda, "The Spanish Text Message That Has Uganda Up in Arms," *Foreign Policy*, June 12, 2012, http://foreignpolicy.com/2012/06/12/the-spanish-text-message-that-has-uganda-up-in-arms.

8. Ibai Trebiño (@ibaitrebino), "Rajoy fascista . . . #UgandaisnotSpain," 6:06 a.m., June 13, 2012, Twitter, https://twitter.com/ibaitrebino/status/212893818113105920.

9. Sara (@greenpeeptoes), "#UgandaIsNotSpain . . .," 1:49 a.m., June 13, 2012, Twitter, https://twitter.com/greenpeeptoes/status/212828982578647041; translations from Spanish by the author, with a little help from Google Translate, Spanishdict.com, and her friends.

10. Xan Rice, "East Africa Finally Joins Broadband Revolution," *Guardian*, July 23, 2009, https://www.theguardian.com/technology/2009/jul/23/east-africa-broadband-revolution.

11. "Network Map: An Overview of SEACOM's Network," SEACOM, http://seacom.mu/network-map, accessed Aug. 2, 2017.

12. Uganda, Internet World Stats, https://www.internetworldstats.com/af/ug.htm, accessed Aug 2, 2017.

13. Xosé Hermida, "Who Is Mariano Rajoy? The Story of a Proper Pontevedran Gentleman," *El País*, Nov. 22, 2011, https://elpais.com/elpais/2011/11/22/inenglish/1321942841_850210.html.

14. Max Fisher, "The Bizarre and Horrifying Story of the Lord's Resistance Army," *Atlantic*, Oct. 17, 2011, https://www.theatlantic.com/international/archive/2011/10/the-bizarre-and-horrifying-story-of-the-lords-resistance-army/246836.

15. Kyra Phillips, CNN Newsroom, transcript from Mar. 9, 2012, http://www.cnn.com/TRANSCRIPTS/1203/09/cnr.03.html.

16. James Rainey, "Group Behind 'Kony 2012' Wins New Respect," *Los Angeles Times*, June 30, 2012, http://articles.latimes.com/2012/jun/30/world/la-fg-invisible-children-20120701.

17. Zack Baddorf, "Uganda Ends Its Hunt for Joseph Kony Empty-Handed," *New York Times*, Apr. 20, 2017, https://www.nytimes.com/2017/04/20/world/africa/uganda-joseph-kony-lra.html.

18. Amanda Lotz, "What Old Media Can Teach New Media," *Spreadable Media*, website for Henry Jenkins, Sam Ford, and Joshua Green, *Spreadable Media: Creating Value and Meaning in a Networked Culture* (New York: New York University Press, 2013), http://spreadablemedia.org/essays/lotz/, accessed Sept. 4, 2017.

19. Jim Edwards, "The Inventor of the Twitter Hashtag Explains Why He Didn't Patent It," *Business Insider*, Nov. 21, 2013, http://www.businessinsider.com/chris-messina-talks-about-inventing-the-hashtag-on-twitter-2013-11.

20. Britney Summit-Gil, "Gif Horse," *Real Life*, Sept. 7, 2016, http://reallifemag.com/wp-content/uploads/2016/12/Ways-of-Speaking.pdf.

CHAPTER 3.2: ENTER THE PANDAMAN

1. "China: Arrests, Disappearances Require International Response," Human Rights Watch, Mar. 31, 2011, https://www.hrw.org/news/2011/03/31/china-arrests-disappearances-require-international-response.

2. Steven Milward, "China Now Has Half a Billion Mobile Web Users, 618 Million Total Internet Users," *Tech in Asia*, Jan. 16, 2014, https://www.techinasia.com/cnnic-china -500-million-mobile-web-users-and-618-internet-users-2013.

3. Sandra Fu, "Chen Guangcheng on Sina Weibo: New List of Banned Search Terms," *China Digital Times*, Oct. 26, 2011, http://chinadigitaltimes.net/2011/10/chen-guangcheng -on-sina-weibo-new-list-of-banned-search-terms.

4. Tania Branigan, "Fears Chinese Lawyer Beaten over House Arrest Video," *Guardian*, Feb. 10, 2011, https://www.theguardian.com/world/2011/feb/10/secret-video-chinese -lawyer-chen.

5. Ibid.

6. Jessica Colwell, "We Like This: 'Dark Glasses. Portrait' Campaign to Support Chen Guangcheng," *Shanghaiist*, Oct. 19, 2011, http://shanghaiist.com/2011/10/19/we_like_this _dark_glasses_portrait.php.

7. Crazy Crab, personal interview, June 20–25, 2012. Translation from Mandarin to English by the author.

8. Tania Branigan, "Arrest Fears over Chinese Activist Who Helped Chen Guangcheng Escape," *Guardian*, Apr. 27, 2012, http://www.theguardian.com/world/2012/apr/27/arrest -fears-china-activist-helped-escape.

9. Samuel Wade, "Attempted Visits to Chen Guangcheng Surge," *China Digital Times*, Oct. 24, 2011, http://chinadigitaltimes.net/2011/10/attempted-visits-to-chen-guangcheng -surge.

10. Horace Lu, "Human Rights Lawyer Chen Guangcheng Escapes from House Arrest and Delivers Message to Wen Jiabao on YouTube (with full transcript)," Apr. 27, 2012, http:// shanghaiist.com/2012/04/27/watch_human_rights_lawyer_chen_guan.php.

11. J.M., "The Great Escape," *Economist*, May 2, 2012, https://www.economist.com/blogs /analects/2012/05/chen-guangcheng.

12. Anne Henochowicz, "Sensitive Words: Chen Guangcheng (updated)," *China Digital Times*, Apr. 29, 2012, http://chinadigitaltimes.net/2012/04/ sensitive-words-chen-guangcheng -edition.

13. Nicholas Bequelin, "Legalizing the Tools of Repression," *New York Times*, Feb. 29, 2017, http://www.nytimes.com/2012/03/01/opinion/legalizing-the-tools-of-repression.html.

14. Anthony Kuhn, "After Liu Xiaobo's Death, Concerns Grow for His Widow's Well-Being," *Parallels*, NPR, July 18, 2017, http://www.npr.org/sections/parallels/2017/07/18 /537879388/after-liu-xiaobos-death-concerns-grow-for-his-widows-well-being.

CHAPTER 3.3: THE HOODIE THAT SPARKED A MOVEMENT

1. Chris Williams, "Justice for Trayvon: Dream Defenders Take the Lead," *Ebony*, July 29, 2013, http://www.ebony.com/news-views/justice-for-trayvon-dream-defenders-take -the-lead-304.

2. Sari Horwitz and Stephanie McCrummen, "Trayvon Martin Documents Reveal New Details in Case," *Washington Post*, May 17, 2012, https://www.washingtonpost.com/politics /trayvon-martin-autospy-report-indicates-struggle/2012/05/17/gIQAxw6HXU_story.html.

3. E.G., "The Injustice," *Economist*, Mar. 12, 2012, https://www.economist.com/democracy -in-america/2012/03/21/the-injustice.

4. Susan Jacobson, "Boy, 17, Shot to Death in Sanford During 'Altercation,' Police Say," *Orlando Sentinel*, Feb. 29, 2012, http://articles.orlandosentinel.com/2012-02-29/news/os-fatal -shooting-sanford-townhomes-20120226_1_gated-community-death-sunday-night-shot.

5. Erhardt Graeff, Matt Stempeck, and Ethan Zuckerman, "The Battle for 'Trayvon Martin': Mapping a Media Controversy Online and Off-line," *First Monday* 19, no. 2 (Feb. 3, 2014), http://firstmonday.org/article/view/4947/3821.

6. Krissah Thompson and Scott Wilson, "Obama on Trayvon Martin: 'If I Had a Son, He'd Look Like Trayvon,'" *Washington Post*, Mar. 23, 2012, https://www.washingtonpost.com /politics/obama-if-i-had-a-son-hed-look-like-trayvon/2012/03/23/gIQApKPpVS_story.html.

7. Williams, "Justice for Trayvon."

8. An Xiao Mina, "A Tale of Two Memes: The Powerful Connection Between Trayvon Martin and Chen Guangcheng," *Atlantic*, July 12, 2012, https://www.theatlantic.com /technology/archive/2012/07/a-tale-of-two-memes-the-powerful-connection-between -trayvon-martin-and-chen-guangcheng/259604.

9. Linton Weeks, "Tragedy Gives the Hoodie a Whole New Meaning," NPR.org, Mar. 24, 2012, http://www.npr.org/2012/03/24/149245834/tragedy-gives-the-hoodie-a-whole -new-meaning.

10. L'Heureux Lewis-McCoy, "Do Hoodies and Sagging Pants Deserve Justice?," *Ebony*, Apr. 2, 2012, http://www.ebony.com/news-views/do-hoodies-and-sagging-pants-deserve -justice.

11. The original video is no longer available on YouTube. A reference to Maree's video may be found at Elahe Izadi, "Trayvon Martin and How 'A Million Hoodies' Began," *DCentric*, Mar. 22, 2012, http://dcentric.wamu.org/tag/daniel-maree/index.html.

12. Ryan Devereaux, "Trayvon Martin's Parents Speak at New York March: 'Our Son Is Your Son,'" *Guardian*, Mar. 22, 2012, https://www.theguardian.com/world/2012/mar/22 /trayvon-martin-million-hoodie-march-new-york.

13. Jeff Jarvis, "Networked Journalism," *BuzzMachine*, July 5, 2006, https://buzzmachine .com/2006/07/05/networked-journalism.

14. Brenna Ehrlich, "Trayvon Martin: How Social Media Became the Biggest Protest," *MTV News*, July 15, 2013, http://www.mtv.com/news/1710582/trayvon-martin-social-media -protest/.

15. MJ Lee, "Geraldo Sorry for 'Hoodie' Comment," *Politico*, Mar. 27, 2012, http://www .politico.com/story/2012/03/geraldo-apologizes-for-hoodie-comment-074529.

16. Know Your Meme contributors, "Planking," Know Your Meme, May 25, 2011, http://knowyourmeme.com/memes/planking.

17. Know Your Meme contributors, "Owling," Know Your Meme, July 12, 2011, http:// knowyourmeme.com/memes/owling.

18. Dan Hanzus, "'Tebowing' Becomes Most Predictable Internet Meme in History," NFL.com, Oct. 27, 2012, http://www.nfl.com/news/story/09000d5d823868ff/article/tebowing -becomes-most-predictable-internet-meme-in-history; Alexander Frandsen, "A Brief History of the Dab," *Boston Globe*, Jan. 4, 2017, https://www.bostonglobe.com/lifestyle/2017/01/04 /brief-history-dab/OXPR8sTnDYo4MQqYf257CN/story.html.

19. Nicholas Demas, "Trayvoning: The Sickening New Social Media Trend You Shouldn't Attempt," *Mic*, July 16, 2013, https://mic.com/articles/54875/trayvoning-the-sickening-new -social-media-trend-you-shouldn-t-attempt.

20. Tim Wu, *The Attention Merchants: The Epic Scramble to Get Inside Our Heads* (New York: Knopf, 2016), 315.

21. Ibid.

22. Ibid., 314.

23. Greg Botelho and Holly Yan, "George Zimmerman Found Not Guilty of Murder in Trayvon Martin's Death," CNN, July 14, 2013, https://www.cnn.com/2013/07/13/justice /zimmerman-trial/index.html.

24. Transcribed in Sarah Florini, "This Week in Blackness, the George Zimmerman Acquittal, and the Production of a Networked Collective Identity," Communication Arts Courses, https://courses.commarts.wisc.edu/449/wp-content/uploads/sites/67/2015/02/W7 -Florini-2015-TWiB-GZ-Acquittal-and-Networked-Collective-ID.pdf, accessed Aug. 1, 2017.

25. Kathleen McGrory, "Dream Defenders End Sit-in Protest at Capitol in Tallahassee," *Miami Herald*, Aug. 15, 2013, http://www.miamiherald.com/news/state/article1954155.html.

26. Patrisse Cullors, "Black Lives Matter," PatrisseCullors.com, http://patrissecullors .com/black-lives-matter, accessed Aug. 2, 2017.

27. Patrisse Cullors and Tarana Burke, "Patrisse Cullors and Tarana Burke: Anger, Activism, and Action," *Elle*, Mar. 13, 2018, https://www.elle.com/culture/career-politics/a19180106/patrisse-cullors-tarana-burke-black-lives-matter-metoo-activism.

CHAPTER 4: NARRATING OUR WAY TO POWER
1. Lotz, "What Old Media Can Teach New Media."

CHAPTER 4.1: ATTENTION TO NARRATIVE
1. Chimamanda Ngozi Adichie, "The Danger of a Single Story," TED.com, July 2009, https://www.ted.com/talks/chimamanda_adichie_the_danger_of_a_single_story/transcript?language=en.
2. Roy Peter Clark, "How 'Narrative' Moved from Literature to Politics and What This Means for Covering Candidates," Poynter, Feb. 20, 2012, https://www.poynter.org/2012/how-narrative-moved-from-literature-to-politics-what-this-means-for-covering-candidates/162834.
3. Frederick Mayer, "Competing Narratives in U.S. Television News," *Yale Climate Connections*, May 7, 2012, https://www.yaleclimateconnections.org/2012/05/competing-narratives-in-us-television-news.
4. Adichie, "The Danger of a Single Story."
5. Sasha Costanza-Chock, *Out of the Shadows, Into the Streets!* (Cambridge, MA: MIT Press, 2014), 195.
6. An Xiao Mina, "#iranelection: An Interview with Negar Mottahedeh on Protest, Play, and the 2009 Green Movement," *Los Angeles Review of Books*, May 28, 2016, https://lareviewofbooks.org/article/iranelection-interview-negar-mottahedeh-protest-play-2009-green-movement/#!.

CHAPTER 4.2: STORIES AND HISTORIES
1. Tim O'Neil, "Look Back 250: Slavery Was a Fact of Life in St. Louis from the Beginning," *St. Louis Post-Dispatch*, May 17, 2014, http://www.stltoday.com/news/local/govt-and-politics/look-back-slavery-was-a-fact-of-life-in-st/article_aec80774-80a2-52e9-b0e9-7a0c5522c66c.html.
2. "History of Dred Scott," Washington University Digital Gateway, http://digital.wustl.edu/dredscott/history.html, accessed Sept. 2, 2017.
3. "Black Panther Party: A Black Power Alternative," *Picture This: California Perspectives on American History*, Oakland Museum of California, accessed Sept. 2, 2017, http://picturethis.museumca.org/pictures/rally-front-alameda-county-court-house-0.
4. *L.A. Burning: The Riots 25 Years Later*, A&E, Apr. 18, 2017.
5. Jake Halpern, "The Cop," *New Yorker*, Aug. 10–17, 2017, https://www.newyorker.com/magazine/2015/08/10/the-cop.
6. David Hunn and Kim Bell, "Why Was Michael Brown's Body Left There for Hours?," *St. Louis Post-Dispatch*, Sept. 14, 2014, http://www.stltoday.com/news/local/crime-and-courts/why-was-michael-brown-s-body-left-there-for-hours/article_0b73ec58-c6a1-516e-882f-74d18a4246e0.html.
7. German Lopez, "The 2014 Ferguson Protests over the Michael Brown Shooting, Explained," *Vox*, Jan. 27, 2016, https://www.vox.com/cards/mike-brown-protests-ferguson-missouri/mike-brown-shooting-facts-details.
8. Deen Freelon, Charlton D. McIlwain, and Meredith Clark, *Beyond the Hashtags: #Ferguson, #Blacklivesmatter, and the Online Struggle for Offline Justice* (Washington, DC: Center for Media and Social Impact, Feb. 29, 2016), http://cmsimpact.org/wp-content/uploads/2016/03/beyond_the_hashtags_2016.pdf.
9. "About Us," Movement for Black Lives, https://policy.m4bl.org/about, accessed Aug. 10, 2017.

10. "About," Black Lives Matter, https://blacklivesmatter.com/about, accessed Sept. 17, 2017.

11. Mitch Smith, "Minnesota Officer Acquitted in Killing of Philando Castile," *New York Times*, June 16, 2017, https://www.nytimes.com/2017/06/16/us/police-shooting-trial-philando -castile.html; Debbie Nathan, "What Happened to Sandra Bland?," *Nation*, Apr. 21, 2016, https://www.thenation.com/article/what-happened-to-sandra-bland.

12. Hong Qu, "Social Media and the Boston Bombings: When Citizens and Journalists Cover the Same Story," Nieman Lab, Apr. 17, 2013, http://www.niemanlab.org/2013/04 /social-media-and-the-boston-bombings-when-citizens-and-journalists-cover-the-same-story.

13. Alicia Garza, "A Herstory of the #BlackLivesMatter Movement by Alicia Garza," Oct. 7, 2014, http://www.thefeministwire.com/2014/10/blacklivesmatter-2.

14. Juan Cartagena, "Las vidas negras importan," *El Diario*, Nov. 3, 2015, https:// eldiariony.com/2015/11/03/las-vidas-negras-importan.

15. Iris Hyon, "Initiating the Dialogue: How 'Letters for Black Lives' Sparked Conver- sations About Asian American Identity," Pulitzer Center, Mar. 15, 2017, http://pulitzercenter .org/reporting/initiating-dialogue-letters-for-black-lives-spark-conversations-asian-american -identity.

16. Adam Dietrich, Varun Bajaj, and Kellan Marvin, dirs., *Concerned Student 1950*, Field of Vision, Mar. 12, 2016, https://fieldofvision.org/concerned-student-1950.

17. "Can a Museum Help America Heal?," *Atlantic*, Oct. 28, 2016, https://www.the atlantic.com/video/index/505694/can-a-museum-help-america-heal.

18. An Xiao Mina, "Challenging Tropes of Native American Representation, Hashtag by Hashtag," *Civic Beat Reader*, Aug. 10, 2014, http://thecivicbeat.com/2014/08/challenging -tropes-of-native-american-representation-hashtag-by-hashtag.

19. Jacqueline Keeler, personal interview, July 25, 2017.

20. Françoise Mouly and Mina Kaneko, "Cover Story: Bruce McCall's 'First Thanksgiv- ing,'" *New Yorker*, Nov. 21, 2014, https://www.newyorker.com/culture/culture-desk/cover -story-2014-12-01.

21. Christabel Nsiah-Buadi, "April Reign Is Changing the Social Conversation," *Global- Post*, Feb. 8, 2018, https://www.pri.org/stories/2018-02-08/april-reign-changing-social -conversation.

22. Kyle Buchanan, "How Did *Moonlight* Win Best Picture?," *Vulture*, Feb. 27, 2017, http://www.vulture.com/2017/02/oscars-2017-how-did-moonlight-win-best-picture.html; Academy of Motion Picture Arts and Sciences, "Academy Takes Historic Action to Increase Diversity," press release, Jan. 22, 2016, http://www.oscars.org/news/academy-takes-historic -action-increase-diversity.

23. Lawrence Lessig, "The Laws of Cyberspace," draft 3, https://cyber.harvard.edu /works/lessig/laws_cyberspace.pdf, accessed Sept. 8, 2017.

24. Monica Anderson and Paul Hitlin, "3. The Hashtag #BlackLivesMatter Emerges: Social Activism on Twitter," Pew Research Center, Aug. 15, 2016, http://www.pewinternet .org/2016/08/15/the-hashtag-blacklivesmatter-emerges-social-activism-on-twitter.

25. Peter Moskowitz, "Should America's Cops Be Protected by Hate Crime Laws?," *Vice*, May 22, 2016, https://www.vice.com/amp/en_us/article/nnkje8/%7B%7Bcontributor.public _url%7D%7D.

26. Reena Flores, "Democratic Debate: Do Black Lives Matter?," *CBS News*, Oct. 13, 2015, https://www.cbsnews.com/news/democratic-debate-do-black-lives-matter; Anders Hagstrom, "ACLU Doubling Down Against State and Federal 'Blue Lives Matter' Bills," *Daily Caller*, July 2, 2017, http://dailycaller.com/2017/07/02/aclu-doubling-down-against -state-and-federal-blue-lives-matter-bills.

27. Brad Knickerbocker, "What Is the 'Tea Party' and How Is It Shaking Up American Politics?," *Christian Science Monitor*, Sept. 15, 2010, https://www.csmonitor.com/USA /Elections/2010/0915/What-is-the-tea-party-and-how-is-it-shaking-up-American-politics.

28. Know Your Meme contributors, "Tea Party Protests," Know Your Meme, http://knowyourmeme.com/memes/events/tea-party-protests, accessed Sept. 17, 2017.

CHAPTER 4.3: SYMBOLS OF ITERATION

1. Gabriel Rockhill, "Is Censorship Proof of Art's Political Power?," *Philosophical Salon*, June 6, 2016, http://thephilosophicalsalon.com/is-censorship-proof-of-arts-political-power.

2. Elizabeth Barber, "Umbrellas Banned During Xi Jinping's Arrival in Macau," Time .com, Dec. 18, 2014, http://time.com/3641579/xi-jinping-macau-umbrellas.

3. Jonathan Kaiman, "Who Guides Hong Kong's 'Umbrella Revolution' Pro-Democracy Movement?" *Guardian*, Sept. 30, 2014, https://www.theguardian.com/world/2014/sep/30/hong-kong-pro-democracy-protest-leaders-occupy.

4. An Xiao Mina, "Hong Kong Citizens' Online, Memetic Protest," *88 Bar*, Sept. 11, 2012, http://www.88-bar.com/2012/09/hong-kong-citizens-online-memetic-protest.

5. Marshall Ganz, "Public Narrative, Collective Action, and Power," in *Accountability Through Public Opinion: From Inertia to Public Action*, ed. Sina Odugbemi and Taeku Lee (Washington, DC: World Bank, 2011), https://dash.harvard.edu/bitstream/handle/1/29314925/Public_Narrative_Collective_Action_and_Power.pdf, 273–89.

6. Richard C. Bush, "China's Decision on Universal Suffrage in Hong Kong," Brookings Institution, Sept. 2, 2014 , https://www.brookings.edu/blog/up-front/2014/09/02/chinas-decision-on-universal-suffrage-in-hong-kong.

7. J.C., "Class Struggle," *Economist*, Sept. 25, 2014, https://www.economist.com/analects/2014/09/25/class-struggle.

8. Tania Branigan and Jonathan Kaiman, "Hong Kong Police Use Teargas and Pepper Spray to Disperse Protesters," *Guardian*. Sept. 28, 2014, https://www.theguardian.com/world/2014/sep/28/kong-kong-police-teargas-pepper-spray-pro-democracy-protesters.

9. *Umbrella Dreams: Fighting for Hong Kong Democracy*, Hank Leukart, dir. (2014), http://withoutbaggage.com/umbrella-dreams.

10. Sebastian Bertoli, Sameena, Thomas Hardiman, and Sirak Tegegn, "The Hong Kong Protests Through the Eyes of Weibo," Digital Methods Initiative, https://digitalmethods.net/Dmi/TheHongKongProtestsThroughTheEyesOfWeibo, accessed Sept. 17, 2017.

11. Jason Li, "How the Umbrella 'Revolution' Meme Hurt the Movement in Hong Kong," *88 Bar*, Oct. 5, 2014, http://www.88-bar.com/2014/10/how-the-umbrella-revolution-meme-hurt-the-movement-in-hong-kong.

12. Becky Sun, "Umbrella Movement," *Victoria and Albert Museum Blog*, Oct. 14, 2014, http://www.vam.ac.uk/blog/disobedient-objects/umbrella-movement.

13. Benjamin Haas and Eric Cheung, "'We Did Nothing Wrong': Banned Hong Kong Politician on Oath-taking Protest," *Guardian*, Nov. 15, 2016, https://www.theguardian.com/world/2016/nov/15/we-didnt-do-anything-wrong-banned-hong-kong-politician-yau-wai-ching-oath-taking-protest; Chris Lau, "Hong Kong Lawmakers Accused of Setting Aside Solemnity in Taking Oaths," *South China Morning Post*, Dec. 2, 2016, http://www.scmp.com/news/hong-kong/politics/article/2051266/hong-kong-lawmakers-accused-setting-aside-solemnity-taking.

14. Henry Wei Leung, email interview, Sept. 7, 2017.

15. Bertoli et al., "The Hong Kong Protests Through the Eyes of Weibo."

16. "Instagram Appears Blocked in China," *BBC News*, Sept. 29, 2014, http://www.bbc.com/news/technology-29409533.

17. Chung-hong Chan and King-wa Fu, "The Relationship Between Cyberbalkanization and Opinion Polarization: Time-Series Analysis on Facebook Pages and Opinion Polls During the Hong Kong Occupy Movement and the Associated Debate on Political Reform," *Journal of Computer-Mediated Communication* (Aug. 4, 2017), https://doi.org/10.1111/jcc4.12192.

18. Jasmine Siu, "Joshua Wong and Other Jailed Hong Kong Student Leaders See Political Careers Halted," *South China Morning Post*, Aug. 17, 2017, http://www.scmp.com/news/hong-kong/politics/article/2107216/occupy-activists-joshua-wong-and-nathan-law-jailed-hong-kong.

19. Henry Wei Leung, "City Without Solitude," *Offing*, Dec. 1, 2015, https://theoffingmag.com/essay/city-without-solitude.

20. Francesca Polletta, "Contending Stories: Narrative in Social Movements," *Qualitative Sociology* 21, no. 4 (Dec. 1998): 419–46.

21. Rockhill, "Is Censorship Proof of Art's Political Power?"

CHAPTER 5: CHAOS MAGIC

1. Garry Kasparov (@Kasparov63), "The point of modern propaganda . . .," 11:08 a.m., Dec. 13, 2016, Twitter, https://twitter.com/kasparov63/status/808750564284702720.

CHAPTER 5.1: THE MEME ELECTION

1. Arlie Russell Hochschild, "I Spent 5 Years with Some of Trump's Biggest Fans. Here's What They Won't Tell You," *Mother Jones*, Sept./Oct. 2016, https://www.motherjones.com/politics/2016/08/trump-white-blue-collar-supporters.

2. Angie Drobnic Holan, "In Context: Hillary Clinton and the 'Basket of Deplorables,'" *Politifact*, Sept. 11, 2016, http://www.politifact.com/truth-o-meter/article/2016/sep/11/context-hillary-clinton-basket-deplorables.

3. Carolina Miranda, "From Clinton's Shimmy to Pepe the Frog: Memes and the LOLcat Effect on the 2016 Election," *Los Angeles Times*, Oct. 20, 2017, http://www.latimes.com/entertainment/arts/miranda/la-ca-cam-memes-political-art-election-20161005-snap-htmlstory.html.

4. Nick Bilton, "Political GIFs Are the New Sound Bites This Campaign Season," *New York Times*, Jan. 6, 2016, https://www.nytimes.com/2016/01/07/fashion/gifs-donald-trump-hillary-clinton-campaign-season.html.

5. "Pepe the Frog," ADL Hate Symbols database, https://www.adl.org/education/references/hate-symbols/pepe-the-frog, accessed Sept. 17, 2017.

6. "Alt-Right," Southern Poverty Law Center, https://www.splcenter.org/fighting-hate/extremist-files/ideology/alt-right, accessed June 15, 2018; Graeme Wood, "His Kampf," *Atlantic*, June 2017, https://www.theatlantic.com/magazine/archive/2017/06/his-kampf/524505; Alice Marwick and Rebecca Lewis, "Media Manipulation and Disinformation Online," *Data and Society*, 2016, https://datasociety.net/output/media-manipulation-and-disinfo-online.

7. Andrea Freeman, "Milk, a Symbol of Neo-Nazi Hate," *Conversation*, Aug. 30, 2017, http://theconversation.com/milk-a-symbol-of-neo-nazi-hate-83292; Joseph Bernstein, "The Trump Internet Keeps Making Fake Hate Symbols, and People Keep Falling for It," *BuzzFeed*, Apr. 29, 2017, https://www.buzzfeed.com/josephbernstein/the-trump-internet-keeps-making-fake-hate-symbols-and.

8. Clark Mindock, "What Is a 'Cuck?': Origin of Insult from Alt-Right, White Nationalists Who Support Trump," *International Business Times*, Nov. 28, 2016, http://www.ibtimes.com/what-cuck-origin-insult-alt-right-white-nationalists-who-support-trump-2451694; Dave Neiwert, "What the Kek: Explaining the Alt-Right 'Deity' Behind Their 'Meme Magic,'" Southern Poverty Law Center, May 8, 2017, https://www.splcenter.org/hatewatch/2017/05/08/what-kek-explaining-alt-right-deity-behind-their-meme-magic; Jessica M. Goldstein, "The Surprising History of 'Snowflake' as a Political Insult," *ThinkProgress*, https://thinkprogress.org/all-the-special-snowflakes-aaf1a922f37b, accessed Sept. 17, 2017.

9. Know Your Meme contributors, "Pepe the Frog," Know Your Meme, http://knowyourmeme.com/memes/pepe-the-frog, accessed Sept. 17, 2017.

10. An Xiao Mina, "Pepe, Nasty Women, and the Memeing of American Politics," *Beacon Broadside*, Nov. 1, 2016, http://www.beaconbroadside.com/broadside/2016/11/pepe-nasty-women-and-the-memeing-of-american-politics.html.

11. JTA, "Pepe the Frog's Creator and ADL Pushing to Remove Antisemitic Association," *Jerusalem Post*, Oct. 15, 2016, http://www.jpost.com/Diaspora/Pepe-the-Frogs-creator-and-ADL-pushing-to-remove-antisemitic-association-470155.

12. Lorelei Laird, "'Pepe the Frog' Creator Wins Copyright Lawsuit Against Author of Conservative Children's Book," *ABA Journal*, Sept. 1, 2017, http://www.abajournal.com/news/article/pepe_the_frog_creator_wins_copyright_lawsuit_against_author_of_conservative.

13. Caroline Sinders, email correspondence, Sept. 4, 2017.

14. Marwick and Lewis, "Media Manipulation and Disinformation Online."

15. Maya Kosoff, "Mitt Romney's 'Binders Full of Women' Are Real—and They Weigh 15 Pounds," *Vanity Fair Hive*, Apr. 11, 2017, https://www.vanityfair.com/news/2017/04/mitt-romneys-binders-full-of-women.

16. Monica Anderson, "U.S. Technology Device Ownership: 2015," Pew Research Center, Oct. 29, 2015, http://www.pewinternet.org/2015/10/29/technology-device-ownership-2015.

17. Marley-Vincent Lindsey, "Parting Ways with Pepe? Anti-Semitism and the Medium of Memes," Cyborgology, Oct. 8, 2016, https://thesocietypages.org/cyborgology/2016/10/08/parting-ways-with-pepe-anti-semitism-and-the-medium-of-memes.

18. Lee Moran, "Tweeters Give Their Favorite Books a Hilarious Donald Trump Twist," *Huffington Post*, Oct. 24, 2016, http://www.huffingtonpost.com/entry/trumpanovel-twitter-election_us_580dba6ee4b02444efa3fe9b.

19. Nicole Puglise, "#TrumpBookReport: Great Literature Reimagined as a Tweet from the Donald," Oct. 20, 2016, https://www.theguardian.com/us-news/2016/oct/20/donald-trump-book-report-twitter-debate.

20. Sam Sanders, "#MemeOfTheWeek: Hillary Clinton, Not Quite an Abuela," NPR, Dec. 26, 2015, http://www.npr.org/2015/12/26/461116160/-memeoftheweek-hillary-clinton-not-quite-an-abuela.

21. Hochschild, "I Spent 5 Years with Some of Trump's Biggest Fans. Here's What They Won't Tell You."

22. Karen Tumulty, "How Donald Trump Came Up with 'Make America Great Again,'" *Washington Post*, Jan. 17, 2017, https://www.washingtonpost.com/politics/how-donald-trump-came-up-with-make-america-great-again/2017/01/17/fb6acf5e-dbf7-11e6-ad42-f3375f271c9c_story.html.

23. Heather Long, "Donald Trump Trademarks 'Make America Great Again,'" *CNN Money*, Oct. 8, 2015, http://money.cnn.com/2015/10/08/investing/donald-trump-make-america-great-again-trademark/index.html.

24. "GOP Convention Theme: Make America ___ Again!," *CBS News*, July 18, 2016, https://www.cbsnews.com/news/theme-for-the-gop-convention-donald-trump-make-america-again.

25. José Antonio Vargas (@joseiswriting), "You can get your own Immigrants Make America Great hat . . .," 3:47 p.m., Feb. 20, 2017, Twitter, https://twitter.com/joseiswriting/status/833825323833769984.

26. Yara Simón, "Someone Already Created a 'Taco Trucks on Every Corner' Hat," Remezcla.com, Sept. 7, 2016, http://remezcla.com/culture/taco-trucks-on-every-corner-hat.

27. Thomas E. Patterson, "News Coverage of the 2016 General Election: How the Press Failed the Voters," Shorenstein Center on Media, Politics, and Public Policy, Dec. 7, 2016, https://shorensteincenter.org/news-coverage-2016-general-election; Thomas E. Patterson, "News Coverage of Donald Trump's First 100 Days," Shorenstein Center on Media, Politics, and Public Policy, May 18, 2017, https://shorensteincenter.org/news-coverage-donald-trumps-first-100-days.

28. Stef W. Kight, "78% of Republicans Approve of Trump," *Axios*, Nov. 1, 2017, https://www.axios.com/78-of-republicans-approve-of-trump-1513306592–05c02c07-f56e-4ee4-a24b-60df98e5d916.html.

29. An Xiao Mina, "Learning the Politics of 'Digital Dissensus,'" *Civicist*, Feb. 5, 2018, https://civichall.org/civicist/learning-the-politics-of-digital-dissensus.

30. A. C. Thompson and Ken Schwencke, "Hate Crimes Are Up—But the Government Isn't Keeping Good Track of Them," *ProPublica*, Nov. 15, 2016, https://www.propublica.org/article/hate-crimes-are-up-but-the-government-isnt-keeping-good-track-of-them.

31. John Bacon, "Racist Graffiti Greets Trump Win Across USA," *USA Today*, Nov. 10, 2016, https://www.usatoday.com/story/news/nation/2016/11/10/racist-graffiti-greets-trump-win-across-usa/93584210.

32. "The Revolution Starts at Noon," *This American Life*, Jan. 20, 2017, https://www.thisamericanlife.org/radio-archives/episode/608/transcript.

33. Know Your Meme contributors, "Shitposting," Know Your Meme, Mar. 5, 2014, http://knowyourmeme.com/memes/shitposting.

34. Paul Spencer, "Trump's Occult Online Supporters Believe 'Meme Magic' Got Him Elected," *Motherboard*, Nov. 18, 2016, https://motherboard.vice.com/en_us/article/pgkx7g/trumps-occult-online-supporters-believe-pepe-meme-magic-got-him-elected.

35. Donald Trump, "The Inaugural Address," Whitehouse.gov, Jan. 20, 2017, https://www.whitehouse.gov/inaugural-address.

CHAPTER 5.2: BODIES AND MINDS
1. Simon Denyer, "China's Plan to Organize Its Society Relies on 'Big Data' to Rate Everyone," *Washington Post*, Oct. 22, 2016, https://www.washingtonpost.com/world/asia_pacific/chinas-plan-to-organize-its-whole-society-around-big-data-a-rating-for-everyone/2016/10/20/1cdodd9c-9516–11e6-ae9d-0030ac1899cd_story.html.

2. Henri Neuendorf, "Chinese Artist Arrested for Joke Images of President Xi Jinping," *ArtNet*, June 1, 2015, https://news.artnet.com/art-world/china-artist-arrested-mocking-president-xi-jinping-303088.

3. Laura C. Mallonee, "Artist Detained for Meme-ing Chinese President," *Hyperallergic*, June 1, 2015, https://hyperallergic.com/210896/artist-detained-for-meme-ing-chinese-president.

4. Gwynn Guilford, "In China, Being Retweeted 500 Times Can Get You Three Years in Prison," *Quartz*, Sept. 9, 2013, https://qz.com/122450/in-china-500-retweets-of-a-libelous-statement-can-get-you-three-years-in-prison.

5. Associated Press, "Chinese Panic-Buy Salt over Japan Nuclear Threat," *Guardian*, Mar. 17, 2011, https://www.theguardian.com/world/2011/mar/17/chinese-panic-buy-salt-japan.

6. David Bamman, Brendan O'Connor, and Noah A. Smith, "Censorship and Deletion Practices in Chinese Social Media," *First Monday* 17, no. 3 (Mar. 5, 2012), http://firstmonday.org/article/view/3943/3169.

7. "China: New Ban on 'Spreading Rumors' About Disasters," Human Rights Watch, Nov. 2, 2015, https://www.hrw.org/news/2015/11/02/china-new-ban-spreading-rumors-about-disasters.

8. Rebecca MacKinnon, "Networked Authoritarianism in China and Beyond: Implications for Global Internet Freedom," presentation, Liberation Technology in Authoritarian Regimes, Oct. 11–12, 2010, http://rconversation.blogs.com/MacKinnon_Libtech.pdf.

9. Tricia Wang and An Xiao Mina, "Real-Name Registration Threatens the Lively World of China's Microblogs," *Wired*, Mar. 15, 2012, https://www.wired.com/2012/03/opinion_anxiaochinamicroblog.

10. An Xiao Mina, "Real Name Registration One Month Later," *88 Bar*, Apr. 23, 2017, http://www.88-bar.com/2012/04/real-name-registration-one-month-later.

11. Denyer, "China's Plan to Organize Its Society Relies on 'Big Data' to Rate Everyone."

12. Jessica McKenzie, "Chinese Netizens Get Revenge on Official Who Arrested 16-Year-Old Blogger," *TechPresident*, Sept. 25, 2013, http://techpresident.com/news/wegov /24369/netizens-get-revenge-official-who-arrested-16-year-old-blogger; Jonathan Kaiman, "Chinese Police Chief Suspended After Online Storm over Teenager's Detention," *Guardian*, Sept. 24, 2013, https://www.theguardian.com/world/2013/sep/24/chinese-police-chief -suspended-yang-hui-detention?CMP=twt_gu.

13. Catherine Cray, "Winnie-the-Pooh Politics: The Ingenuity of Chinese Memes," *Politic*, Oct. 6, 2015, http://thepolitic.org/winnie-the-pooh-politics-the-ingenuity-of-chinese -memes/.

14. "U of T's Citizen Lab Exposes Censorship on Popular Chat App, WeChat," *University of Toronto News*, Dec. 1, 2016, https://www.utoronto.ca/news/u-t-s-citizen-lab-exposes -censorship-popular-chat-app-wechat; Jason Q. Ng, "Politics, Rumors, and Ambiguity: Tracking Censorship on WeChat's Public Accounts Platform," Citizen Lab, July 20, 2015, https://themediatedimage.com/2015/07/24/july-24th-2015.

15. Ng, "Politics, Rumors, and Ambiguity."

16. Garry Kasparov, "Trump, Putin, and the Dangers of Fake News," *Parallax*, Jan. 16, 2017, https://www.the-parallax.com/2017/01/16/kasparov-trump-putin-fake-news.

17. Gary King, Jennifer Pan, and Margaret E. Roberts, "How the Chinese Government Fabricates Social Media Posts for Strategic Distraction, Not Engaged Argument," *American Political Science Review* 111, no. 3 (2017): 484–501, available online at http://gking.harvard .edu/50c.

18. Ibid.

19. Wu, *The Attention Merchants*.

20. Austin Ramzy, "Chinese Leader Gets a Cartoon Makeover," *New York Times*, Oct. 17, 2013, https://sinosphere.blogs.nytimes.com/2013/10/17/chinese-leader-gets-a-cartoon-makeover.

21. Austin Ramzy, "Musical Ode to Xi Jinping and His Wife Goes Viral," *New York Times*, Nov. 25, 2014, https://sinosphere.blogs.nytimes.com/2014/11/25/musical-ode-to-xi -jinping-and-his-wife-goes-viral.

22. The "Streisand Effect" was named for the American singer and actor Barbra Streisand, whose effort to prevent photos being taken of her Malibu, California, home resulted in more attention being driven to photos of her home.

CHAPTER 5.3: FAKE, FAKE, FAKE, FAKE

1. Whitney Phillips, "Putting the Folklore in Fake News," *Culture Digitally*, Jan. 24, 2017, http://culturedigitally.org/2017/01/putting-the-folklore-in-fake-news.

2. Spencer S. Hsu, "Comet Ping Pong Pizza Case," *Washington Post*, Jan. 24, 2017, https://www.washingtonpost.com/local/public-safety/us-prosecutors-offer-unspecified-plea -deal-in-comet-ping-pong-pizza-case/2017/01/24/db300f2a-e245-11e6-ba11-63c4b4fb5a63 _story.html?utm_term=.0b4d79b44d58.

3. "Guns in the US: The Statistics Behind the Violence," *BBC News*, Jan. 5, 2016, http:// www.bbc.com/news/world-us-canada-34996604.

4. German Lopez, "Pizzagate, the Fake News Conspiracy Theory That Led a Gunman to DC's Comet Ping Pong, Explained," *Vox*, Dec. 8, 2016, https://www.vox.com/policy-and -politics/2016/12/5/13842258/pizzagate-comet-ping-pong-fake-news.

5. Marc Fisher, John Woodrow Cox, and Peter Hermann, "Pizzagate: From Rumor, to Hashtag, to Gunfire in D.C.," Oct. 6, 2017, https://www.washingtonpost.com/local/pizzagate -from-rumor-to-hashtag-to-gunfire-in-dc/2016/12/06/4c7def50-bbd4-11e6-94ac-3d324840106c _story.html.

6. Tim Stelloh, "'Pizzagate' Gunman Surrendered After Finding No Evidence of Fake Conspiracy: Court Docs," *NBC News*, Dec. 5, 2016, https://www.nbcnews.com/news/us-news /pizzagate-gunman-surrendered-after-finding-no-evidence-fake-conspiracy-court-n692321.

7. Craig Silverman, "How the Bizarre Conspiracy Theory Behind 'Pizzagate' Was Spread," *BuzzFeed*, Dec. 5, 2016, https://www.buzzfeed.com/craigsilverman/fever-swamp-election.

8. Craig Silverman and Lawrence Alexander, "How Teens in the Balkans Are Duping Trump Supporters with Fake News," *BuzzFeed*, Nov. 3, 2016, https://www.buzzfeed.com/craigsilverman/how-macedonia-became-a-global-hub-for-pro-trump-misinfo.

9. Terrence McCoy, "Inside a Long Beach Web Operation That Makes Up Stories About Trump and Clinton: What They Do for Clicks and Cash," *Los Angeles Times*, Nov. 22, 2016, http://www.latimes.com/business/technology/la-fi-tn-fake-news-20161122-story.html; Eric Lubbers, "There Is No Such Thing as the Denver Guardian, Despite That Facebook Post You Saw," *Denver Post*, Nov. 5, 2016, http://www.denverpost.com/2016/11/05/there-is-no-such-thing-as-the-denver-guardian.

10. Claire Wardle, "Fake News. It's Complicated," *First Draft News*, Feb. 16, 2017, https://medium.com/1st-draft/fake-news-its-complicated-d0f773766c79.

11. Claire Wardle, "Internet Memes: Misinformation Machines or Vectors of Truth?," International Journalism Festival, Apr. 6, 2017, https://www.journalismfestival.com/programme/2017/internet-memes-misinformation-machines-or-vectors-of-truth.

12. Wardle, "Fake News. It's Complicated."

13. Marwick and Lewis, "Media Manipulation and Disinformation Online."

14. Clay Shirky, "How Both Parties Became Host Bodies for Third-Party Candidates," *Civicist*, Feb. 19, 2016, https://civichall.org/civicist/clay-shirky-on-the-whys-behind-current-us-presidential-election-cycle.

15. Chris Hayes, "The New Right-Wing Smear Machine," *Nation*, Oct. 25, 2007, https://www.thenation.com/article/new-right-wing-smear-machine.

16. Touré, "Racism Is Fun?," *Time*, Oct. 27, 2011, http://ideas.time.com/2011/10/27/racism-is-fun.

17. Barack Obama, *Dreams from My Father: A Story of Race and Inheritance* (New York: Broadway Books, 2004).

18. Carl Huse, "Ted Cruz and John McCain Share History in Questions over 'Natural Born' Status," *New York Times*, Jan. 7, 2016, https://www.nytimes.com/politics/first-draft/2016/01/07/ted-cruz-and-john-mccain-share-history-of-facing-natural-born-questions.

19. David Mikkelson, "Birth Certificate," *Snopes*, Aug. 27, 2011, http://www.snopes.com/politics/obama/birthers/birthcertificate.asp.

20. David Jackson, "Trump Finally Says Obama Born in U.S., Blames Clinton for Controversy," *USA Today*, Sept. 16, 2016, https://www.usatoday.com/story/news/politics/elections/2016/2016/09/16/donald-trump-barack-obama-hillary-clinton-presidential-campaign-birtherism/90471868.

21. CredibilityCoalition.org, www.credibilitycoalition.org.

22. Phillips, "Putting the Folklore in Fake News."

23. Henry Jenkins, "Fandom, Participatory Culture, and Web 2.0—A Syllabus," personal blog, Jan. 9, 2010, http://henryjenkins.org/blog/2010/01/fandom_participatory_culture_a.html.

24. Nausicaa Renner, "Memes Trump Articles on Breitbart's Facebook Page," *Columbia Journalism Review*, Jan. 30, 2017, https://www.cjr.org/tow_center/memes-trump-articles-on-breitbarts-facebook-page.php.

25. Yochai Benkler, Robert Faris, Hal Roberts, and Ethan Zuckerman, "Study: Breitbart-Led Right-Wing Media Ecosystem Altered Broader Media Agenda," *Columbia Journalism Review*, Mar. 3, 2017, https://www.cjr.org/analysis/breitbart-media-trump-harvard-study.php.

26. Christina Xu, "Watching the Election from the Post-Truth Future," *Medium*, Nov. 17, 2016, https://medium.com/@xuhulk/watching-the-election-from-the-post-truth-future-97a0d66bdcfe.

27. Adrian Chen, "The Agency," *New York Times*, June 2, 2015, https://www.nytimes.com/2015/06/07/magazine/the-agency.html.

28. Russell Brandom, "Robert Mueller Charges Russian 'Troll Farm' with Election Interference," *Verge*, Feb. 16, 2018, https://www.theverge.com/2018/2/16/17020774/robert -mueller-russia-troll-internet-research-agency-election-interference.

29. Claire Wardle and Hossein Derakhshan, *Information Disorder: Toward an Interdisciplinary Framework for Research and Policy Making* (Strasbourg Cedex: Council of Europe, 2017), https://rm.coe.int/information-disorder-toward-an-interdisciplinary-framework-for -researc/168076277c.

CHAPTER 6.1: WHERE THE WIND BLOWS

1. Chris Buckley, "Documentary on Air Pollution Grips China," *New York Times*, Mar. 2, 2015, https://cn.nytimes.com/china/20150302/c02documentary/en-us.

2. Alastair Jamieson, "Beijing Olympics Were the Most Polluted Games Ever, Researchers Say," *Telegraph*, June 22, 2009, http://www.telegraph.co.uk/sport/olympics/london-2012 /5597277/Beijing-Olympics-were-the-most-polluted-games-ever-researchers-say.html.

3. "Pant by Numbers: The Cities with the Most Dangerous Air—Listed," *Guardian*, Feb. 13, 2017, https://www.theguardian.com/cities/datablog/2017/feb/13/most-polluted-cities -world-listed-region.

4. Alan Clark, "China's Environmental Clean-up to Have Big Impact on Industry," *Financial Times*, May 22, 2017, https://www.ft.com/content/e22dd988-3ed9-11e7-9d56-25f963e998b2.

5. Annie Gowen and Simon Denyer, "As U.S. Backs Away from Climate Pledges, India and China Step Up," *Washington Post*, June 1, 2017, https://www.washingtonpost.com/world /asia_pacific/as-us-backs-away-from-climate-pledges-india-and-china-step-up/2017/06/01 /59ccb494-16e4-4d47-a881-c5bd0922c3db_story.html; Beth Gardiner, "Three Reasons to Believe in China's Renewable Energy Boom," *National Geographic*, May 12, 2017, http:// news.nationalgeographic.com/2017/05/china-renewables-energy-climate-change-pollution -environment.

6. "Fine Particles (PM 2.5) Questions and Answers," New York State Department of Health website, https://www.health.ny.gov/environmental/indoors/air/pmq_a.htm, accessed Aug. 15, 2017.

7. "Air Pollution in Northern Chinese City Surpasses WHO Guideline by 100 Times," Reuters, Dec. 19, 2016, https://www.reuters.com/article/us-china-pollution/air-pollution-in -northern-chinese-city-surpasses-who-guideline-by-100-times-idUSKBN1480XM.

8. Barbara Demick and John Lee, "Severe Beijing Smog—or Fog?—Leads to Long Airport Delays," *Los Angeles Times*, Dec. 6, 2011, http://latimesblogs.latimes.com/world_now /2011/12/severe-beijing-smog-or-fog-leads-to-long-airport-delays-.html.

9. David Roberts, "How the US Embassy Tweeted to Clear Beijing's Air," *Wired*, Mar. 6, 2015, https://www.wired.com/2015/03/opinion-us-embassy-beijing-tweeted-clear-air.

10. Xinhua News Agency, "Urban Residents' Average Gross Salary Up 17% in 2008," China.org.cn, Apr. 10, 2009, http://www.china.org.cn/china/news/2009-04/10/content _17580841.htm.

11. Fengshi Wu, "Environmental Civil Society in China: 15 Years in Review," Harvard-Yenching Institute Working Paper Series, Jan. 2009, https://www.researchgate.net/profile /Fengshi_Wu/publication/297345772_Environmental_Civil_Society_in_China_15_Years_in _Review/links/56de7d6108aedf2bfoc8c2de.pdf.

12. Anna Brettell, "Channeling Dissent: The Institutionalization of Environmental Complaint Resolution," in *China's Embedded Activism: Opportunities and Constraints of a Social Movement*, ed. Peter Ho and Richard Louis Edmonds (New York: Routledge, 2008).

13. Steven Millward, "'DirtyBeijing' App Courts Controversy, Warns Smartphone Users of Crazybad Air," Tech in Asia, Nov. 20, 2011, https://www.techinasia.com/dirtybeijing-app.

14. Ellery Biddle, "Fog or Fiction? Tips on Misinformation and the Social Web," MisinfoCon, Nieman Foundation for Journalism at Harvard, Feb. 24, 2017, https://vimeo .com/205621757.

15. Kristie Lu Stout, "Kites Untether China's Grip on Air Pollution Data," CNN.com, Aug. 24, 2012, http://www.cnn.com/2012/08/24/world/asia/china-kites-pollution-stout/index.html.

16. Davey Alba, "This Wearable Detects Pollution to Build Air Quality Maps in Real Time," *Wired*, Nov. 19, 2014, https://www.wired.com/2014/11/clarity-wearable.

17. Steven Schwankert, "Chai Jing's Environmental Documentary 'Under the Dome' Goes off the Air," *Beijinger*, Mar. 7, 2015, https://www.thebeijinger.com/blog/2015/03/07/chai-jings-environmental-documentary-under-dome-goes-air.

18. Buckley, "Documentary on Air Pollution Grips China."

19. Ari Phillips, "China's Surprising Reaction to an Online Video Exposing the Country's Extreme Pollution Problem," *ThinkProgress*, Mar. 2, 2015, https://thinkprogress.org/chinas-surprising-reaction-to-an-online-video-exposing-the-country-s-extreme-pollution-problem-6a8df1ab2e85.

20. Nooshin Soluch and Kerry Allen, "Defying the Online Censors with Jokes About Chinese Smog," *BBC News*, Dec. 9, 2015, http://www.bbc.co.uk/news/blogs-trending-35044681; Xiong Lei, "How Social Media Is Taking on the Environment in China, *Huffington Post*, updated Dec. 6, 2017, http://www.huffingtonpost.com/xiong-lei/china-social-media-environment_b_6875432.html.

21. Mark MacKinnon, "Think China's Air Is Breathable? Think Again," *Globe and Mail*, Sept. 27, 2011, https://www.theglobeandmail.com/news/world/think-chinas-air-is-breathable-think-again/article4247966.

22. Lei Xie, "China's Environmental Activism in the Age of Globalization," *Asian Politics and Policy* 3, no. 2 (Apr. 2011), http://onlinelibrary.wiley.com/doi/10.1111/j.1943-0787.2011.01256.x/full.

23. Charles Zhu, "A Visual Guide to Chinese Air Pollution," *Atlantic*, Oct. 17, 2012, https://www.theatlantic.com/international/archive/2012/10/a-visual-guide-to-chinese-air-pollution/263698.

24. Anthony Kuhn, "For Some in China's Middle Class, Pollution Is Spurring Action," *Parallels*, NPR, Mar. 2, 2017, http://www.npr.org/sections/parallels/2017/03/02/518173670/for-some-in-chinas-middle-class-pollution-is-spurring-action.

25. Costanza-Chock, *Out of the Shadows, Into the Streets!*

26. Biddle, "Fog or Fiction? Tips on Misinformation and the Social Web."

27. Elizabeth Plantan and Chris Cairns, "Hazy Messaging: Framing Air Pollution on Chinese Social Media," symposium, "Everyday Politics of Digital Life in China," University of Pittsburgh, Oct. 7–8, 2016, http://www.chrismcairns.com/uploads/3/0/2/2/30226899/hazy_messaging_plantan_and_cairns.pdf. Cited with author's permission.

28. Natalie Gyenes, email correspondence, Sept. 18, 2017.

29. Mary Hennock, "China Combats Air Pollution with Tough Monitoring Rules," *Guardian*, Mar. 1, 2012, https://www.theguardian.com/world/2012/mar/01/china-air-pollution-tough-rules.

30. Jeffrey N. Wasserstrom and Maura Elizabeth Cunningham, *China in the 21st Century: What Everyone Needs to Know*, 2nd ed. (2010; New York: Oxford University Press, 2013), 151.

31. Barbara Demick, "Dead Pigs by the Thousands Float Down Chinese River," *Los Angeles Times*, Mar. 11, 2013, http://articles.latimes.com/2013/mar/11/world/la-fg-wn-china-dead-pigs-river-20130311.

32. Sophie Brown, "Shanghai Teens Top International Education Ranking, OECD Says," CNN.com, Dec. 3, 2013, https://www.cnn.com/2013/12/03/world/asia/pisa-education-study/index.html.

33. Matt Schiavenza, "Dead Swine-Gate: Anatomy of a Chinese Scandal," *Atlantic*, Apr. 2, 2013, https://www.theatlantic.com/china/archive/2013/04/dead-swine-gate-anatomy-of-a-chinese-scandal/274549; Mandy Zuo, "Cradle of Communist Party at Centre of Dead Pig

Fiasco," *Guardian*, May 7, 2013, http://www.scmp.com/news/china/article/1204193/cradle-communist-party-centre-dead-pig-fiasco.

34. Peter Ho, "Embedded Activism and Political Change in a Semiauthoritarian Context," *China Information* 2, no. 2 (July 26, 2016): 177–209, http://journals.sagepub.com/doi/abs/10.1177/0920203X07079643.

35. Zheping Huang, "Mark Zuckerberg Went Jogging in Smoggy Beijing—and Everyone Has Something to Say About It," *Quartz*, Mar. 18, 2016, https://qz.com/642545/mark-zuckerberg-went-jogging-in-smoggy-beijing-and-everyone-has-something-to-say-about-it.

36. David Stanway and Sue-Lin Wong, "Smoke and Mirrors: Beijing Battles to Control Smog Message," Reuters, Feb. 15, 2017, https://www.reuters.com/article/us-china-pollution-censorship/smoke-and-mirrors-beijing-battles-to-control-smog-message-idUSKBN15U2UY.

37. Data Team, "Why China's Air Pollution Is on the Rise Again," *Economist*, Jan. 4, 2017, https://www.economist.com/blogs/graphicdetail/2017/01/daily-chart-1.

CHAPTER 6.2: THE STATE OF AFFAIRS

1. Gisela Pérez de Acha, video chat interview, Mar. 21, 2018.

2. #RexisteMX, "Pinta monumental 'Fue El Estado' en el Zócalo de México," http://rexiste.org/post/107326632417/pinta-monumental-fue-el-estado-en-el-zócalo-de, accessed Mar. 4, 2018.

3. Sam Jones, "Paint Remover: Mexico Activists Attempt to Drone Out Beleaguered President," *Guardian*, Oct. 14, 2015, https://www.theguardian.com/global-development/2015/oct/15/mexico-droncita-rexiste-collective-president-enrique-pena-nieto.

4. "Mexican Students Protest for Greater Democracy, 1968," Global Nonviolent Action Database, https://nvdatabase.swarthmore.edu/content/mexican-students-protest-greater-democracy-1968, accessed May 2, 2018.

5. "Ayotzinapa. Have You Seen," Street Art SF, Mar. 2, 2015, https://www.streetartsf.com/ayotzinapa-have-you-seen/; Dean Terasaki, "Mural for the Ayotzinapa 43," Sept. 13, 2015, https://www.flickr.com/photos/28isnormal/21743420678.

6. Francisco Goldman, "Crisis in Mexico: The Disappearance of the Forty-Three," *New Yorker*, Oct. 24, 2014, https://www.newyorker.com/news/news-desk/crisis-mexico-disappearance-forty-three.

7. Kirk Semple, "Missing Mexican Students Suffered a Night of 'Terror,' Investigators Say," *New York Times*. Apr. 24, 2016, https://www.nytimes.com/2016/04/25/world/americas/missing-mexican-students-suffered-a-night-of-terror-investigators-say.html.

8. "Mexico's Disappeared: The Enduring Cost of a Crisis Ignored," Human Rights Watch, Feb. 20, 2013, https://www.hrw.org/report/2013/02/20/mexicos-disappeared/enduring-cost-crisis-ignored.

9. Ginger Thompson, "How the U.S. Triggered a Massacre in Mexico," *ProPublica*, June 12, 2017, https://www.propublica.org/article/allende-zetas-cartel-massacre-and-the-us-dea.

10. "Latin America's Disappeared," *Telesur*, Aug. 29, 2014, https://www.telesurtv.net/english/analysis/Latin-Americas-Disappeared-20140829-0068.html.

11. *They Took Them Alive*, Emily Pederson, dir., Field of Vision, Nov. 17, 2016, https://fieldofvision.org/they-took-them-alive.

12. Elizabeth Rivera, "Mexicans Demand President Peña Nieto Resign with Trending Twitter Hashtag," *Global Voices*, Oct. 20, 2014, https://globalvoices.org/2014/10/20/mexicans-demand-president-pena-nieto-resign-with-trending-twitter-hashtag.

13. Ayotzinapavive, Instagram, https://www.instagram.com/ayotzinapavive, accessed Aug. 3, 2017.

14. Julie Schwietert Collazo, phone interview, Aug. 24, 2017.

15. David Sim, "Illustrators with Ayotzinapa: Artists' Moving Portraits of Mexico's 43 Missing Students," *International Business Times*, Nov. 21, 2014, http://www.ibtimes.co.uk/illustrators-ayotzinapa-artists-moving-portraits-mexicos-43-missing-students-1473520.

16. Arturo Conde, "'Semillas' Uses Dance, Art to Grow Ayotzinapa Awareness," *NBC News*, Feb. 26, 2016, http://www.nbcnews.com/news/latino/semillas-uses-dance-art-grow-ayotzinapa-awareness-n525721.

17. "With Art and Music, Latinos in US Respond to Ayotzinapa," *Latin Correspondent*, Nov. 26, 2014, accessed Sept. 5, 2017; Felipe Nery, "Performance Ayotzinapa. Estudiantes de Artes Escenicas, UNISON," YouTube, Oct. 22, 2014, https://www.youtube.com/watch?v=fIWOuc_SSsk; Ann Ochoaa, "Performance 'Vivos se los llevaron, vivos los queremos'—Escuela Nacional de Arte Teatral," YouTube, Oct. 16, 2014, https://www.youtube.com/watch?v=ivJulIYWuQs.

18. Saskia Sassen, *Globalization and Its Discontents: Essays on the New Mobility of People and Money* (New York: New Press, 1999).

19. "Globalization," *National Geographic Encyclopedia*, https://admin.nationalgeographic.org/encyclopedia/globalization, accessed Sept. 10, 2017.

20. "Mexico Internet Users," Internet Live Stats, http://www.internetlivestats.com/internet-users/mexico/, accessed Aug. 10, 2017.

21. Bernardo Gutiérrez, "#Ayotzinapa: La expansión global de una causa," *Horizontal*, Sept. 25, 2015, https://horizontal.mx/ayotzinapa-la-expansion-global-de-una-causa.

22. Emily Pederson, "No Están Solos: Mexico and Its Diaspora Mobilize for Change After Ayotzinapa," *NACLA Report on the Americas* 48, no. 1 (May 4, 2016), http://www.tandfonline.com/doi/abs/10.1080/10714839.2016.1170306.

23. Gisela Pérez de Acha, video chat interview, Mar. 21, 2018.

24. Klint Finley, "Pro-Government Twitter Bots Try to Hush Mexican Activists," *Wired*, Aug. 23, 2015, https://www.wired.com/2015/08/pro-government-twitter-bots-try-hush-mexican-activists.

25. Aviv Ovadya, "What's Worse Than Fake News? The Distortion of Reality Itself," *Washington Post*, Feb. 22, 2017, https://www.washingtonpost.com/news/theworldpost/wp/2018/02/22/digital-reality.

26. Robert Gotwa, "Spreading Fake News Becomes Standard Practice for Governments Across the World," *Oxford Internet Institute Blog*, July 18, 2017, https://www.oii.ox.ac.uk/blog/spreading-fake-news-becomes-standard-practice-for-governments-across-the-world.

27. Freedom House, "Manipulating Social Media to Undermine Democracy," Freedom on the Net 2017, https://freedomhouse.org/report/freedom-net/freedom-net-2017, accessed Feb. 2, 2017.

28. Alejandro Jaramillo, "In Pictures: These Are the Faces of the Caravana 43 for the Disappeared Students of Ayotzinapa, Mexico," Africa Is a Country, Apr. 30, 2015, http://africasacountry.com/2015/04/photos-these-are-the-faces-of-the-caravana-43-for-ayotzinapa.; Anita Chabria, "Parents of Missing Mexican Students Tour US to Push for New Investigation," *Guardian*, Apr. 10, 2015, https://www.theguardian.com/world/2015/apr/10/parents-missing-mexican-students-united-states-caravana-43-tour.

29. Tara McKelvey, "Michelle Obama's Hashtag Quest to Rescue Nigerian Girls," *BBC News*, Apr. 14, 2016, http://www.bbc.com/news/world-us-canada-35948362.

30. Homa Khaleeli, "#SayHerName: Why Kimberlé Crenshaw Is Fighting for Forgotten Women," *Guardian*, May 30, 2016, https://www.theguardian.com/lifeandstyle/2016/may/30/sayhername-why-kimberle-crenshaw-is-fighting-for-forgotten-women.

31. Alejandro Gómez Escorcia, email interview, Mar. 21, 2018.

32. Ibid.

33. Jenkins, Ford, and Green, *Spreadable Media*.

34. Ryan Devereaux, "Three Years After 43 Students Disappeared in Mexico, a New Visualization Reveals the Cracks in the Government's Story," *Intercept*, Sept. 7, 2017, https://theintercept.com/2017/09/07/three-years-after-43-students-disappeared-in-mexico-a-new-visualization-reveals-the-cracks-in-the-governments-story.

35. Laura Carlsen, "Ayotzinapa's Message to the World: Organize!," *CounterPunch*, Sept. 28, 2016, http://www.counterpunch.org/2016/09/28/ayotzinapas-message-to-the-world-organize.

36. Thomas Olesen, *Global Injustice Symbols and Social Movements* (London: Palgrave Macmillan, 2015).

37. "Mexico's Drug War Makes Everyone a Target," Global Voices Advocacy, June 26, 2017, https://advox.globalvoices.org/2017/06/26/mexicos-drug-war-makes-everyone-a-target-especially-journalists.

38. Collazo, phone interview.

39. "#NosFaltan43: se gradúa la generación de los normalistas desaparecidos de Ayotzinapa," *Animal Politico*, July 13, 2018, https://www.animalpolitico.com/2018/07/graduacion-generacion-normalistas-ayotzinapa.

40. Ibid.

41. Gisela Pérez de Acha, video chat interview, Mar. 21, 2018.

CHAPTER 6.3: POWER PLAY

1. Lin Prøitz, "Visual Social Media and Affectivity: The Impact of the Image of Alan Kurdi and Young People's Response to the Refugee Crisis in Oslo and Sheffield," *Information, Communication & Society* 21, no. 4 (2018).

2. Favianna Rodriguez, "Change the Culture, Change the World," *Creative Time Reports*, Apr. 1, 2013, http://creativetimereports.org/2013/04/01/change-the-culture-change-the-world.

3. Ibid.

4. Jeronimo Saldaña, phone interview, July 26, 2017.

5. Donald Trump, "Executive Order Protecting the Nation from Foreign Terrorist Entry into the United States," White House Press Office, Mar. 6, 2017, https://www.whitehouse.gov/the-press-office/2017/03/06/executive-order-protecting-nation-foreign-terrorist-entry-united-states.

6. Rachael Revesz, "Donald Trump's New 'Muslim Ban' Still Does Not Include Countries That Have Produced Terrorists," *Independent*, Mar. 6, 2017, http://www.independent.co.uk/news/world/americas/donald-trump-muslim-travel-ban-countries-terrorists-immigration-order-a7614701.html.

7. Alexander Burns, "2 Federal Judges Rule Against Trump's Latest Travel Ban," *New York Times*, Mar. 15, 2017, https://www.nytimes.com/2017/03/15/us/politics/trump-travel-ban.html.

8. Jessica Taylor, "Trump Calls for 'Total and Complete Shutdown of Muslims Entering' U.S.," NPR, Dec. 7, 2015, http://www.npr.org/2015/12/07/458836388/trump-calls-for-total-and-complete-shutdown-of-muslims-entering-u-s.

9. Marcus Benigno, phone interview, Aug. 16, 2017.

10. George Lakoff, "Trump's Twitter Distraction," personal blog, Mar. 7, 2017. https://georgelakoff.com/2017/03/07/trumps-twitter-distraction.

11. "Alan Kurdi's Family Holds Memorial in Vancouver Today," *CBC News*, Sept. 6, 2015, http://www.cbc.ca/news/canada/british-columbia/alan-kurdi-syrian-refugee-memorial-1.3217074.

12. "Alan Kurdi Family to Reunite in Vancouver Area," *CBC News*, Dec. 28, 2015, http://www.cbc.ca/news/canada/british-columbia/reunion-of-alan-kurdi-relatives-in-metro-vancouver-to-be-bittersweet-1.3382034.

13. Reuters, "Europe Is Facing the Worst Refugee Crisis Since World War II—and There's No End in Sight," *Business Insider*, Aug. 28, 2015, http://www.businessinsider.com/r-migrant-tragedies-on-land-and-sea-claim-hundreds-of-lives-2015-8.

14. Ismail Küpeli, "We Spoke to the Photographer Behind the Picture of the Drowned Syrian Boy," *Vice*, Sept. 4, 2015, https://www.vice.com/en_us/article/zngqpx/nilfer-demir-interview-876.

15. Francesco D'Orazio, "Journey of an Image: From a Beach in Bodrum to Twenty Million Screens Across the World," in *The Iconic Image on Social Media: A Rapid Research Response to the Death of Aylan Kurdi*, Visual Social Media Lab, Dec. 2015, http://visualsocialmedialab .org/projects/the-iconic-image-on-social-media.

16. Farida Vis and Olga Goriunova, eds., "The Iconic Image on Social Media: A Rapid Research Response to the Death of Aylan Kurdi," Visual Social Media Lab, Dec. 2015, http://visualsocialmedialab.org/blog/the-iconic-image-on-social-media-a-rapid-response-to -the-death-of-aylan-kurdi

17. "The 1951 Refugee Convention," UNHCR, http://www.unhcr.org/1951-refugee -convention.html, accessed Aug. 16, 2017.

18. Mukul Devichand, "Did Alan Kurdi's Death Change Anything?" BBC Trending, Sept. 2, 2016, http://www.bbc.com/news/blogs-trending-37257869.

19. US Holocaust Memorial Museum, "Immigration to the United States 1933–1941," https://www.ushmm.org/wlc/en/article.php?ModuleId=10008297, accessed Aug. 16, 2017; Helen Barnett, "#RefugeesWelcome Hashtag Sees Celebs and Politicians Pile Pressure on David Cameron," *Express*, Sept. 3, 2015, http://www.express.co.uk/news/uk/602727 /RefugeesWelcome-migrants-viral-Twitter-hashtag-Stan-Collymore-David-Miliband.

20. Scott Gold, "The Artist Behind the Iconic 'Running Immigrants' Image," *Los Angeles Times*, Apr. 4, 2008, http://www.latimes.com/local/la-me-outthere4apr04-story.html.

21. Prøitz, "Visual Social Media and Affectivity."

22. Ray Drainville, "The Visual Propaganda of the Brexit Leave Campaign," *Hyperallergic*, July 12, 2016, https://hyperallergic.com/310631/the-visual-propaganda-of-the-brexit -leave-campaign.

23. *The Journey*, Matthew Cassel, dir., Field of Vision, 2016, https://fieldofvision.org /the-journey.

24. Ryan M. Milner, "The World Made Meme: Discourse and Identity in Participatory Media," PhD diss., University of Kansas, May 8, 2012, https://kuscholarworks.ku.edu /handle/1808/10256.

25. "The 5 Awkward Questions They Won't Answer About the Drowned Boy, Syria and Our 'Moral Duty,'" *Breitbart*, Sept. 8, 2015, http://www.breitbart.com/london/2015 /09/08/the-5-awkward-questions-they-wont-answer-about-the-drowned-boy-syria-and-our -moral-duty.

26. Charlotte Alfred and Daniel Howden, "Expert Views: The E.U.-Turkey Deal After Two Years," Refugees Deeply, Mar. 20, 2018, https://www.newsdeeply.com/refugees/community /2018/03/20/expert-views-the-e-u-turkey-deal-after-two-years; Gabriela Meléndez Olivera, "Decoding Trump's Latest Anti-Immigrant Attacks," ACLU, Apr. 27, 2018, https://www .aclu.org/blog/immigrants-rights/decoding-trumps-latest-anti-immigrant-attacks.

CHAPTER 7: FIELDS

1. Rodriguez, "Change the Culture, Change the World."

CHAPTER 7.1: THE RISE OF THE GOAT

1. Catie L'Heureux, "Read Janet Mock's Women's March Speech on Trans Women of Color and Sex Workers," *Cut*, Jan. 21, 2017, https://www.thecut.com/2017/01/read-janet-mocks -speech-at-the-womens-march-on-washington-trans-women-of-color-sex-workers.html.

2. Yasin Mugerwa, "30,000 Uganda Government Goats Go Missing," *East African*, Apr. 26, 2011, http://www.theeastafrican.co.ke/news/30000-Uganda-Government-goats-missing /2558–1151062-tfk2bg/index.html.

3. An Xiao Mina, "The Chickens and Goats of Uganda's Internet," *Ethnography Matters*, Mar. 25, 2013, https://ethnographymatters.net/blog/2013/03/25/the-chickens-and-goats-of -ugandas-internet.

4. All citations from this exhibition appear with thanks to Jason Eppink, curator of *How Cats Took Over the Internet* at the Museum of the Moving Image. Eppink invited me and the Civic Beat, the global research collective I cofounded with Jason Li, to organize the world animal-meme map to take up a significant section of the space. The map has since been shown again at the Institute for the Future and the Victoria and Albert Museum, among other venues.

5. Goats of Bangladesh, Facebook, Aug. 24, 2017, https://www.facebook.com/realgoatstoriesbd/photos/a.800649733291860.1073741828.800626583294175/1512407285449431.

6. Ibid.

7. "Decorated Cave of Pont d'Arc, Known as Grotte Chauvet-Pont d'Arc," UNESCO, http://whc.unesco.org/en/list/1426, accessed Sept. 17, 2017.

8. Carol Hills, "Was European Cave Art the Earliest Form of Cinema?," *The World*, PRI, June 14, 2012, https://www.pri.org/stories/2012-06-14/was-european-cave-art-earliest-form-cinema.

9. Zach Zorich, "Early Humans Made Animated Art," *Nautilus*, Mar. 27, 2014, http://nautil.us/issue/11/light/early-humans-made-animated-art.

10. Alexis Madrigal, "Happy Birthday, Eadweard Muybridge, You Have a Lot of GIFs to Answer For," *Atlantic*, Apr. 9, 2013, https://www.theatlantic.com/technology/archive/2013/04/happy-birthday-eadweard-muybridge-you-have-a-lot-of-gifs-to-answer-for/274832.

11. Andrew Blum, *Tubes: A Journey to the Center of the Internet* (New York: Ecco, 2013), 198.

12. Tom Standage, *The Victorian Internet: The Remarkable Story of the Telegraph and the Nineteenth Century's On-line Pioneers* (New York: Bloomsbury, 2014.)

13. "Submarine Cable Map," https://www.submarinecablemap.com, accessed Aug. 30, 2017.

14. With thanks to Marc Mayer, senior educator of contemporary art, at the Asian Art Museum, San Francisco.

15. Latoya Peterson, Personal Democracy Forum, June 5, 2014, New York.

16. Kate Miltner, Victoria & Albert Museum, June 30, 2017, London.

17. Saudis kissing their camels were not featured in the world animal-meme map. This fact comes from Rami Alhames, "Why Are Saudis Kissing Their Camels?," *Global Voices*, May 21, 2014, https://globalvoices.org/2014/05/21/why-are-saudis-kissing-their-camels.

18. Emily D. Parker, "In Praise of Echo Chambers," *Washington Post*, May 22, 2017, https://www.washingtonpost.com/news/democracy-post/wp/2017/05/22/in-praise-of-echo-chambers.

19. Farida Vis, "Internet Memes: Misinformation Machines or Vectors of Truth?," International Journalism Festival, Apr. 6, 2017, Perugia, Italy.

20. Rebecca Hersher, "Key Moments In The Dakota Access Pipeline Fight," NPR, Feb. 22, 2017, https://www.npr.org/sections/thetwo-way/2017/02/22/514988040/key-moments-in-the-dakota-access-pipeline-fight.

21. Jacqueline Keeler, "On 'More Important Things' and #NotYourMascot and #NoDAPL," *TiyospayeNow*, Nov. 4, 2016, http://tiyospayenow.blogspot.com/2016/11/on-more-important-things-and.html.

22. Meaghan Beatley, "Meet the Argentine Women Behind Ni Una Menos, the Feminist Collective Angela Davis Cites as Inspiration," Remezcla, Mar. 9, 2017, http://remezcla.com/features/culture/ni-una-menos-collective-argentina-founders.

23. Sandra Dibble, "Baja California's First Femicide Case," *San Diego Union-Tribune*, Apr. 4, 2015, http://www.sandiegouniontribune.com/news/border-baja-california/sdut-baja-california-femicide-feminicide-mexico-abuse-2015apr04-story.html.

24. L'Heureux, "Read Janet Mock's Women's March Speech on Trans Women of Color and Sex Workers."

25. Jacqueline Keeler, personal interview, July 25, 2017.

CHAPTER 7.2: SIGNS AND SEEDS

1. Barry Popik, "They Tried to Bury Us, But They Didn't Know We Were Seeds," Big Apple, Nov. 2, 2015, http://www.barrypopik.com/index.php/new_york_city/entry/they_tried _to_bury_us_but_they_didnt_know_we_were_seeds.

2. Jane Srivastava, "The Auspicious Swastika," *Hinduism Today*, https://www.hinduism today.com/modules/smartsection/item.php?itemid=1411, accessed Aug. 24, 2017.

3. Mukti Jain Campion, "How the World Loved the Swastika—Until Hitler Stole It," BBC.com, Oct. 23, 2014, http://www.bbc.com/news/magazine-29644591.

4. Parth Shah, "Diwali Dilemma: My Complicated Relationship with the Swastika," *Codeswitch*, NPR, Oct. 28, 2016, http://www.npr.org/sections/codeswitch/2016/10/28 /499475248/diwali-dilemma-my-complicated-relationship-with-the-swastika.

5. Campion, "How the World Loved the Swastika—Until Hitler Stole It."

6. Sara J. Bloomfield, "White Supremacists Are Openly Using Nazi Symbols. That's a Warning to All of Us," *Washington Post*, Aug. 22, 2017, https://www.washingtonpost.com /news/posteverything/wp/2017/08/22/white-supremacists-are-openly-using-nazi-symbols -thats-a-warning-to-all-of-us.

7. Holly Yan, Kristina Sgueglia, and Kylie Walker, "'Make America White Again': Hate Speech and Crimes Post-Election," CNN.com, Dec. 22, 2016, http://www.cnn.com/2016 /11/10/us/post-election-hate-crimes-and-fears-trnd/index.html.

8. Jonathan Zalman, "How to Transform a Swastika into Something Fluffy," Nov. 15, 2016, http://www.tabletmag.com/scroll/217978/how-to-transform-a-swastika-into -something-fluffy.

9. "Hate Groups Increase for Second Consecutive Year as Trump Electrifies Radical Right," Southern Poverty Law Center, Feb. 15, 2017, https://www.splcenter.org/news/2017 /02/15/hate-groups-increase-second-consecutive-year-trump-electrifies-radical-right.

10. Lorraine Boissoneault, "The Man Who Brought the Swastika to Germany, and How the Nazis Stole It," *Smithsonian Magazine*, Apr. 6, 2017, http://www.smithsonianmag.com /history/man-who-brought-swastika-germany-and-how-nazis-stole-it-180962812.

11. "History of the Swastika," *Holocaust Encyclopedia*, US Holocaust Memorial Museum, https://www.ushmm.org/wlc/en/article.php?ModuleId=10007453, accessed Aug. 24, 2017.

12. "Coining a Word and Championing a Cause: The Story of Raphael Lemkin," *Holocaust Encyclopedia*, US Holocaust Memorial Museum, https://www.ushmm.org/wlc/en/article .php?ModuleId=10007050, accessed Aug. 24, 2017.

13. Mark Sinclair, "The Untold Story of the Peace Sign," *Fast Company*, Oct. 2, 2014, https://www.fastcodesign.com/3036540/the-untold-story-of-the-peace-sign.

14. Andrew Grant Jackson, "November 19: Allen Ginsberg Invents 'Flower Power,'" on *1965: The Most Revolutionary Year in Music* book blog: Nov. 5, (book published New York: Thomas Dunne, 2015), https://1965book.com/2014/11/05/november-19-the-berkeley-barb -publishes-allen-ginsbergs-essay-demonstration-or-spectacle-as-example-as-communication -or-how-to-make-a-marchspectacle-which-extols-the-use-of-flowers-in-pro, Ben Cosgrove, "V for Victory: Celebrating a Gesture of Solidarity and Defiance," *Time*, July 4, 2014, http:// time.com/3880345/v-for-victory-a-gesture-of-solidarity-and-defiance.

15. Geoff Wood, "We Shall Overcome: How a Hymn Became an Anthem," ABC, June 30, 2015, http://www.abc.net.au/radionational/programs/rhythmdivine/we-shall-overcome: -how-a-hymn-became-an-icon/6576506.

16. "Keep Your Hand on the Plow" (lyrics), Genius, https://genius.com/Mahalia-jackson -keep-your-hand-on-the-plow-lyrics, accessed Sept. 17, 2017.

17. "Keep Your Eyes on the Prize" (lyrics), Genius, https://genius.com/Robert-parris -moses-keep-your-eyes-on-the-prize-lyrics, accessed Sept. 17, 2017.

18. Marissa Fessenden, "The Ku Klux Klan Didn't Always Wear Hoods," *Smithsonian*, Jan. 13, 2016, http://www.smithsonianmag.com/smart-news/ku-klux-klan-didnt-always-wear -hoods-180957773.

19. Michael W. Twitty, "Cultural Appropriation in America Can Be Audacious. Just Look at the Ku Klux Klan," *Guardian*, July 18, 2015, https://www.theguardian.com/commentisfree /2015/jul/18/ku-klux-klan-history-african-tradition-terrorize-black-americans.

20. Lessig, "The Laws of Cyberspace."

21. Jeff Chang, "Art of Change: Jeff Chang on How Culture Can Influence Politics," Ford Foundation, https://vimeo.com/132458668, accessed Sept. 17, 2017.

22. Popik, "They Tried to Bury Us, But They Didn't Know We Were Seeds."

23. Alexandra Boutopoulou, email correspondence, Mar. 1, 2018.

24. Susan Benesch, "The New Law of Incitement to Genocide: A Critique and a Proposal," paper, Hate Speech and Group-Targeted Violence: The Role of Speech in Violent Conflicts, US Holocaust Museum seminar, Feb. 2009, https://www.ushmm.org/confront -genocide/speakers-and-events/all-speakers-and-events/speech-power-violence.

INDEX

Academy of Motion Picture Arts and Sciences, 86
acceptable public discourse, 122–23
ACLU (American Civil Liberties Union), 156, 157
activism: creative media, 76–77; evading censorship by, 45–46; attention activist, 117
actors, intersecting range of, 82–83
Adichie, Chimamanda Ngozi, 74, 75
ADL (Anti-Defamation League), 100, 101, 102
Adobe Photoshop, 33
affirmation, memes as, 27
affirmation superhighway, 127
Africa, long-running narrative about countries in, 75
"Against Brainwashing" protest, 89
aggregate, impact of, 34–35
air filters, 133, 140
air pollution in China, 132–41; blaming government for, 137, 138
airport-based protests, 156
air sensors, 135, 140
ai weilai (爱未来), 9
Ai Weiwei, 8–10, 42, 57, 188
Albright, Madeleine, 98
Alexander, Michelle, 84
algorithms: and fake news, 123; keyword search, 44, 46
#AllLivesMatter, 86, 97
alternative narratives, 97, 115, 133, 140, 187
alternative reality, 115
alternative right (alt-right), 100–102, 109, 122
alternative sources of information in China, 140

alternative "truth," fog-smog narrative as, 133
amateur media, sharing of, 44–45
Amazon, 154
American Civil Liberties Union (ACLU), 156, 157
amplification of message, 25, 62, 81–82, 123
Andrews, Penny, 107–8, 164
Angry Birds, 61, 138–39
Angry Pigs, 139
animal memes, 168–77; and globalism and intersectionality, 175–77; goat, 168–71, 172–73; grass mud horse, 38–43, 45, 46, 114–15, 118, 122; grounded in societies from which they arise, 174–75; and infrastructure of the internet, 171–72; and Paleolithic art, 170–71; world map of, 169, 173–74. *See also* cat memes
Animal Planet, 23
Anti-Defamation League (ADL), 100, 101, 102
antifa (antifascist activists), 190
antiwar movement, 181
Arab Spring, 57, 91, 143
architecture as constraint on human behavior, 86
Arellano, Juan, 173
Argentina, #NiUnaMenos in, 176
Arizona Tea and Trayvon Martin, 64, 69, 163
"Armaria, nãm," 170
art(s): activist, 76–77; as cultural memory, 152; political and social power of, 95; and visionary ideas, 153
Art 2.1, 7

ABOUT THE AUTHOR

AN "AN XIAO" MINA is an American technologist, writer, and artist. She leads the product team at Meedan, where they build tools for global journalism and translation, and she is a cofounder of the Credibility Coalition, an effort to develop standards for online content credibility through rigorous research, in partnership with Hacks/Hackers and the W3C Credible Web Community Group.

At Harvard University, Mina is an affiliate researcher at and former fellow of the Berkman Klein Center for Internet and Society and a 2016 Knight Visiting Fellow at the Nieman Foundation for Journalism. Around the world, she has given keynotes and led workshops on the topic of media and the internet, in venues ranging from Creative Mornings to the World Economic Forum, and to groups from the ACLU to the Aspen Institute. She has contributed writing to publications including the *Atlantic*, *Quartz*, *the Los Angeles Review of Books*, the *Economist*, and *Hyperallergic*, and has contributed commentary for the *BBC World Service*, *Refinery29*, *AJ+ Español*, and the *Harvard Political Review*. She has served as a contributing editor for the book *Ai Weiwei: Spatial Matters*.

Mina is the cofounder of the Civic Beat, a global research collective focused on the creative side of civic technology. They have led workshops and exhibitions in spaces such as the Victoria and Albert Museum, the Mozilla Festival Open Artist Studio (curated by the V&A Museum and Tate Modern), the Asian Art Museum, and the Museum of the Moving Image, and they've been producing what Net Monitor called "the cutest map of the internet"—a world map of animal memes, in collaboration with over a dozen internet culture researchers.

She serves as contributing editor to *Civicist*, advisory editor to *Hyperallergic*, board member at China Residencies, and cochair at the Online News Association's SF Bay Area chapter. She loves cats, dogs, and llamas, but she not-so-secretly wants a pet pig.

Find her ongoing commentary at www.memestomovements.com.